ROMANTIC

JEALOUSY

Also by Ayala M. Pines

Keeping the Spark Alive: Preventing Burnout in Love and Marriage

Career Burnout: Causes and Cures (with Elliot Aronson)

Experiencing Social Psychology (with Christina Maslach)

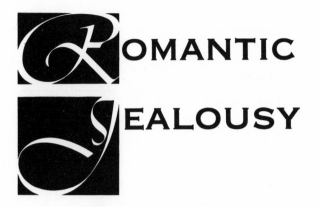

ROMANTIC JEALOUSY

UNDERSTANDING

AND CONQUERING

THE SHADOW

OF LOVE

•

AYALA M. PINES, PH.D.

ST. MARTIN'S PRESS

NEW YORK

ROMANTIC JEALOUSY. Copyright © 1992 by Ayala M. Pines, Ph.D. All rights reserved. Printed in the United States of America. No part of this book may be used or reproduced in any manner whatsoever without written permission except in the case of brief quotations embodied in critical articles or reviews. For information, address St. Martin's Press, 175 Fifth Avenue, New York, N.Y. 10010.

DESIGN BY JUDITH A. STAGNITTO

PRODUCTION EDITOR: MARIE FINAMORE

Library of Congress Cataloging-in-Publication Data

Pines, Ayala M.
    Romantic jealousy : understanding and conquering the shadow of love / Ayala M. Pines.
        p.   cm.
    ISBN 0-312-07106-X
    1. Jealousy.   2. Jealousy—Case studies.   I. Title.
BF575.J4P47   1992
152.4—dc20   91-37994
                                                        CIP

First Edition: March 1992
10 9 8 7 6 5 4 3 2 1

For Israel

CONTENTS

Acknowledgments

I would like to thank my friends and colleagues who read this book and helped improve it with their thoughtful comments. These include Dr. Gordon Clanton, Dr. Bernie Zilbergeld, Dr. Clair Rabin, Dr. Loise Shawver, Dr. Laura Stechel, and Kathy Knopoff (on her way to a brilliant career in psychology). Discussions with Professors Elliot Aronson, Murray Bilmes, Jack Block, and Troy Duster, as well as with Tsafi Gilad and Israel Segal helped crystallize my ideas about jealousy.

I owe special thanks to my agent, Judith Weber, who besides being a dear friend is a wonderful editor and an intelligent and insightful reader who helped improve the book greatly both in content and in style. Wanda Cuevas, a member of the Sobel Weber Associates professional staff, also provided valuable feedback and support.

Anne Savarese, my editor at St. Martin's Press, has gone through every version of the book with thoroughness I have never encountered before. The result is an invaluable contribution to the book, for which I am extremely grateful.

The greatest thanks, however, are reserved for the people in my private practice and participants in my workshops and research, who opened their hearts to me and shared some of their most painful and difficult experiences with jealousy. This book could never have been written without their contribution.

PREFACE

On the summer of 1978, I flew back to San Francisco from Toronto, where I had attended an American Psychological Association convention. On the plane I sat next to Elliot Aronson, one of the leading social psychologists in the country and a friend I admire greatly. We were chatting about various things when he said, "What do you know about jealousy?"

"Jealousy?" I responded, surprised. He explained, "I was asked to write an article called 'What We Don't Know About Jealousy' for a new behavioral science magazine. The problem is that I don't know much about jealousy—hence the title. But I thought if you were interested in the subject, we could pool our ignorance and have some fun writing the article together." While I definitely had my own personal experience with jealousy, I had never given much thought to it as a subject for study. I knew as much about it as Elliot did, but the offer was such a great compliment that I said yes right away.

The next day, in Berkeley, I went to the university library and did a computer search to find out what had been written about jealousy.

There was quite a lot. I buried myself in literature on the subject by novelists, poets, philosophers, anthropologists, sociologists, psychiatrists, and psychologists. While the volumes written were numerous, many questions were left unanswered. This was the subject of the article Elliot and I wrote.

Although the magazine folded before the article could be published, I became hooked on jealousy, and for the following twelve years I continued to study it. I've worked with jealous individuals and couples in my private practice, I've led jealousy workshops and collected questionnaires from close to a thousand people. I've worked in prison with male inmates serving time for "crimes of passion," and collected questionnaires from female inmates in another prison. I've worked with couples in open relationships. I've studied two urban communes practicing open relationships: one in which members succeeded in overcoming their jealousy, the other in which jealousy was a major problem and eventually caused the break-up of the commune. I've also reviewed the extensive literature on jealousy. This book is based on these experiences, research, and clinical work.

The book describes five different approaches to jealousy: The *psychodynamic* approach views jealousy as the result of unresolved childhood traumas. The *systems* approach views it as the result of the dynamics within a particular relationship. The *behavioral* approach views it as a learned response that can be unlearned. The *social-psychological* approach views it as the result of culture, which determines when jealousy is experienced and how it is expressed. The *sociobiological* approach views it as innate, the result of evolutionary processes that are different for men and women.

While these approaches are considered by many to be contradictory, I use all five of them in my work. I believe anything that helps a person with a jealousy problem can and should be used. This book reflects that conviction.

WHAT THE BOOK IS ABOUT

This book is for anyone who seeks better understanding of romantic jealousy, which I call the shadow of love. It was written with two kinds of readers in mind. One is the person currently struggling with a jealousy problem or with the jealousy problem of a mate, who hopes to find answers and cures. The other is the intellectually curious person who might have had an encounter with jealousy in the past, and who is interested in learning more about it. Each chapter has something for both types of readers.

Whether or not you currently have a jealousy problem, you are likely to benefit from answering the jealousy questionnaire in the appendix beginning on page 247. You can answer the questionnaire again after reading the book to see if any of your answers changed as a result of what you've learned.

The first chapter of the book serves as an introduction, defining romantic jealousy and explaining the differences between jealousy and envy, and between normal and abnormal jealousy. It also explains the title of the book.

In the second chapter you will be presented with a series of questions aimed at helping you explore your own romantic jealousy, and you will be able to compare your responses to those given by more than seven hundred people to the same questions.

The third chapter explores the unconscious roots of jealousy from the perspective of the psychodynamic approach, which views jealousy as a problem in the mind of the jealous individual that is best treated by individual therapy. This chapter can help you understand how childhood events may have influenced your jealousy.

The fourth chapter presents the systems approach, which proposes that jealousy occurs within the dynamic of a particular relationship, and can best be treated through couple therapy. Whether or not you are currently in a relationship with a jealousy problem, the chapter can provide you with some valuable insights about the way couples collude to keep a jealousy problem alive.

The fifth chapter, titled "Men Get Angry, Women Get Depressed," presents the sociobiological approach, in which jealousy is seen as an innate response resulting from evolutionary forces that are different for men and women. Examining this approach can help you realize that part of your jealousy problem is not unique to you and your mate, but is a universal problem for couples.

The sixth chapter discusses jealousy in different cultures and presents the social-psychological approach. According to this approach, our culture determines when we feel jealous and how we express our jealousy. In this chapter you will be encouraged to shift your explanation for your jealousy from "I'm a jealous person" to "I get jealous in certain situations."

Chapters seven and eight examine the range of responses to romantic jealousy. While most readers will resort neither to violence nor to an open relationship, reading about people who did can broaden our understanding of jealousy. Chapter seven presents the views of people who believe that jealousy is a learned response that can be unlearned successfully.

While the book looks at jealousy as the shadow of love instead of as a green-eyed monster, chapter eight addresses the most "monstrous" response to jealousy: violence. From this discussion you can gain an appreciation for the explosive potential in jealousy and learn how to defuse it in your own relationship.

Chapter nine is devoted to coping with jealousy. It presents the behavioral approach, in which jealousy is seen as a learned response that, if inappropriate, can be unlearned and replaced with a more appropriate response. The chapter offers a variety of behavioral techniques for coping with a jealousy problem. It also makes reference to techniques and exercises inspired by the other approaches presented throughout the book. The goal of these coping techniques is to help individuals and couples protect their relationships in positive and constructive ways so that something good can come out of jealousy.

My view that jealousy can be a growth-enhancing force is explored in chapter ten and demonstrated through the analysis of an unusual triangle relationship.

Beyond the benefits to be gained from each chapter, my hope is that the book as a whole will help readers turn romantic jealousy into a useful signal they can use to improve themselves and their relationships.*

I have enjoyed my work on jealousy immensely and loved writing this book. I hope my excitement about the subject comes through.

---

*Everything I say in this book about male-female relationships can be applied to male-male or female-female relationships as well.

ROMANTIC JEALOUSY

THE GREEN-EYED MONSTER
OR THE SHADOW OF LOVE?

*O, beware my lord of jealousy! It is the green eyed
monster, which doth mock the meat it feeds on.*
—SHAKESPEARE, OTHELLO

He that is not jealous is not in love.
—ST. AUGUSTINE

*Jealousy is the dragon in paradise: the hell of
heaven: and the most bitter of emotions because it
is associated with the sweetest.*
—A. R. ORAGE, ON LOVE

I found myself sitting all curled up in the bushes
following every movement seen through the curtains
in her lit-up window. I knew her boyfriend was there,
and the knowledge caused me an excruciating pain.
It was a cold winter night, and once in a while it
would drizzle. I said to myself, "I know I am a sane,
well-adjusted, responsible adult. What in the world is
happening to me? Have I totally lost my mind?" And
yet I continued sitting in those bushes for hours. I
didn't leave until the light in the window was gone.
A force larger than myself held me hypnotized to the
light and to her. I have never in my life felt so close
to madness.

* * *

Although I knew that our relationship was over, I still had very strong feelings toward him. Then, one day, I saw him at the corner store we used to shop at when we lived together. He was with this Los Angeles–type bleached blonde, the kind who spends hours choosing her outfit. She had heavy makeup perfectly put on, and every hair on her head was in just the right place. I knew that I looked like a bag lady, my nose was red from a cold, my hair was unwashed and greasy. I think I simply went mad. I went up to him, kicked him in the balls, snapped the hat he was holding in his hand, and ran outside. I went into his car—which for some reason he left unlocked—and started crying uncontrollably. I've never cried like that in my life. I felt I was going out of my mind.

The man in the first paragraph and the woman in the second are describing powerful experiences that have several things in common. The experiences are extreme and unusual, involve loss of control, and result in a sense that one is going mad. Indeed, these are three notable features of jealousy.

WHAT IS ROMANTIC JEALOUSY?

The word *jealous* is derived from the Greek word *zelos*, which signifies emulation, zeal, and jealousy, and denotes intensity of feelings.

In this book the focus is not on jealousy in general, but on *romantic* jealousy: the jealousy that emerges in the context of a romantic relationship.

The phrase "romantic jealousy" means different things to different people. It evokes a variety of images, explanations, and definitions. Here are some examples: "It's a hard-to-control emotion that results from fear of losing an important person to someone else." "It's a feeling you have when you're afraid you're losing an important relationship." "It's the feeling of being betrayed by someone you trust." "It's when somebody else looks at a person I love the way I do." "It's when you are insecure about your relationship or about yourself, and you feel that you are not man enough." "When you love someone, but the love they felt for you is gone."

What is your own definition of romantic jealousy?

I've presented this question to close to a thousand people and received as many definitions as there were respondents. The personal definitions I just presented, for example, were suggested by inmates serving time in prison for committing crimes related to jealousy.

Since it's clear that we can't simply assume everyone knows what jealousy is, I would like to offer the following definition: *Jealousy is a reaction to a perceived threat to a valued relationship or to its quality.*[1]

Jealousy is a complex *reaction* that has both internal and external components. The internal component of jealousy includes certain emotions, thoughts, and physical symptoms that often are not visible to the outside world.

The emotions associated with jealousy may include pain, anger, rage, envy, sadness, fear, grief, and humiliation. The thoughts associated with jealousy may include resentment ("How could you have lied to me like this?"), self-blame ("How could I have been so blind, so stupid, so trusting?"), comparison with the rival ("I'm not as attractive, sexy, intelligent, successful."), concern for one's public image ("Everyone knows, and laughs at me."), or self-pity ("I'm all alone in the world, nobody loves me."). The physical symptoms associated with jealousy may include blood rushing to the head, sweaty and trembling hands, shortness of breath, stomach cramps, feeling faint, a fast heartbeat, and trouble falling or staying asleep.

The external component of jealousy is more clearly visible to the outside world, and is expressed in some kind of behavior: for example, talking openly about the problem, screaming, crying, making a point of ignoring the issue, using humor, retaliating, leaving, or becoming violent.

The fact that jealousy has both an internal and an external component has an important implication for coping. Even if we can modify the internal component to some extent, we have relatively little control over it, especially over our emotional and physical responses: "I wish I could be cool and rational about it, but the pain is simply too big." "I stood there like an idiot, blood rushing to my face, and couldn't do a thing to stop it." We have somewhat more control over our thoughts. Actually, the premise of cognitive therapy, which will be presented in chapter nine, is that we can change our feelings by changing our thoughts.

We have much more control over the external component of jealousy than over the internal component. We don't always realize this (and even when we realize it, we don't always want to admit it), but we can choose to talk about our feelings, make fun of the whole thing, cry our hearts out, suffer silently and covertly or loudly and visibly, lash out in anger, get out of the relationship, make our mate jealous, or throw dishes.

We will return to this point in chapter nine, during the discussion of the various techniques for coping with jealousy. For now, suffice it to say that when you are feeling overwhelmed by jealousy, remember that while we may not be able to completely control our jealous feelings, by changing our thoughts we can keep the feelings from controlling us. Furthermore, we have significant control over what we decide to do about our jealousy.

The jealous response is triggered when there's a perceived threat to a relationship. The perceived threat may be real or imagined, just as the relationship itself can be real or imagined. If a man thinks that his wife is interested in other men, even if the threat is a result of his own wild imagination, he is going to respond with intense jealousy. (We will return to this example in the discussion of normal and abnormal jealousy.) On the other hand, if a woman has a close friendship with another man, but her husband feels secure in their marriage and does not feel threatened by this friendship, he is not likely to respond with jealousy.

A couple with whom I worked recently provides an example of jealousy as a response to an imaginary threat. The husband, a rather plain-looking man, married a beautiful woman thirteen years younger than himself. He was convinced that every man who looked at his wife desired her. Since he did not feel secure in his own attractiveness, he was terrified every time she left the house, thinking that she would find someone else and leave him. His wife was faithful and committed to the marriage; when they first met, she loved the fact that he put her on a pedestal, and welcomed his intense attraction to her. With time, however, she found his jealousy increasingly bothersome and suffocating. When the couple came to me for help, she said she needed to get away from him—not because he lacked attractiveness, not because she had found a more attractive man, but because of his suffocating jealousy.

Another couple provides an example of how *not* perceiving a situation as a threat can act as a buffer against jealousy. The husband in this case was a swinger. He loved swingers' parties, even orgies. His wife did not. For years he used to go to these sexual encounters alone, with the full knowledge of his wife. The wife, for her part, disliked the idea of sexual promiscuity, but accepted the fact that this was something extremely important for her husband, and something he did not intend as a threat to their marriage or to herself. After years of this arrangement, the wife had an affair. The husband's way of dealing with it was to befriend her lover and accept him as part of the family. He said the lover wasn't a threat to his marriage. Furthermore, the fact that his wife had a lover made him feel freer to continue his own sexual exploits. Even if one doubts the husband's claim that he felt no jealousy, it's clear that his response to what is for most people a powerful jealousy trigger was very mild.

The relationship that triggers the jealous response has to be *valuable*. It can be valuable in different ways. If a woman can't stand her husband and he arouses in her only feelings of disgust, the knowledge that he is having an affair is not likely, in and of itself, to trigger much jealousy. Yet for this woman, losing her husband to another woman may threaten her public image, as well as her standard of living and general lifestyle. The marriage may not be valuable for her emotionally, but it may have economic or social value.

The following is a case in point. It demonstrates that the potential for jealousy can exist in a relationship that has only extraneous value, even after that relationship has ended.

A wealthy woman who wanted desperately to get out of her marriage finally managed to do so, at great financial cost. She had to leave the house to her husband, but said she was glad to be rid of him. Then, one night as she drove past the house, she saw a shadow of a woman on the curtain and was overcome by tremendous jealousy.

Did she perceive a threat to her marriage? Obviously not, since the marriage was over. Was her marriage emotionally valuable to her as a love relationship? Obviously not, since she was the one who worked so hard, and sacrificed so much, to get out of it. Yet she felt jealous when she saw the shadow of the woman. Jealousy, as we know, is a response to a perceived threat to a valued relationship *or to its quality*. The woman was responding to the threat against her perception of her relationship with her husband.

In her mind she saw herself as superior to her husband and as having more power in their relationship. After all, wasn't she the one who kicked *him* out of the marriage and out of her life? And here the worthless bum had already found someone else to be with, while she was still alone. What enraged her even more was that the two of them were "in" and she was "out" of "her" house. The other woman presented a threat not to her actual marriage but rather to her perception of her marriage.

The above example illustrates the complexity of the jealous response. The wealthy woman experienced possessiveness (this was "her" husband and "her" house), exclusion (they were "in" and she was "out"), competitiveness (her husband had someone and she didn't), and envy (she wanted to have a relationship like the one he had).

For some people, the strongest component of jealousy is a fear of being abandoned: "He is going to fall in love with her and leave me and then I'll be all alone." For some, the primary component is loss of face: "How could you humiliate me in front of everyone by flirting openly with this slut?" For some, the most painful aspect is the betrayal: "How could someone I trusted lie to me and betray me in this way?" For some, the primary component is competitiveness: "If she fell in love with him, he must be a better lover than I am"; or, "How could she fall for this sleazeball?" And there are those for whom the primary component is envy: "I wish I were as skinny and gorgeous as she is," or "as successful professionally as he is."

When people describe intense jealousy, they often confuse their response with the degree of threat actually present in the situation. They may, for example, respond as if their mate's "outrageous" flirting at the party indicated that their mate would leave them for that other person, when in fact all that the flirting causes is embarrassment. When they confront the threat realistically ("How likely is it that your husband will leave you for this other woman?"), the intensity of their jealousy invariably diminishes.

PREDISPOSITION TO JEALOUSY

Although jealousy occurs in different forms, and exists in varying degrees of intensity, it always results from *an interaction between a certain predisposition and a particular triggering event.*

Predisposition to jealousy is influenced by *the culture we live in*; some cultures encourage jealousy while others discourage it. It is influenced by *our family background*: a man whose mother was unfaithful to his father or whose parents had violent outbursts of jealousy is likely to have a far greater predisposition to jealousy than a man whose father and mother felt secure in each other's love. It is influenced by our *family constellation*: a woman who was outshone by a prettier or brighter sister is likely to have a greater predisposition to jealousy than a woman who was the favorite child in the family. It is also influenced by *our experiences with intimate relationships*: a person who was betrayed by a trusted mate is likely to develop a greater predisposition to jealousy in the future.

A predisposition to jealousy may never express itself unless a triggering event brings it out. For a person with an unusually high predisposition to jealousy, such a triggering event can be as minor as a partner's glance at an attractive stranger passing by. For most people, however, a jealousy trigger is a much more serious event, such as discovering that their mate is having an illicit affair. For a person with an unusually low predisposition to jealousy, almost no event, short of the end of the relationship, can activate the jealous response.

Throughout the book, as mentioned in the preface, five approaches to romantic jealousy will be presented. Each emphasizes a different aspect of the predisposition to jealousy.

The psychodynamic approach focuses on the question, Why do certain people have an unusually high or low predisposition to jealousy? It assumes that the answer can be found in people's childhood experiences.

The systems approach asks, What is it about certain relationships that increases or decreases couples' predisposition to jealousy? It assumes that the answer can be found in the repeated patterns in these couples' interactions.

The behavioral approach asks, What increases the individual's predisposition to behave in a jealous way? It assumes that the answer can be found in learned behaviors.

The social-psychological approach asks, What effects does the culture have on people's predisposition to jealousy? It assumes that the answer can be found in cultural norms, which define what people perceive as threatening and what responses are considered appropriate.

The sociobiological approach asks, How have evolutionary forces of natural selection shaped men's and women's innate predisposition to jealousy? It assumes that the answer can be found in universal sex differences that exist in most human societies as well as in the animal world.

JEALOUSY AND ENVY

In defining jealousy, it's important to distinguish it from envy. Despite the frequent confusion between the two in everyday use, jealousy and envy are very different psychologically. Envy usually involves two people. The envious person wants something that belongs to the other person, and doesn't want the other person to have it. The object of envy can be the other person's mate, a good relationship, a desirable trait such as beauty or intelligence, a possession, success, or popularity. Jealousy, on the other hand, usually involves three people. The jealous person is responding to a perceived threat to a valued relationship posed by a third person. This is true even when the third person exists only in the imagination of the jealous person.

Envy and jealousy are keyed to two of the most basic conditions of human existence. Envy is connected with not having. Jealousy is connected with having.[2]

People tend to mistake envy for jealousy, but not the other way around. Would you tell your husband that seeing him with his old girlfriend makes you envious, or that it makes you jealous? Would you say that you are jealous, or envious, of a friend who has just inherited a large amount of money? If you are like most people, you would describe yourself in both cases as jealous, although what you actually feel in the second case is envy.

This transposition often occurs because envy tends to have a more negative connotation than jealousy; envy is less mitigated by love than is jealousy.[3] While jealousy is a response to a threat to a valued relationship, envy is an expression of hostility toward a perceived superior and a desire not only to possess the advantage, but destroy the superior.

The different attitudes toward jealousy and envy are found in many countries. A study comparing responses to jealousy and envy in seven countries (Hungary, Ireland, Mexico, the Netherlands, the USSR, Yugoslavia, and the United States) shows similar responses to jealousy and envy in all of them.[4]

If jealousy and envy are so distinct, why do people confuse them so often? Part of the reason lies in the fact that the jealous response includes, in many cases, a component of envy. A man who is jealous because his wife is having an affair with his best friend, for example, is likely to feel envious of his friend's success with his wife.

Jealousy and envy also originate in different stages of our psychological development. As we will see in chapter three, during the discussion of its unconscious roots, jealousy originates primarily in emotional experiences children have during the Oedipal stage, when they are about three years old. Envy, on the other hand, originates much earlier, during the first weeks of the child's life.

According to Freud, during the Oedipal stage children experience the first stirrings of sexuality. Their sexual urge is directed toward the closest person of the opposite sex. In the case of a boy, that means his mother. In the case of a girl, her father. The boy wants Mother to himself. Unfortunately he has a very powerful competitor for her love: Father. The competitor is bigger and stronger and has other advantages too, so that the boy "loses" the contest. (Through a similar process, the girl "loses" Father to Mother.) When the child becomes an adult, every time a third person presents a threat to a valued romantic relationship, the old painful wound is reopened and experienced as jealousy.[5]

Envy, according to the child analyst Melanie Klein, develops during the period from birth through the first year of life, in response to the baby's total helplessness and dependence on Mother. "From the beginning of life, the infant turns to Mother for all his needs," Klein writes. The mother's breast, toward which all the infant's desires are directed, is instinctively felt to be not only the source of nourishment but of life itself.

An element of frustration, however, is bound to enter into the infant's earliest relation to Mother, because "even a happy feeding situation cannot altogether replace the prenatal unity with the mother." The frustration and helplessness the hungry baby experiences are the roots of envy. The baby "envies" Mother for her power to nurse him or deprive him of nourishment. In his frustration, he wants to devour the source of his nourishment and her power—the breast.

Even if we don't accept Klein's idea that the baby "envies" his mother's power to feed him, we can still accept her idea that the early bond with Mother contains the fundamental elements of the baby's future relationship to the world. When the bond is loving and satisfying, the baby will develop a basic sense of security and trust toward people. When the bond is not loving and not satisfying, deep-seated insecurity and envy will develop and the baby will grow up to be an envious adult. Whenever envy is triggered in such an adult, it reopens the early childhood wounds with all their destructive power.[6]

Klein believes that jealousy is based on envy, but is different from it nonetheless. Her distinction between the two is similar to the one presented here: "Envy is the angry feeling that another person possesses and enjoys something desirable—the envious impulse being to take it away or to spoil it." Jealousy, on the other hand, involves the person's relationship to at least two other people, and "is mainly concerned with love which the individual feels is his due and which has been taken away, or is in danger of being taken."[7]

Envy, as Klein describes it, is an earlier, more primitive, and more destructive emotion than jealousy. It is different from the jealous desire to protect the relationship or get the beloved back. When there is a component of envy in a jealousy situation, it is expressed in an impulse to destroy the person who has the advantage—either the rival or the beloved, who has the power to make us happy and chooses not to.

NORMAL AND ABNORMAL JEALOUSY

After defining romantic jealousy and distinguishing it from envy, we need to make yet another important distinction, between normal and abnormal jealousy. The discussion of abnormal jealousy will lead us to some of the most extreme forms that jealousy can take, and some of its more dramatic consequences.

Jealousy has produced pain, drama, and tragedy throughout history. A wide range of hostile, bitter, and painful events have been attributed to jealousy: murder, aggression, hatred, lowered self-esteem, depression, suicide and suicide attempts, wife-battering, the destruction of romantic relationships, marital problems, and divorce.[8] A nationwide survey of marriage counselors indicates that jealousy is a problem in one-third of all couples coming for marital therapy.[9]

Most people describe jealousy as an extremely painful, "crazy" experience. A woman who participated in one of my jealousy workshops said that jealousy was the most painful thing she had ever experienced:

> I tried everything in an attempt to gain some control over it, but nothing, nothing works. Now the only thing left for me is lobotomy. And believe me, I am tempted. I don't think I can live with this much pain any longer.

Even when people who experience extreme jealousy have enough self-control not to resort to actual acts of violence, they often fantasize about such acts. A woman who saw her ex-husband with his new wife, a woman who used to be her best friend, recalls:

> One day, as I was parking my car, I saw them in his new sports car parked right in front of me. It was a car he never let me drive but was letting her use. Everything went white with rage in front of my eyes. I sat there trying to get hold of myself. I imagined myself putting my car in gear, accelerating, pushing my foot all the way down on the gas pedal and slamming into them at full speed, full force. I could feel the impact of the crash in my body, and hear the sound of metal and glass crashing. . . . I don't know what force helped me control the urge to destroy everything.

Most of us have faced jealousy at some point in our lives, even if we don't consider it a problem.[10] Anyone who has experienced intense jealousy is well aware of its power and potential destructiveness. This helps explain our fascination with stories about the wild things some people are driven to do out of jealousy. One such story involves a middle-aged woman whose husband left her for a younger woman. With the help of a friend, the outraged wife kidnapped her rival at gunpoint, shaved her head, stripped her naked, covered her with tar and feathers, and released her at the city dump. I read the story in the newspaper and subsequently heard it repeated over and over again, with great delight, by women who identified with the revenge of the deposed wife.

We tend to show more understanding toward people who commit "hot-blooded" crimes motivated by jealousy than we do toward people who commit "cold-blooded" crimes motivated by greed. We may feel a certain identification with the betrayed lover who "had his revenge," who dared do something most of us can only imagine as a fitting revenge for our unfaithful mate or the interloper who stole our mate's heart.

Even the law in certain countries treats "crimes of passion" with relative leniency. In a famous case that happened some years ago in Italy, a man who suspected his wife of infidelity bought a gun and drove all the way from Rome, where he lived, to Milan, where he had reason to suspect that his wife was spending time with her lover. He arrived in Milan, caught his wife and her lover together in bed, shot them both, and was tried and found not guilty on grounds of temporary insanity.

In chapter eight, which is devoted to a discussion of jealousy and violence, I describe the stories of men who are in prison for crimes motivated by jealousy. The special circumstances of their crimes weren't enough to find them not guilty in the American court.

Is jealousy a form of madness? Getting back to the examples presented at the beginning of this chapter, we can ask, Is a man who is sitting in the bushes on a rainy night, spying on a woman, sane? What about a woman who kicks a man in the groin, or one who covers another woman with tar and feathers? What about a man who kills two people in a jealous rage?

Jealousy, as these examples show, lies somewhere in the gray area between sanity and madness. Some reactions to jealousy are so natural that a person who doesn't show them seems in some way "not normal." Think, for example, about a man whose wife has just informed him that she has fallen in love with another man, and who says in response, "How wonderful for you, darling."

Other reactions seem so excessive that one doesn't need to be an expert to know that they are pathological. A classic example is the man who is so suspicious of his loving and faithful wife that he constantly spies on her, listens in on her phone conversations, checks her underpants for stains, records the mileage in her car for unexplained trips, makes surprise visits, and, despite her repeatedly proven fidelity, continues to suspect her and suffer from tremendous jealousy.

While the responses of these two husbands seem completely different from each other, there is an important similarity between them. Both are very inappropriate. In one case the husband is not responding to a real threat to his marriage: his wife might leave him for the other man. In the other, the husband is responding with jealousy when there's no real threat. Indeed, both cases are considered by clinical psychologists to be abnormal behaviors that indicate certain personality disorders.[11] In chapter three I will discuss the roots of such extreme responses to jealousy.

For most of us, even if jealousy produces tremendous pain and distress, it remains an inner experience that does not cross the boundary to violent action. The woman I described earlier, whose estranged husband started dating her best friend shortly after their separation, said:

> I have daydreams in which I go into her apartment
> with a sledgehammer and start destroying things—
> furniture, records, windows. I can virtually hear the
> glass breaking. . . . These fantasies have a way of calm-
> ing me down, even if I know I will never carry them
> out.

Does that seem like an appropriate response? What if the other woman were not her best friend? What if she knew that her husband left her because of that "best friend"? What if, instead of imagining the sledgehammer destruction, she were actually to do it?

The more a response seems (in Freud's words) to "derive from the actual situation" and be "proportionate to the real circumstances," the more "normal" it is.[12] Freud, and modern-day therapists who subscribe to the psychodynamic approach, differentiate "normal" from "delusional" jealousy. Normal jealousy has its basis in a real threat to the relationship. Delusional jealousy, on the other hand, persists despite the absence of any real or even probable threat. The husband who suspects and spies on his wife, despite her faithfulness and devotion to him, presents a good example of delusional jealousy.

Why would someone "choose" to suffer the incredible pains of jealousy if there is no basis for it in reality? One explanation, which I will present in chapter three, is that through jealousy the person is trying to deal with an unresolved childhood trauma of betrayal. In chapter four I will present another explanation that focuses on couples' interactions that help maintain such a jealousy problem. In chapter nine I will present a third explanation that sees the roots of the jealousy problem in behaviors that were learned at some earlier point in life, and which persist even though they are no longer appropriate.

In addition to the distinction between a real and an imagined threat, another distinction is often made between an appropriate ("normal") and an inappropriate ("abnormal") response to the jealousy-producing threat. In chapter six, which describes the way romantic jealousy is experienced and expressed in different cultures, we will see that "normal" is simply that which is accepted as an appropriate response in a particular culture.[13] No matter how abnormal a certain response to jealousy may seem to you, chances are that it is (or was) considered normal somewhere.

Another distinction made between normal and abnormal jealousy has to do with the effect the two have on relationships. While normal jealousy is a protective response that can save a marriage, abnormal jealousy is a destructive obsession that hurts people and relationships.[14]

Instead of emphasizing the negative and judgmental connotation implied in the ordinary usage of the word *abnormal* (that is, pathological, morbid, crazy, sick), it is more useful to think of *normal* as a statistical term that describes what is typical or average. People experience as broad a range of jealous responses as they possess different physical and emotional characteristics. The vast majority fall in the middle range and are defined as normal. A small minority fall in the lowest part of the scale and are defined as abnormally low. A similar minority fall in the highest part of the scale and are defined as abnormally high.[15]

Think about such a thing as height, for example. Most people are of "normal" height, a small percentage are "abnormally" short, and a similar minority are "abnormally" tall. *Abnormal* in this case does not mean crazy or sick—it simply means the lowest and highest ends of the scale.

The same thing that can be said about height, weight, strength, or beauty can be said about jealousy. The majority of people are in the middle (that is, the "normal") range of the jealousy scale. The few that are at the highest end of the scale, who see a threat even when none exists, are "abnormally" jealous; the few in the lowest part of the scale, who don't see a threat when it's obviously there, are "abnormally non-jealous."

This point is more than a semantic distinction. All too often, people who experience jealousy are so shaken by the intensity of their emotions and by the things they find themselves doing or wishing they could do—such as spying on an ex-lover or daydreaming about destroying a house with a sledgehammer—that they jump to the conclusion "I must be crazy!" This conclusion is not very useful, and is also very likely incorrect. Most "normal" people experience intense jealousy when a valued relationship is threatened.

This is not to say there aren't cases of abnormal jealousy, but they are very few. We hear so much about them precisely because they are truly outside the "normal" range, and are therefore particularly fascinating.

Most abnormal cases of jealousy have one or both of the following features: (a) they are not related to a real threat to a valued relationship, but to some inner trigger of the jealous individual, and (b) the jealous response is dramatically exaggerated or violent.

Having said that, I would also like to note that some social scientists, whose views will be presented in chapter six, reject altogether the notion of abnormal jealousy as it applies to the individual. They believe that what is normal or abnormal is defined by the culture, and that the individual has little to do with it.

If you are concerned about whether you or your mate is "abnormally jealous," you might find chapter two and the jealousy questionnaire in the appendix especially helpful. In the latter you'll be presented with a series of questions aimed at helping you diagnose your own (or your mate's) jealousy. Filling out the jealousy questionnaire may be interesting even if you don't have a jealousy problem. It will make reading the rest of the book, and especially the following chapter, more personally relevant.

I named this first chapter "The Green-Eyed Monster or the Shadow of Love?" Now that we have seen some of the extreme forms that jealousy takes as, in Shakespeare's words, "the green-eyed monster," we can move on to a discussion of jealousy as the shadow of love.

ROMANTIC JEALOUSY AS THE SHADOW OF LOVE

Whatever it is that draws two lovers to each other will create the character of the jealousy they may experience. Let me demonstrate this statement with an exercise:

Think back to the time you first met or got to know your mate, and try to recall as best you can the way you felt. What was it that most attracted you? What was it that made you think (right away, or at some point later) that this was the person with whom you wanted to share your life? What was the most important thing the relationship gave you? A feeling of security? Of being respected and listened to? Of being desired or adored?

Now switch back to the present, and consider the primary component of your jealousy, the most painful thoughts and feelings associated with your jealousy or that of your mate. Is it a fear of being abandoned? It is humiliation and loss of face? Is it loss of self-esteem?

The third part of this exercise is the most challenging, and the most significant. Think: could there be some connection between the things that the relationship gave you initially and the primary components of your jealousy? For example, a woman who fell in love with her husband because he made her feel she had "finally come home" to a safe and secure place described the most painful aspect of her jealousy as "feeling abandoned and all alone in the world."

The opposite example, mentioned earlier, is the woman who fell in love with her husband because he made her the center of his world. After twenty years of marriage she wanted a divorce because his jealousy was suffocating her. Her husband fell in love with her because she was beautiful—the kind of woman he only dared dream about as a shy adolescent. His jealousy focused on his feelings of inferiority and insecurity.

Why is it so important to note the connection between what attracted us to our mate—the most valuable thing the relationship gave us initially—and the primary components of our jealousy? Because it proves that jealousy is indeed the shadow of love. Furthermore, it's a reminder that we didn't just happen to be in this relationship. We *chose* to be in it. Something in us attracted us to our mate. Something in us makes us experience jealousy the way we do. That something is our romantic image.

Psychologists have invested a great deal of effort in studying who falls in love with whom.[16] They have discovered similarities among couples across a wide range of variables including personality characteristics, family background, education, income and social status of parents, religious affiliation, sex of siblings, attitude toward parents, happiness of their parents' marriage, tendency to be a "lone wolf" or socially gregarious, preference to "stay at home" or be "on the go," drinking and smoking habits, number of friends, intelligence, attractiveness, various physical attributes, mental health, and psychological maturity.

Even if you and your mate are similar in several of the traits mentioned in the list, you probably still feel that these were not the *real* reasons you fell in love with your mate. Yet, after you made your choice, these were the things that told you that your choice was right. Your emotional choice—the spark you felt—was based on your internalized romantic image.[17]

We develop our romantic images very early in life, based on powerful experiences we had during childhood. Our parents and other adults involved in raising us influence the development of our romantic images in two primary ways: (a) by the way they express, or don't express, love toward us, and (b) by the way they express, or don't express, love toward each other.

Think back to the earliest time in your life you can remember. (It may be helpful to think about a house you lived in or a particular event that sticks in your memory.) Who took care of you? Who taught you the meaning of love? Was it your mother, your father, an older sibling, a grandparent? Who else was important in your childhood? Try to remember as much as you can about these people—not the way they are now, but the way you experienced them in your childhood. What were their most important traits, both good and bad? What was the most notable characteristic of their relationship with each other? What was the most important thing they gave you? What was the thing you most wanted but didn't get? Were they unfaithful to each other? Were they jealous?

The positive and negative features of the people who raised us are the building blocks of our romantic images. But while our romantic image is influenced by our mother, our father, and other people who reared us, there is an important difference between their negative and positive traits. The negative traits tend to have more influence on our romantic image. The reason for this is not (as one psychologist has suggested) that we choose to marry our worst nightmare, but that these are traits with which we still have "unfinished business."[18] If a girl's father was unfaithful to her mother, his unfaithfulness will become an important component of the girl's romantic image. If a boy's mother had frequent fits of jealousy, this will become an important component of his romantic image.

As adults we look for a person who will fit our romantic image in a significant way. When we meet such a person, we project our internalized image onto him or her. This is why, when we fall in love, we often say, "I feel as if I've known you all my life." This is also why we are so often surprised after the infatuation is over. It's as if we didn't see the person, but only the projection of our own romantic image.

The person who fits our romantic image is also the person who is best able to help us work through our childhood traumas. For example, although it would seem to make sense for the woman whose father was unfaithful to look for a man who is sure to be faithful, this is not what usually happens. In fact, a woman like this most often falls in love with playboys just like her father—not because she needs to repeat her childhood trauma, but because only a man who resembles her father can give her what she didn't get from her father. The paradox is that she marries such a man because he resembles her father, yet what she wants most desperately is for him *not* to behave the way her father did. She wants him—a sexy, flirtatious man, with women always flocking around him—to be a faithful husband and give her the security she didn't get as a child. Even if this does not happen, by repeating her childhood trauma as an adult with some measure of control over her life, she can—and often does—achieve a healing effect.

The effects of a romantic image are not always that direct and straightforward. A boy who witnessed his mother's unfaithfulness to his father may choose to marry a woman whose most redeeming quality is her faithfulness. How will he then be able to "work" on his childhood trauma? By suspecting his faithful wife of infidelity. The repeated proof of her innocence helps heal his wound. It shows that, unlike his father, he is number one with his wife.

Because the person we choose to fall in love with has such an important influence on our inner life, the discovery of such a person is a powerful event. When we fall in love and our love is reciprocated, we are completely happy. We are sure we have found our "match made in heaven." Loneliness is gone. Love gives our whole life a sense of meaning.

When someone gives meaning to our entire life, the threat of losing that person can be devastating. Indeed, the results of a recent study on love and jealousy show that people who invest such existential significance in love relationships tend to be particularly sensitive to the threat of their loss.[19]

Most of us have some unresolved conflicts we carry from our childhood. Some of us have more of them, some have fewer. For some of us these conflicts are serious and problematic, for others they are less so. We experience these conflicts as vulnerabilities, insecurities, or fears. When we fall in love and our love is reciprocated, these vulnerabilities, fears, and insecurities seem to vanish. We are loved despite our imperfections. We feel whole, we feel safe. But when this love is threatened, the fears and insecurities that we thought had gone forever come back full force. If this person whom we love—the person who we thought loved us despite our flaws—is going to leave us for another, then there is no hope for us, ever! We no longer feel secure even in those things we previously loved in ourselves. As glowing as the love was, so dark is the shadow of its possible loss.

As we will see in the next chapter, even those whose upbringing was loving and relatively problem-free, and who are burdened by few unresolved conflicts, respond to the threat or the actual loss of love in a similar way. Their response, however, is likely to be appropriate, and proportionate to the situation.

Since these people had less-serious childhood traumas to deal with, their romantic image is based on more-positive traits of their primary caretakers, and on the experiences of love they either had themselves or observed between their parents. When they meet someone who fits that internalized romantic image, they too fall in love and feel that they've known the person all their lives. But instead of feeling that they are loved despite all their flaws, they feel loved for the things they love in themselves.

These people are not as desperately dependent on this love as is someone who is trying to work through a childhood trauma; they are less likely to perceive a threat when none exists, and an actual threat seems less overwhelming to them. They too respond with jealousy, however, when a third person threatens a romantic relationship for which they care deeply.

If even well-adjusted people who had a happy childhood experience jealousy, then we can assume that *everyone* experiences jealousy at some point in life. This seems a logical conclusion considering the origins of jealousy discussed earlier. All of us were infants once, and as a result we all carry certain vulnerabilities and fears. As loving as our parents may have been, we all were left hungry at times and thus had an opportunity to feel fear of abandonment. Similarly, at one time or another we all have had to compete for the exclusive love of a parent or a caretaker, and have lost. Since these experiences are universal, say psychologists like Freud, then jealousy is universal.

Jealousy need not be the green-eyed monster that destroys people and relationships. Recognizing it as the shadow of love gives couples an opportunity to examine two important questions:

- What is the essence of your love? What was it that attracted you to each other initially, and what is the most important thing the relationship has given each one of you?

- What is the shadow that your love casts when threatened? What is the threat or the loss that the jealous person is responding to? Even if the jealousy is not grounded in reality, what is it focused on: a loss of love? of face? of self-worth?[20]

Jealousy has been described as an eruption that can be transcended only through awareness. As we move with awareness into the core of our jealousy, we discover ungrounded expectations, projections, envy, loss of self-esteem, and infantile fears and insecurities.[21]

These are not "nice" discoveries. In fact, they may be so unpleasant that some people will try hard to avoid them. Unfortunately, avoiding a problem and even suppressing it from our consciousness doesn't make it go away. To solve a jealousy problem, a much more effective approach is an open and honest examination of the issues involved. Such an examination can do more than help relieve the jealous person's perceived threat. It can also help enhance the relationship and deepen both mates' commitment to each other. The next chapter offers an opportunity for just this kind of examination.

Are You a Jealous Person?

Thou tyrant, tyrant jealousy. Thou tyrant of the mind.

—JOHN DRYDEN, THE SONG OF JEALOUSY

Are you a jealous person? When I asked this question of 728 people in three different studies, slightly more than half (54 percent) answered "Yes, I am a jealous person." Close to half (46 percent) answered "No, I am not a jealous person."[1]

Nearly all of the people who described themselves as not jealous have experienced jealousy at some point in their lives. Furthermore, their experiences were rather similar to those of the people who described themselves as jealous. But as we shall see, the difference in self-perception between people who define themselves as "a jealous person" and those who don't has far-reaching implications for coping.

THE EXPERIENCE OF JEALOUSY

Try to recall the event that produced your most extreme jealousy. Even if this is difficult, recall the event with as much vividness and as many details as possible. What related incidents preceded it? What was your relationship like prior to it? Where and when did it take place? What was the trigger? Who was the interloper? When it happened, how did your mate look? How did you feel? What did you think? Ideally, you should recall enough details to be able to reproduce the event on stage or on a movie screen.

Once you have the event firmly in your memory, try to recall how intensely you experienced each of the following physical, emotional, and cognitive (thought-related) components of jealousy. Did you experience the particular component very intensely, moderately, or not at all?

If you are like the 728 people who answered the questionnaire, you probably experienced many of these components of jealousy to some extent, and experienced those at the top of each list more intensely than those at the bottom. If you experienced all the items in the list very intensely, or didn't experience any at all, you belong to that small minority that is either "abnormally jealous" or "abnormally not jealous." Abnormal, as noted in chapter one, doesn't mean pathological, but outside the middle range where the majority of responses fall. What to do about it depends on you. If the intensity of your jealousy is such that you find it difficult to handle, and if the techniques recommended in this book are not enough, you may want to consider professional help.

It is important to note that the experience of jealousy reported by people who described themselves both as "jealous" and as "not jealous" was similar; the only difference was in intensity. Those who described themselves as "a jealous person" reported experiencing feelings of pain, grief, inferiority, aggression, and resentment "intensely," while those who described themselves as "not jealous" reported experiencing them "moderately." In all other cases the differences between the two groups were even smaller. This indicates that despite its complexity, jealousy has some universal and identifiable features.

COMPONENTS OF JEALOUSY

	INTENSITY		
	Very intense	Moderate	Not at all
PHYSICAL COMPONENTS:			
emptiness in stomach	———	———	———
trouble falling or staying asleep	———	———	———
nervousness and shakiness	———	———	———
heart beating fast	———	———	———
loss of appetite	———	———	———
hands sweaty or trembling	———	———	———
blood rushing to head	———	———	———
feeling faint	———	———	———
EMOTIONAL COMPONENTS:			
grief	———	———	———
pain	———	———	———
aggression	———	———	———
rage	———	———	———
helplessness	———	———	———
envy	———	———	———
fear	———	———	———
humiliation	———	———	———
COGNITIVE COMPONENTS:			
thoughts about your inferiority	———	———	———
self-pity	———	———	———
self-blame	———	———	———
possessiveness	———	———	———
resentment	———	———	———
thoughts about being excluded	———	———	———
thoughts about revenge	———	———	———
defeatist thoughts	———	———	———

SITUATIONS THAT TRIGGER JEALOUSY

You probably would not be surprised to discover that the intensity of our experience with jealousy is related to the circumstances in which it is aroused. The following situations were presented to the people who participated in my research. All of them were real situations that happened to real people. How much jealousy would you experience when . . .

- during a party, your mate is flirtatious and spends a great deal of time dancing intimately and behaving provocatively with someone else?

- your mate spends a great deal of time during a party dancing with someone else?

- your mate spends a great deal of time during a party talking to someone else?

- you are at a party and your mate disappears for a long period of time?

- you are at a party, and for a brief time you realize you don't know where your mate is?

- your phone rings and the caller either says, "Sorry, wrong number," or simply hangs up?

- you call your mate and the line is busy?

If you are like the others who responded, you would be most jealous in the first situation—when your mate is behaving provocatively. You would not feel jealous in the last three situations—when the phone is busy, someone hangs up on you, or you don't know where your mate is during a party. If these last situations cause you jealousy, you are "abnormally" jealous. This can be a temporary condition caused by the recent discovery of an affair or a more permanent condition. If the first situation doesn't cause you jealousy, you are "abnormally" non-jealous.

The majority of people who answered this question felt jealous even in situations less extreme than having their mate dance intimately with someone else; for many, such behavior is a good enough reason to get out of the relationship, not just the party. Seeing one's mate spend a lot of time during a party dancing with someone else ("only because s/he is such a wonderful dancer, and for no other reason") is enough to make most people jealous. The same goes for seeing one's mate spend a great deal of time during a party talking to someone else ("only because he or she is working in the same company and it's good politics"). If you find yourself in such a situation, and your mate "can't understand" why you are making such a big fuss over an "innocent" dance or conversation, you can comfort yourself (and enlighten your mate) with the knowledge that most people would have responded the same way. In other words, you are not "abnormally" jealous.

Let us examine some other common jealousy triggers.

Would you (or do you) experience jealousy when your mate . . .

- has a lover?

- has an intimate friend who is single and available?

- has an intimate friend?

- is associating with single available people?

- expresses appreciation and interest in a casual acquaintance?

- expresses appreciation of an attractive stranger passing by?

- expresses admiration of a film or television star?

For most people, jealousy is most likely when their mate has an affair. For good reason—research suggests that the majority of marriages in which there is an affair end in divorce.[2] An affair is a major threat to an intimate relationship, and the jealousy it triggers reflects that. Appreciation of a movie star, however, doesn't trigger jealousy in most people. If you are jealous even in such a situation, you are "abnormally" jealous. If you are not jealous even when your mate has a lover, you either no longer value the relationship or are "abnormally" non-jealous.

Clearly, the situation most likely to produce jealousy is one's mate having a lover. But it turns out that there are variations even here. How much jealousy would you experience when . . .

- your mate announces he or she has fallen in love with someone else and is thinking about leaving you?

- your mate has a serious, long-term love affair?

- your mate has an affair, but assures you it is a result of his or her need for variety and in no way affects your relationship?

- your mate is open to, and frequently has, casual sexual experiences?

- you discover that your mate recently had a casual "one-night stand"?

- you discover that your mate had a love affair many years ago, when the two of you were already a couple?

- you discover that your mate had a love affair many years ago, before the two of you were a couple?

- you discover that your mate had a love affair many years ago, when the two of you were already a couple, with a person who is now deceased?

- you discover that your mate had a love affair many years ago, before the two of you were a couple, with a person who is now deceased?

All the people who answered this question described the most intense jealousy in response to their mate announcing that he or she has fallen in love with another person and is leaving them. This is the nightmare that triggers the most intense jealousy, even in situations that don't really pose this kind of threat. The reason is obvious: this situation represents the worst possible threat to a valued love relationship—its unwanted, unexpected, and painful end.

In one of my workshops, a woman told what happened when she found herself in this exact situation.

> My husband came home one night looking very grim. When I asked him what the problem was, he said he had fallen in love with another woman, that he had been having an affair with her for a while, and had finally decided to leave me and go live with her. I went wild. I jumped at him and started hitting his face with my bare hands. He is much bigger and stronger than I am, but there was no way he could stop me. I didn't stop until his face was covered with blood.

Years after the incident, she was still not over it. She shook and sobbed when she described it in the workshop, still unable to comprehend how she, a calm, sane, nonviolent person, could have done what she did. Professionals, however, know that the situation she was in is the most likely to produce violence. The person who is left for another is pushed against the wall without having any recourse to prevent the impending catastrophe. The violence is a response to the helpless frustration, pain, rage, and despair. (We will return to this point in chapter eight, during the discussion of the relationship between romantic jealousy and violence.)

For most people questioned, the idea of their mate leaving them for another was almost too much even to contemplate. Other situations involving a current affair—even a casual one-night stand—also caused great jealousy. On the other hand, an affair that happened many years ago, especially if it happened before they were a couple, caused little or no jealousy.

The reason? This kind of an affair no longer poses a threat to the relationship. On the rare occasions when it does—as in the case of the wife who doesn't stop telling her new husband how wonderful her late husband was—it is likely to trigger jealousy. This is true despite the fact that the "other person" no longer presents a "real" threat to the relationship.

A past relationship can cause a "perceived" threat even without such an obvious provocation. A woman described her jealousy when seeing her husband's ex-wife for the first time:

> We were sitting in the football stadium waiting for the game to start when my husband said, "There's Meg," and pointed to a woman who sat across the aisle from us. I felt the blood rush to my head and thought I was going to faint. The fact that they had a terrible divorce that happened before my time didn't matter. All I could think about was that they were high-school sweethearts, something we could never be, and that he was madly in love with her in those early days.

Even an affair that happened many years ago with a person who is now deceased can occasionally cause jealousy, despite the obvious fact that this person can't possibly present a real threat, because the dead person poses a threat to the quality of the relationship.

A powerful example of such a situation is described in James Joyce's short story "The Dead."[3] After a lavish dinner party, Gabriel is feeling amorous toward his wife, Gretta. But she is distracted; a song played at the party reminded her of a young man she knew in her youth. Gabriel, who wants to get her out of her strange mood so they can make love, is feeling a twinge of jealousy:

> He tried to keep up his tone of cold interrogation but his voice when he spoke was humble and indifferent.
> —I suppose you were in love with this Michael Fury, Gretta, he said.

—I was great with him at that time, she said.

Her voice was veiled and sad. Gabriel, feeling now how vain it would be to try to lead her with what he had purposed caressed one of her hands and said also sadly:

—And what did he die of so young, Gretta? Consumption, was it?

—I think he died for me, she answered.

A vague terror seized Gabriel at this answer as if, at that hour when he had hoped to triumph, some impalpable and vindictive being was coming against him, gathering forces against him in its vague world. But he shook himself free of it with an effort of reason and continued to caress her hand.

Gabriel's reason tells him that he has nothing to worry about. Yet he knows full well that the dead Fury has defeated him in the battle for Gretta's love.

Just as a past relationship can still present a threat, embarrassing circumstances in which an affair is discovered can pose an additional threat not only to the relationship itself, but also to the image that the couple presents to other people.

How much jealousy would you experience in each one of the following situations: no jealousy at all? moderate jealousy? extreme jealousy? Once again, these are all situations that actually happened to people.

You discover that your mate has a love affair and . . .

- your mate is extremely indiscreet about it, a scandal erupts in the middle of a big party, you are cast in the role of the betrayed lover, and are expected to respond?

- your mate is extremely indiscreet about it, a scandal erupts, you are cast in the role of the betrayed lover, and hear about it when you are alone?

- everyone else but you has known about it for a long time, but no one has said anything?

- everyone knows about it?

- only you and a few close and trusted friends know about it?

- your mate is very discreet, the three of you are the only ones who know about it, and they know that you know?

- your mate is very discreet, no one else knows about it, and your mate doesn't know that you know?

Based on the responses of those surveyed, the worst trigger of jealousy is not the situation in which a scandal erupts in the middle of a big party. A woman who found herself in this situation describes the experience:

> I wanted to leave the party, and since I couldn't find my husband, I decided to leave alone. I went to get my coat, together with some other guests who were ready to leave. I opened the bedroom where the coats were put, with the other guests right behind me. There, on top of all the coats, was my husband fucking this slut he had been flirting with all night long. . . . I felt the blood running out of my face, and my knees started wobbling. But I knew everyone was looking at me and waiting for me to respond. So I just said, "Good night, dear. I'm going home," and left.

Behaving in this cool manner gave her a measure of control in the situation. This and other people's similar experiences suggest that in public, people are more likely to minimize their jealous responses. The courageous face that they put on helps them control their reactions, at least to some extent, and manage their jealousy better than they would otherwise.

When you discover that your mate had an affair for years that everyone else but you knew about, you don't have the comfort such a public performance can provide. A man who had gone through this devastating experience describes it:

> We were married thirty-seven years and I was sure we had a wonderful marriage. One day I came home early and discovered my wife in the bedroom with a man I considered one of my best friends. I was devastated. Then I discovered to my horror that this had been going on for years and all our friends and acquaintances knew about it, but no one had said anything. I felt betrayed and humiliated. I could imagine them talking behind my back, laughing. . . .

The man felt that the situation would have been easier to bear if only the three people involved knew about it.

One could argue that an affair that has gone on for years doesn't pose much of a threat to a marriage, especially if everyone, including the unfaithful mate, has tried to protect the marriage by keeping the affair a secret. Although the discovery of "the slut on the coats" may be more embarrassing at the time, a long-term secret affair presents a far more serious threat. Both incidents, however, undermine the foundation of trust in the marriage.

Why is our response to such "public" situations so extreme? The reason is that these situations threaten the public image of our relationship. We are socialized to believe that people fall in love with their "match made in heaven" and live with that one and only, "happily ever after." Part of the pain associated with the discovery that our mate is having an affair comes from the realization that we can no longer apply this idealized image to ourselves. When other people know about the affair, the image of our relationship in the public eye is destroyed. Their knowledge takes away our option of pretending to the world that "everything's fine."

PEOPLE WHO TRIGGER JEALOUSY

Thus far we've focused on the different situations that can trigger jealousy. But the effects these situations can have depend on the people involved. It is possible, for example, that the woman who discovered her husband on the pile of coats was able to keep her cool because she didn't consider the other woman a serious rival, but instead a worthless "slut." The man who discovered his wife with his best friend, on the other hand, not only had a serious rival, but the added pain of betrayal by the two people he most loved and trusted.

Who are the people who most elicit *your* jealousy? Try to imagine how much jealousy you would experience if you found out that your mate has been having an affair with . . .

- someone you don't know personally and of whom you have a low opinion?

- someone you don't know personally and know nothing about?

- someone you don't know personally and of whom you think very highly?

- someone you know personally and distrust?

- someone you know personally and find very similar to you?

- someone you know personally, trust, and consider a friend?

- a family member?

- your best friend and confidant?

- someone you know personally and are envious of?

Most people who answered this question said that a person they had a low opinion of and didn't know personally triggered the least amount of jealousy. The "slut on the coats" is one example. A "hostess" in a hotel bar with whom your husband had a one-night stand is another example. Having a low opinion about these kinds of people as well as not knowing them personally are the two elements that help reduce the threat that involvement with them implies for the partner who was betrayed. It's important to note, however, that even this kind of "low-life," unknown person elicits some jealousy.

The most jealousy-provoking "third person" for all respondents was someone they knew personally and whom they envied: someone they found brighter or more attractive than themselves, or else more successful in exactly the ways they would have liked to be. Your mate's affair with this type of person produces the greatest perceived threat because if you think the person is better than you, why shouldn't your mate?

HOW JEALOUS ARE YOU?

After considering these different situations and the possible responses to them, along with your own probable response, how jealous do you think you are? Not at all? Moderately? Extremely? Almost all of my respondents described themselves as moderately jealous. The few people who described themselves as either extremely jealous or not jealous at all were those we would describe as either abnormally jealous or abnormally non-jealous.

Earlier in this chapter I asked you to recall your most intense experience of jealousy. Going back to this experience again, how long did it last? Minutes? Days? Months? Years? Most people report that an extreme experience of jealousy lasts for days. In a few cases, when the experience is especially traumatic or the person is especially prone to jealousy, it can last for months and even years without losing its intensity.

Jane, an attractive and elegant woman, was happily married for thirty-five years until she discovered that her husband had had an affair with a younger woman he knew through his job. Seven months after she discovered the affair—long after her husband had ended it—Jane was still unable to get over her intense jealousy. She couldn't stop thinking about the other woman and started spying on her. The first time she was able to check her out was at an opera matinee. Seeing her rival in an outrageous backless dress sent Jane into a decline for weeks.

Finding out that your husband of thirty-five years, a man you considered your best and most trusted friend, has betrayed you is no doubt a justifiable cause for extreme jealousy. "Abnormally jealous" people, however, experience extreme jealousy in response to far milder triggers, and far more often. "Abnormal jealousy" may stem from choosing a mate who is likely to make you jealous (because of your mate's personality, your own lack of confidence, or the dynamic of your interaction). It can be caused by imagining threats even where there are none: "Every attractive woman I see walking down the street is a threat. Thinking about the women he is meeting in his work can make me insane with jealousy."

How often do you experience extreme jealousy? Never? Rarely? Occasionally? Often? All the time? For most people, intense jealousy is a rare experience. People who are "abnormally non-jealous" never experience intense jealousy. Some manage to protect themselves by avoiding involvement with someone they are passionately in love with. Others do it simply by "not seeing," or ignoring, the threat.

Jealousy can be an extremely painful experience, but making it stop is not easy. Question: Can you make yourself stop being (feeling, thinking, acting) jealous? Definitely? To a certain degree? Definitely not? Most people are able to stop themselves from being jealous— but only to a certain degree. When one is in the midst of a jealousy crisis it is especially hard. Chapter nine provides suggestions on how this can be done.

Jane said she couldn't stop herself from being jealous. No matter how hard she tried, she couldn't stop thinking about the other woman—the way she looked at the theater in her backless dress, the way she sounded on the answering machine ("so unnaturally cheerful"), the way she must have behaved with Jane's husband (free, daring). Jane couldn't stop going over again and again in her mind every detail of the affair.

Only through therapy was Jane able to overcome her intense jealousy. She came to realize that she played a role in enabling the affair by being away and unavailable when her husband needed support and assurance of his manhood. She also realized that her husband's affair was only part of the reason for her obsession with the other woman. Her thoughts and feelings were related to her own sense of disappointment with the choices she made in her life. The other woman had a successful career and had achieved many of the things Jane herself wanted. As a free and independent woman, her rival could afford to come to the theater dressed in an outrageously sexy outfit. She could also do other things (such as have affairs) that Jane herself, as a married woman and homemaker with many family responsibilities, could never afford to do. Jane's own life was devoted to her husband and children. She never had time for her own interests, but her devotion seemed to go unappreciated. Once Jane understood the roots of her obsession, she could direct the energy that fueled her jealousy into discovering ways to find meaning in her own life.

THE JEALOUS PERSON AND THE JEALOUSY-PRODUCING RELATIONSHIP

Until her husband's affair, Jane had never considered herself a jealous person. The affair made her change her self-perception. She "discovered" she was jealous. Question: Has your mate ever been unfaithful to you? If your answer is yes, chances are that you too describe yourself as jealous. Indeed, the more unfaithful people's mates are— in other words, the more they experience jealousy-producing situations—the more likely they are to describe themselves as jealous.

Unfaithfulness damages one's sense of security in a relationship. It makes one realize that even a good marriage can be threatened. And security, it turns out, buffers against jealousy. The more insecure you feel in your relationship, the more likely you are to be jealous.

Another question: How long do you expect the relationship to last? The longer you expect your relationship to last, the less likely you are to be jealous. It is revealing that the length of the relationship in and of itself was not at all related to jealousy—both young and old couples (in terms of the time they had been together) described themselves as jealous, and both young and old couples described themselves as non-jealous. The length that the relationship was *expected* to last, which is a measure of security and commitment, did correlate with jealousy: the more commitment, the less jealousy.

Commitment to a relationship doesn't develop in a vacuum. It's a reflection of the way a couple feels about each other and about the relationship. The more satisfied people are with their mate and the relationship, the data show, the less jealous they tend to be. Question: How do you feel about your mate and the relationship in general? The more satisfied you feel, the less jealous you are likely to be.

Does jealousy cause the dissatisfaction, or does dissatisfaction cause the jealousy? It can be argued that jealousy, with its ensuing drama, conflict, and unhappiness, is the cause of the insecurity and the dissatisfaction. On the other hand, it can be argued that unstable, insecure, and unsatisfactory relationships make people more sensitive to threats and consequently more likely to be jealous. One interpretation focuses on the jealous person, the other on the jealous relationship. Which is correct? In the next two chapters both perspectives are elaborated, and we will see that both are correct.

As noted in chapter one, people don't just fall into a certain kind of a relationship. They play an active role in shaping their relationships as well as their problems. Some create relationships in which jealousy is not very likely to be triggered. Others choose mates and take part in building relationships in which jealousy is likely to be triggered often. Once a relationship is established, both mates have to collude to keep a jealousy problem going.

Do you believe in monogamy for yourself? Most people, it turns out, believe that monogamy is the best type of relationship. This is true even for those who don't practice it.[4] While people who insist on exclusivity in their intimate relationships tend to be more jealous than people for whom exclusivity is not that important, monogamous people tend to seek like-minded mates and consequently have relationships in which their jealousy is not likely to be triggered.[5]

If the connection between belief in monogamy and jealousy doesn't seem obvious, let me point to a much more obvious connection, between what we do to others and what we fear they might do to us. Have you ever been unfaithful to your mate sexually? (Never? Once? Very few times? Many times? All the time?) The more unfaithful you yourself have been, the more jealous you are likely to be. The more lies you have told, the more attuned your ear becomes to lies, at times hearing them even when they have not been spoken. The more schemes you have pulled off to be able to get together with your lover, the more suspicious you become of situations that might be such schemes.

"Projected jealousy" derives either from one's own actual unfaithfulness or from impulses toward it that have been repressed.[6] Have you ever fantasized about sexual involvement with someone other than your mate? Most people have at times had such fantasies. What is revealing is that those who fantasize most often about being with someone else are also those who describe themselves as most jealous.[7] Since they themselves are attracted to other people and possibly have thoughts about wild love affairs, they naturally assume that their mate has such thoughts, too. Just as they think at times about eloping with a passionate lover, they are sure that their mate has such thoughts too. Projecting their own impulses onto their mate makes them jealous.

Jealousy can be projected onto other people besides one's mate. Indeed, individuals who describe themselves as jealous tend to think that more people in the general population are jealous than do people who describe themselves as not jealous.

Furthermore, people who describe themselves as jealous prefer their mates to be jealous, and in general tend to see jealousy as a more positive personality characteristic. They are likely, for example, to see jealousy as a normal reaction that accompanies love, or as an instinctive reaction to a threat. They are less likely to see it as a defect.

It is possible that people who see themselves as less likely to control their jealous response need to believe that jealousy is not such a negative trait. The need to justify their own jealousy is so great that it keeps them from seeing the negative effect jealousy can have on intimate relationships. In fact, the more people described themselves as jealous, the more likely they were to have intimate relationships end because of their jealousy.

IS THERE A "JEALOUS PERSONALITY"?

People who have several intimate relationships end because of their jealousy usually describe themselves as having been jealous from a very young age. This has made some personality psychologists argue that such a thing as a "jealous personality" actually exists. The differences between people in the propensity to respond with jealousy, they claim, are not only valid and reliable over time—they even run in families.[8]

My own experience leads me to believe that labeling certain individuals as having "jealous personalities" doesn't do them any good, and can even be damaging. It is much more helpful to look at people as having different predispositions to jealousy. As we saw in chapter one, jealousy originates very early in life. It is triggered again whenever there is a threat of losing a valued love relationship. People whom personality psychologists label "jealous personalities" tend to have had a more traumatic experience associated with unfaithfulness, jealousy, or loss of love in their childhood, and consequently they have more of a predisposition to respond with jealousy in later stages of their lives.

How jealous were *you* during the earlier stages of your life?

- during childhood?
- during adolescence?
- during young adulthood?
- during adulthood?

Of the people I surveyed, the majority reported being most jealous during adolescence. It is possible that during this stormy period all experiences, including jealousy, are more intense. It is also possible that adolescents are most likely to fear losing their beloved because a lack of mutual commitment characterizes relationships at that stage of life.

People report decreasing levels of jealousy after adolescence (less during young adulthood than during adolescence, and less during advanced adulthood than during young adulthood). There are several ways to interpret these findings. It is possible that over time, people develop better coping strategies for dealing with their jealousy. It is possible that, with experience, people avoid relationships in which their jealousy is likely to be triggered often. It is possible that with age most people become more sure of themselves and thus are less likely to be threatened by certain jealousy triggers.[9] It is possible that over time most couples develop a sense of security in their relationship and thus are less likely to view jealousy-triggering incidents as serious threats. And it is possible that the growing openness of society in general and the institution of marriage in particular has caused a general decline in jealousy.[10]

The fact that people who were more jealous than others in childhood also tend to be more jealous than others later in life supports the notion that people have stable predispositions for jealousy. Such a predisposition is influenced by one's family constellation. Developmental psychologists see roots of adult jealousy in sibling rivalry. The psychological pattern of reacting to jealousy triggers in later life, they argue, is determined by the child's first experiences of jealousy when his desire for exclusivity with his mother is threatened by a sibling.[11]

In my research, the more older brothers people had, the more jealous they were likely to be. The more younger brothers they had, the less jealous they were likely to be. The number of sisters was not related to jealousy. This suggests that it's not the presence of a sibling in and of itself that triggers jealousy. The trigger has to be a sibling who is in a position of advantage (an older brother has both an age and a sex advantage in our patriarchal society). Adult jealousy is influenced by childhood envy of the older sibling's advantage and by the childhood jealousy triangle with one's sibling and mother.[12]

If we indeed have a predisposition to jealousy, we can expect people around us to notice it at some point. And they do. Do most people who know you well consider you a jealous person? The more jealous you are (or consider yourself to be), the more likely it is that people who know you well will consider you jealous. It's hard to hide the torment of jealousy.

If jealousy is hard to hide from people who know us, it is doubly hard to hide from our intimate partners. They are the ones most likely both to trigger and to witness our jealousy. People are less likely to exhibit jealous behavior in public or in casual relationships, and more likely to exhibit it in intimate relationships. One obvious reason is that jealousy is more likely to be triggered in an intimate relationship than in a less valued casual relationship. Another reason is that jealous behavior is generally considered socially unacceptable in our culture.

Do people with whom you've had an intimate relationship consider you jealous? The more jealous you feel, the more likely it is that your mate will consider you jealous (far more so than other people who know you well). The reason seems simple enough: You are jealous, and your mate can't help but notice it and "tell it like it is." Correct? Not necessarily. It is also possible that the more your mate considers you jealous, the more likely you are to consider yourself jealous. Your mate may call you jealous for many reasons, only one of which is that you truly are jealous. Another reason, as we saw, is that he or she either has fantasies about sexual involvements with other people or has real affairs, and makes you think you're excessively jealous to excuse his or her own behavior.

When I asked people what they thought caused jealousy, one of the two most common responses was "personal insecurity." Some people, as well as some researchers, believe that jealousy is a part of a person's personality, that those who are insecure in general are also insecure about their intimate relationships, and that insecurity manifests itself in jealousy.[13]

Sounds straightforward enough, doesn't it? Yet the second-top-rated explanation was, "Jealousy is the result of being afraid of losing face." Third in the ranking was, "Jealousy is the result of weakness in the relationship." Fourth, "Jealousy is the result of feeling excluded and left out."

Being afraid of losing face, feeling excluded, and having problems in the relationship are not stable parts of a person's personality. Rather, they are related to the dynamics of a particular relationship or situation.

This brings us back to the notion (presented in chapter one) that jealousy always results from an interaction between a certain predisposition and a certain triggering event. The predisposition for jealousy is related to other personality characteristics such as insecurity. Whether or not the predisposition will reveal itself depends on the relationship itself—on problems in the relationship and involvements with other people as well as on the trust and sense of security that mates have in the relationship.

As it turns out, whether or not the predisposition to jealousy will reveal itself also depends in part on your current mental state, which may have nothing to do with jealousy. How would you describe your mental condition? The better your mental state, the less likely you are to suffer the torments of jealousy. Of course, if you're in the midst of a jealousy crisis, it won't have the best effect on your mental state.[14]

How would you describe your physical condition? Poor physical condition, to a lesser degree than mental condition, is also associated with a greater tendency to experience jealousy. The better your physical condition in general, the less likely you are to suffer from jealousy.

Unlike the findings that told us about the early antecedents of jealousy in our childhood, about which we can do little, the findings about the correlation between our mental and physical condition and jealousy can be translated to specific recommendations.

Because chapter nine is devoted to various techniques for coping with jealousy, at this point simply remember that if you are frequently tormented by jealousy, one way to prepare to deal with the problem is to improve your general mental and physical health. You can improve your mental health by going to therapy, by learning relaxation techniques, or by doing things that make you feel good. When you feel better psychologically, you are likely to suffer less from your jealousy, even if other factors contributing to the situation haven't changed. Similarly, if you get into better physical shape, your ability to cope with all the stresses in your life, including jealousy, will improve. If you enjoy dancing, for example, put on music with a good beat and dance for fifteen minutes each day, especially when you're depressed. It will have a positive effect both on your mood and your physical condition—which is likely to help you handle your jealousy more effectively.

A Word about Mild Jealousy

Thus far we've focused on extreme jealousy, the kind that causes tremendous pain and rage. Jealousy is not always that extreme; it comes in milder forms, too. How often do you experience mild jealousy? When you experience mild jealousy, how long does it usually last?

Most people experience mild jealousy far more often than extreme jealousy ("every time I see him flirting with an attractive woman"; "every time she expresses admiration of another man"). The experience lasts a far shorter time (seconds as compared to days), and is much less painful and traumatic. In fact, some people even say that this type of jealousy adds spice to their relationships. A woman who describes herself as happily married explains:

> When I see him flirting with an attractive woman, his eyes shining and his whole face radiating, it reminds me of what a handsome man he is. I feel a twinge of jealousy, but it's not an unpleasant feeling. I can even say that I rather like it. It brings excitement into our relationship, a tease. It makes sure I don't take him for granted. . . . What makes me so cool about it is the fact that I feel secure in his love, and know that when we go home we are going to talk about that other woman, and laugh about it all.

Jealousy is like a hot pepper. Use it mildly, and you add spice to the relationship. Use too much of it and it can burn. Indeed, in one of my studies of marriage burnout I discovered that the more people experienced intense jealousy in their relationship, the more likely they were to burn out.[15] The reverse seems true of mild jealousy.

THE "JEALOUS PERSON" AND THE "NON-JEALOUS PERSON"

Now let's return to the issue of self-definition as jealous or non-jealous. People who describe themselves as jealous also describe themselves as suffering from jealousy more intensely and more frequently than do people who describe themselves as not jealous. The former group's jealousy is more easily triggered and it lasts longer. They consider their jealousy more of a problem and report experiencing more jealousy during all stages of their lives. Other people help validate their perception of themselves as jealous. People who know them well, and people with whom they have had intimate relationships, consider them jealous.

Yet, as we have seen throughout this chapter, people who describe themselves as not jealous also experience jealousy when an important relationship is threatened. Furthermore, they experience it with the same physical, emotional, and cognitive symptoms as people who define themselves as jealous. They experience it in response to similar triggers in a similar rank order: an affair with someone they know and envy triggers the most jealousy, and an affair with someone they don't know and whom they have a low opinion triggers the least.

While the triggers and the actual experience of jealousy are similar in both groups, there are a number of differences between the relationships of self-described jealous and non-jealous people. Non-jealous people feel more secure in their relationship, expect it to last longer, and are more certain that their mates have never been unfaithful to them. By contrast, it appears that even when self-described jealous people have good reasons to feel insecure in their relationships and to experience jealousy, some perceive their jealousy as a personality trait. They don't say, "I am experiencing this jealousy because my husband of thirty-five years has had an affair." They say instead, "I am experiencing this intense jealousy because I am a jealous person." One response implies that the problem is a result of the situation and thus can be changed. The other implies that the problem is built into the individual's personality, and thus is much harder to change.

Given the great agreement among people about what triggers jealousy and how it is experienced, it's amazing that some choose to explain it as a personality trait about which there is little they can do, while others explain it in the context of a particular situation about which they can do quite a lot.

It is possible, of course, that some people view their jealousy as a personality trait *because* it explains behaviors that would otherwise be unacceptable. Sexual jealousy is widely accepted as grounds for moral indignation in our culture. "Feeling jealous" serves as an explanation or excuse for a wide range of hostile, bitter, and violent actions. Without the legitimizing context of jealousy, these same actions would be taken as symptoms of severe pathology and derangement.[16]

Not surprisingly, people who describe themselves as jealous also tend to attribute more positive effects to jealousy and see it more positively overall than do people who describe themselves as not jealous. For example, jealous people tend to believe that jealousy teaches us not to take each other for granted, makes relationships last longer, induces commitment, brings excitement to listless relationships, makes one's partner look more desirable, and makes one examine one's relationship.

But although being "a jealous person" can be effective in excusing certain unacceptable behaviors ("That's why I don't want you to dance with anyone else"; "That's why I had a temper tantrum"), in the long run it causes more problems than it solves. The reason: it greatly reduces our freedom to act and our ability to cope directly with jealousy triggers.

Having said all that, let me return to the question presented at the beginning of this chapter: Are you a jealous person?

Whatever your answer, you'll probably be interested in learning about the unconscious roots of your jealousy—the subject of the next chapter.

3

THE UNCONSCIOUS ROOTS
OF ROMANTIC JEALOUSY

No one who . . . conjures up the most evil of those
half-tamed demons that inhibit the human breast,
and seeks to wrestle with them, can expect to come
through the struggle unscathed.

—SIGMUND FREUD, "DORA" IN COMPLETE
PSYCHOLOGICAL WORKS, 1905

JEALOUSY IS NORMAL AND UNIVERSAL

According to Freud, jealousy is universal not because it is innate, but because it is inevitable. No one can escape it because it originates in painful childhood experiences we all share. These universal childhood traumas are reexperienced whenever our jealousy is evoked in adulthood.

Because everyone experiences it, jealousy is, by definition, normal. Indeed, Freud describes jealousy as "one of those affective states, like grief, that may be described as normal. If anyone appears to be without it, the inference can be justified that it has undergone severe repression and consequently plays all the greater part in his unconscious mental life."[1]

In Freud's view, if you don't experience jealousy when an important relationship is threatened, something is not altogether right about you. It is akin to not feeling grief when someone you care deeply about dies. Such a response most probably means that you are working hard to suppress your feelings or hide them from others, as well as from yourself.

Fifty-six years after the publication of Freud's work on jealousy, a psychiatrist named Emil Pinta published an article entitled "Pathological Tolerance." It describes a clinical syndrome in which a person who should be responding with jealousy does not.[2] Pinta cites several cases in which a husband or a wife accepted a sexual relationship between his or her mate and a third person.

In one case, John (age twenty-five) and Sharon (age thirty-three) were married. Michael (age seventeen), a high school dropout who was originally hired to help with chores on the farm, lived with them and had become Sharon's lover. Sharon insisted that she loved both men, and was unwilling to make a choice between them. John resented having another man in his home making love to his wife, yet was reluctant to leave or to pressure Sharon to decide between himself and Michael.

In another case, Lana (age twenty-six) was married to Jack (age thirty-two). During the year prior to her starting therapy, another woman, Marilyn (age thirty-two) lived with them in their home and shared Jack sexually. Marilyn and Jack worked during the day, leaving Lana at home to baby-sit Marilyn's two children from a previous marriage. Lana described herself as feeling "unappreciated and misunderstood" by Jack, Marilyn, and the children. Her primary reason for entering therapy was to "have the children obey me." She was aware that her relationship with Jack and Marilyn was emotionally destructive, but refused to consider leaving or insisting that Marilyn leave.

Pinta suggests that the dynamics of pathological tolerance are identical to those of pathological jealousy. We will return to the dynamics of pathological tolerance (and to the two triangles) after we examine the dynamics of pathological jealousy. For now, I think most people would agree with Pinta that in both John's and Lana's case, something is not quite "normal" about their lack of jealousy and their entire relationship.

A clinical syndrome similar to pathological tolerance is *psychological scotoma* (blindness), the inability to notice or correctly interpret situations that are obvious jealousy-triggers to virtually everyone else. An illustration of psychological scotoma that you may recall from chapter one is the husband whose wife flirts with every man around and sleeps with anyone willing and able; the husband is the only one who doesn't know and doesn't suspect. A woman who became sexually involved with a man whose wife seemed to be suffering from psychological scotoma describes the strange experience:

> We were dancing so provocatively—practically making out—that I don't think there was anyone at the party who didn't notice that something was going on. Anyone besides his wife, that is. She was chatting with her friends, smiling at us from time to time. I know she doesn't like to dance and her husband says she doesn't like sex either, so she simply doesn't see when he is making out with other women. Since he insists that he has to have sex every single day, and for her once every three months is more than enough, there's a lot for her not to see. Who knows, maybe she is relieved that someone else is doing her "dirty work."

THE PSYCHODYNAMIC APPROACH TO JEALOUSY

The psychodynamic approach emphasizes the unconscious forces operating in jealousy. It assumes that deep in our psyches we all carry drives, desires, fears, and traumatic memories of which we are not aware. Every conscious feeling is accompanied by its unconscious counterpart, which is often its opposite: we may be consciously disgusted by things to which we are unconsciously attracted; we may consciously love people we unconsciously hate.

The emphasis on innate drives and unconscious motives explains behavior that is otherwise difficult to understand, such as why some people stay with a mate who is continuously unfaithful to them, and why some people drive away a mate they love dearly with groundless jealousy. The psychodynamic approach assumes that people play an active (even if unconscious) role in creating their life circumstances as well as their love relationships. It wasn't your bad luck that landed you in a relationship with a "pathologically unfaithful" or a "pathologically jealous" mate. You chose your mate very carefully to fill that role.

Our earliest childhood memories and deprivations, most of them unconscious, have a powerful influence on the way we experience and respond to the world. Childhood experiences also have a great influence on our choice of a mate. That choice is never arbitrary. We choose a person who is best suited to fulfill emotional needs that were not fulfilled in our childhood.

When we find such a person, we project onto him or her the internal image that was shaped during our childhood. A man who saw his mother cheating on his father may, for example, project his internalized image of an unfaithful wife, which was created during the childhood trauma, onto his chaste and faithful wife.

Couples have complementary needs. Each mate chooses someone who represents a repressed part of him- or herself. A man who had to repress the emotional part of himself marries an emotional woman who had to repress the logical part of herself. Their internalized conflict becomes externalized as a marital conflict ("Why isn't he more emotional?" "Why isn't she more logical?"). Conflicts between mates, around issues of jealousy as well as all other issues, are a reenactment of inner conflicts. If, for example, infidelity is a recurring issue in your conflicts with your mate, chances are that both of you have some internal conflict about it.

Childhood experiences of jealousy do not "cause" the adult jealousy. They are re-evoked in similar situations and determine how easily and how intensely we respond to jealousy triggers. The goal of therapy is to bring the unconscious into consciousness. The therapist helps patients gain insight into the "true" causes of their jealousy by making the connection between past experiences and present problems. Once you understand the roots of your jealousy—that is, which past events are replayed in your current jealousy—and what you are gaining by holding on to it, you are considered cured.

THE ROOTS OF JEALOUSY ACCORDING TO FREUD

Freud believed it is "easy to see" that jealousy is composed of:

- grief, the pain caused by the thought of losing someone we love
- the painful realization that we can't have everything we want, even if we want it very badly and feel we deserve to have it
- feelings of enmity against the successful rival
- a greater or lesser amount of self-criticism that hold us accountable for our loss

"Although we may call it normal," he added, "this jealousy is by no means completely rational, that is, derived from the actual situation, proportionate to the real circumstances and under the complete control of the conscious ego." In other words, even in normal jealousy—the kind we all experience—there are always some irrational components. The reason is that jealousy "is rooted deep in the unconscious, and is a continuation of the earliest stirrings of the child's affective life."[3]

As you may recall from the discussion of jealousy and envy in chapter one, Freud believed that jealousy is rooted primarily in childhood events associated with the Oedipal conflict. This takes place during the phallic stage, when the child is about three. At this stage, the sex organ is becoming the child's center of interest and enjoyment. Since boys' and girls' sex organs are different, the issues they have to work through are different. According to Freud's famous dictum, "Anatomy is destiny."

Children spend most of their time with family members. Consequently, family members are their most accessible objects of love and identification. It is only natural for them to direct their first sexual feelings toward someone in the family. The sexual feelings are accompanied by enmity against the person whom the child perceives as a rival. This rivalry is the root of the Oedipal complex in boys and the Electra complex in girls.[4]

Oedipus and Electra are tragic heroes of Greek mythology. Oedipus, unbeknown to himself, killed his father and married his mother. Electra loved her father and hated her mother, who betrayed him and caused his death. To avenge her father's death, Electra persuaded her brother to kill their mother. According to Freud, every child experiences some of Oedipus and Electra's pain. The boy is "in love" with his mother; the girl is "in love" with her father. But both have a formidable rival—for the boy, his father; for the girl, her mother. The boy is afraid of his father's anger at discovering that his son covets his wife. He escapes this anxiety by identifying with his father, and becoming a man like him. The girl envies her mother's advantage, and overcomes it by identifying with the mother. The grief, the pain of loss, the powerlessness, the realization that they can't have everything they want, the enmity against a successful rival that children experience when they "lose" in this original triangle, are all engraved on their psyches, and reemerge in adulthood when they find themselves in a similar triangle.

PROJECTED AND DELUSIONAL JEALOUSY

Freud distinguished "normal" jealousy from "projected" and "delusional" jealousy—both of which he perceived as pathological.

Projected jealousy is derived either from actual infidelity, or from impulses toward infidelity which have been repressed. If you have been unfaithful, or desired someone but didn't act on it, you are likely to "project" that infidelity onto your innocent mate. You will blame your mate for the things *you* did or wanted to do, and will respond to the projected threat with jealousy.

"It is a matter of everyday experience," Freud wrote, "that fidelity, especially that degree of it required in marriage, is only maintained in the face of continual temptations." Even a person who denies these temptations in himself experiences them. How can such a person relieve his guilt over the impulse or the actual infidelity? One way is to "project his own impulses to faithlessness on to the partner to whom he owes faith. He can then justify himself with the thought that the other is not much better than himself."[5]

The jealousy that arises from such projection, says Freud, has an almost delusional character. (Delusion is a belief that persists even with no basis in reality.) Projected jealousy, however, unlike delusional jealousy, often responds well to psychodynamic therapy.

When the jealous person realizes that his jealousy is a result of his own suppressed impulses toward infidelity and that his mate is faithful, the insight is usually enough to solve the jealousy problem. In the case of delusional jealousy, the solution is not so easy.

Delusional jealousy is a form of paranoia. It too has its origin in suppressed impulses toward infidelity, but according to Freud, the object in these cases is of the same sex as the jealous person. (As we will see later, modern psychotherapists tend to disagree with Freud on this point.) Freud said that all of us are bisexual to some degree. Young children, prior to the Oedipal stage, are attracted to the same-sex parent as well as the opposite-sex parent. These feelings are repressed, but may emerge again in the form of conscious or unconscious attraction toward one's rival in adult jealousy. This kind of homosexual attraction, according to Freud, is the primary feature of delusional jealousy. In an attempt to defend himself against his unduly strong homosexual impulse, the jealous man says, in effect, "I don't love him, *she* loves him." Since the homosexual impulse produces much more anxiety than the heterosexual impulse, the defense against it is more likely to involve a serious distortion of reality.

Freud presents as an example of delusional jealousy a young man whose object of jealousy was his impeccably faithful wife. The jealousy came in attacks that lasted several days and appeared regularly on the day after he had had sex with his wife.

Freud's inference was that after satisfying the heterosexual drive, the homosexual drive that was also stimulated by the sexual act "forced an outlet for itself in the attack of jealousy."

The jealous attacks were focused on minute gestures in which his wife's "quite unconscious coquetry, unnoticed to anyone else, has betrayed itself to him." She had unintentionally touched the man sitting next to her; she had turned too much toward him, or had smiled more pleasantly than when at home with her husband.

The husband was unusually sensitive to all these manifestations of her unconscious, and knew how to interpret them. In this he was similar to people suffering from paranoia, who cannot regard anything other people do as indifferent. They too interpret every minute gesture—a person laughed to himself, looked with indifference, even spit on the ground—as directed at them personally.

Our jealous husband perceived his wife's unfaithfulness instead of his own. By paying careful attention to hers and magnifying it enormously, he was able to keep his own unfaithfulness unconscious. Similarly, the hatred that the persecuted paranoid sees in others is a reflection of his own hostile impulses toward them.

As can be expected, Freud finds the reasons for the husband's delusional jealousy in his early childhood history. The husband's youth was dominated by a strong attachment to his mother. Of her many sons he was her declared favorite and developed a marked "normal" jealousy toward her. When he got engaged, his desire for a virgin mother expressed itself in obsessive doubts about his fiancée's virginity. These doubts disappeared after their marriage. The first years of his marriage were free of jealousy. Then he became involved in a long-term affair with another woman. When the affair was over, he started experiencing jealousy again. This time it was projected jealousy, which enabled him to relieve his guilt about his own infidelity. The fact that his father had little influence in the family combined with a "humiliating homosexual trauma in early boyhood" are seen by Freud as the roots of a strong sexual attraction he felt toward his father-in-law, that eventually became a "fully formed jealous paranoia."

Most clinical psychologists working with people who have a jealousy problem agree with Freud that jealousy can vary in degree of pathology all the way from normal jealousy to delusional jealousy. They also agree with Freud that delusional jealousy is a form of paranoia, and is the hardest to treat and cure. Many do not agree, however, that delusional jealousy is primarily the result of repressed impulses toward homosexuality.

An example of the use a modern psychoanalyst is making of Freud's notions about jealousy is provided by Dr. Pinta's analysis of the dynamics of pathological tolerance.[6]

THE DYNAMICS OF PATHOLOGICAL TOLERANCE

Like pathological jealousy, pathological tolerence (those rare cases I describe in chapter one as "abnormally non-jealous") has its origin in the Oedipal conflict. In both, the individual re-creates an early family situation and unconscious Oedipal wishes. In the triangle involving John, Sharon, and Michael, John felt, at the birth of his younger brother, that he had been replaced in his mother's love. An almost identical relationship has been reenacted in his marriage, with Sharon representing his mother, and Michael his brother. In the triangle involving Lana, Jack, and Marilyn, the similarities to Lana's family history are even more striking. Jack and Marilyn work and take on the role of surrogate parents while Lana assumes a "big sister" role to Marilyn's children. In therapy, Lana said she felt just the way she used to feel with her siblings. Also, Jack was openly unfaithful to Lana, just as her father was openly unfaithful to her mother.

Another mechanism seen in pathological tolerence that Freud noted in delusional jealousy is the projection of unconscious homosexual impulses. In the first triangle, John's physical attraction to Michael was quite evident. They established a considerable intimacy, sometimes even to the exclusion of Sharon. In the second triangle, Lana had a history of homosexuality, and her attraction to Marilyn was evident. The close proximity in which sexual relations occurred in the triad strongly implies the gratification of unconscious homosexual impulses.

DIAGNOSING DELUSIONAL JEALOUSY

In the official diagnostic manual of the American Psychiatric Association—the *DSM-III*—delusional jealousy is described as a paranoid disorder. When suffering from it an individual may become convinced, without due cause, that his or her mate is unfaithful. The jealous person may collect small bits of "evidence" such as disarrayed clothing or spots on the sheets and use them to justify the delusion. The person may also become suspicious, resentful, angry, even violent.

The manual provides the diagnostic criteria psychologists are supposed to use for defining a particular case of jealousy as delusional. These criteria may be helpful for those trying to decide whether their own or their mate's jealousy is delusional. The criteria include the following:

- Persistent jealousy, despite evidence that it has no basis in reality.

- Emotion and behavior appropriate to the delusion.

- Duration of the delusion of at least one week.

- No incoherence, hallucinations, or bizarre delusions (e.g., delusions of control, thought broadcasting).

- No organic mental disorder that can explain the delusion.

In simpler words, the jealousy has no basis in reality, yet it persists. When this is true for someone you love or are close to, nothing you say or do will convince the person that you are innocent. The best thing to do in such a case is to seek professional help.

An example in the casebook accompanying the *DSM-III* helps clarify these criteria.[7] A beautiful, successful thirty-four-year-old interior designer is brought to the clinic by her thirty-seven-year-old husband, who is a prominent attorney. The husband complains that for the past three years his wife has made increasingly shrill accusations that he is unfaithful to her. He has done everything in his power to convince her of his innocence, but nothing he says or does can shake her conviction. A careful examination of the facts reveals that indeed there is no evidence to suggest that the husband has been unfaithful. When the wife is asked what her evidence is, she becomes vague and mysterious, yet remains absolutely sure that she is right. She says she can tell such things by a faraway look in his eyes, and seems highly insulted by the suggestion that she is imagining the disloyalty. The woman has no hallucinations, functions well on her job, and has no difficulty in thinking, aside from her conviction of the disloyalty.

Since the evidence seems to suggest that the wife's complaints of infidelity are unfounded, the conclusion is that her jealousy must be delusional. The fact that she has no hallucinations and her speech is organized suggests that her delusion is not a symptom of schizophrenia but of paranoia. As is common in paranoia, this woman's impairment due to her delusion does not involve her daily functioning aside from her relationship with her husband. Let us examine the criteria for diagnosing jealousy in a less extreme case.

SAM AND AMALYA

Amalya told me:

> Sam's jealousy is most likely to flare up when we are making love. It happens often. All of a sudden I feel him withdrawing from me. The first time it happened I didn't know what hit me. We were in Paris having the most wonderful time. Suddenly, in the middle of lovemaking, he stopped and pushed me away. . . . By now I've learned what it means. He is disgusted by me physically. He can't touch me. My body repulses him. When he talks about it, he tells me that he imagines me having sex with other men I was involved with in the past. He imagines me doing with those men all the things we are doing while making love. He can imagine me playing with another man's penis, or the man kissing my nipple, things like that. He thinks my sex with other men was dirty, and it makes him see me as dirty, cheap, despicable,

not worthy of someone as pure and wholesome as he is.

When he had his last jealousy attack he blared, "All women are whores, except Mary." Mary is his ex-wife. He tells me he didn't love her. They rarely had sex. Mary was dependent on him for every-thing—she never put gas in their car (which she was the only one to drive) because she didn't know what to do when she drove into a gas station. When she went shopping, he followed her on his motorcycle, paid, and carried the bags. Why did he stay with her ten years? Because he was sure she was loyal. Mary could never manage without a man around her. She could never manage without him.

Sam's parents had a very unusual marriage. His mother—an excep-tionally beautiful woman—had a love affair with another man for many years. His father, whom Sam describes as passive, weak, impo-tent, and jealous, also had affairs throughout their marriage.

When Sam was fifteen, he and his brother went to get his mother a present for Mother's Day. At the bus stop he saw his mother waiting. She didn't notice him. As he watched, a big car rolled by and stopped next to her. The door opened. His mother went in. Sam could see her kissing the man in the car. Afterward, he saw the same big car parked next to the house many times when his father was away. He knew not to go in.

In the mornings, after his father left the house, the man used to call. His mother would take the telephone into the bathroom and have long erotic conversations with her lover while Sam listened outside the door.

Sam's father must have discovered the affair, because one day he appeared with a gun, while his mother had her women friends over for coffee. He started screaming, "I'm going to kill you, you whore!" Sam was in the house at the time, and had to rescue his mother from his father's rage.

After the jealousy scene, his father collapsed and had to be hospitalized for what appeared to be a heart attack. Sam—forever the family rescuer—was the one who took him to the hospital.

When Sam was sixteen, he fell in love with a beautiful young woman, whom he describes as "the cheap type." He never went to bed with her, yet suffered tremendous jealousy. His first sexual experience was with a married woman neighbor much older than himself. He didn't love this woman, and wasn't jealous of her. He also didn't love Mary, whom he met when he was seventeen. But Mary seemed to love and need him very much, and she wasn't the type to provoke his jealousy, so he married her.

It may be worth noting that Sam's sister, who is ten years older than him, is unhappily married to an abusive man who has frequent jealousy attacks during which he beats her. She has many affairs, but still remains with him—thus replicating her mother's infidelity and reliving her father's jealousy tantrums.

When Sam met Amalya, he had been separated from his wife but had not yet gone through the divorce. While he was certain that he was unhappy in his marriage, he loved his two young boys and was reluctant to give up completely the security the family gave him. But Amalya is an attractive and charming woman (eight years older than he is), and he fell in love with her in a way he never allowed himself before.

When Amalya met Sam, she said right away that he was the man she wanted to marry. She had never said that about another man, and she had dated many. Before Sam, Amalya wasn't exactly discriminating in her choice of men.

The only thing these men seemed to have in common was their unavailability—whether because they were married, or because they were emotionally unavailable. That was just fine with Amalya. Having grown up with a father and mother who had had a suffocating symbiotic relationship, she valued her freedom and independence. Things started changing after her thirty-fifth birthday. Amalya decided she wanted a family. She was ready, and Sam was the man she had been waiting for.

Their affair was passionate. Sam came to Amalya's house every day after work and they made wild, sweet, passionate love for hours. Sex had never been that exciting for Sam, never that sweet for Amalya. Their trip to Paris was the climax of the affair. Sam had always wanted to visit Paris, and for him it was a dream come true. For Amalya, the chance to be together twenty-four hours a day was the most important thing; Paris was just a wonderful addition. Spending all their time together made her realize that this was what she wanted. She told Sam she wanted to get married and have a child. This was the backdrop of Sam's first jealousy attack. As Amalya recounts the event:

> He tells me he can never marry me until he trusts me completely. He is troubled by those dark corners in me that are responsible for my past, that might emerge again in the future. Since I was unfaithful in the past, by going to bed with ex-lovers while I dated other men, what guarantee does he have that I'm not going to be unfaithful in the future? After every jealousy attack he feels guilty and remorseful, and apologizes profusely. He tells me he hopes I have the strength and the patience to cope with his jealousy. He asks for my help in dealing with it himself. He knows that it's his own problem and I have nothing to do with it, but when his jealousy flares up, he has no control.
>
> I try to reassure him in every conceivable way. I tell him that I never had such wonderful sex with anyone else. I tell him that my vast experience with other men should make him feel secure—because I have chosen him, and I love him in a way I never loved before. Since I had all those casual sexual experiences, I know what they are like and I have no desire whatsoever to go back to them. Actually, I say to him, I'm the one who should be concerned, because he has had so few sexual relationships that he may still be

curious and at some point want to experiment. For me, all that is finished.

But nothing I say seems to matter. He knows I love him, but he can't understand my past. How could I have done the things I've done? They seem so unlike the person he thinks he knows. The fact that I did them makes him distrust me. The threat he feels is so immense that nothing I say calms it.

Amalya wants to know where Sam's jealousy is coming from, and, more important, what can be done to cure it. Let's leave Sam and Amalya's story briefly, and examine these questions from the psychodynamic perspective.

THE ROOTS OF DELUSIONAL JEALOUSY

When Sam was an adolescent, he discovered that his mother was having an illicit affair. Adolescence is considered the second Oedipal period. What goes on in the mind of a boy like Sam, in this period of heightened sexuality, when he discovers that his mother is unfaithful to his father? Psychotherapists John Docherty and Jean Ellis describe one possible consequence.[8]

Docherty and Ellis treated three couples whose chief complaint was "obsessive-delusional jealousy" in the husbands. A striking coincidental finding emerged in these couples during the course of treatment. In all three cases the husband had witnessed his mother engaged in extramarital sexual relations during his early adolescence.

The jealous husbands' accusations diverged noticeably from a realistic picture of their wives. In fact, the accusations more appropriately fitted their mothers. In one case, the husband claimed his wife of twenty-seven years was drinking excessively and having sex with undesirable characters. He monitored her telephone calls and examined her purse, and berated her until she knelt at his feet and begged him to trust her. During the course of treatment it became apparent that the man's accusations didn't fit his wife—but did fit his mother.

The mother was an alcoholic; as an adolescent he had had to bring her home on several occasions because she was too drunk to get home on her own. She had worked as a waitress and fraternized with various unsavory customers.

Having noticed these discrepancies, the therapists pursued the matter further until the man recalled a memory that carried a great emotional charge. When he was twelve years old he had returned home unexpectedly early one day and found his mother having sex with a strange man. He had not said a thing about it, even though his mother's affairs became the subject of violent arguments between his parents. It had left him feeling bitter resentment toward his mother and guilty disloyalty toward his father.

In the second case, a couple who had been married for two years sought treatment after the husband became enraged by his wife's suspected infidelities. He had been drinking heavily and had become physically abusive. The husband's suspiciousness had plagued the couple's relationship almost from the start. The wife had learned to be extremely cautious in her interactions with other men. At parties she could only be with her husband or with other women, never with other men. He needed to know her whereabouts at all times.

In the course of treatment the therapists noticed again that the man accused his wife of things that were not true of her, but were true of his mother, such as gross negligence in her household duties. This led them to pursue the question of the mother's sexual activities. The husband remembered that when he was a young teenager, he had seen his mother at a neighborhood tavern with other men. On one occasion he had come home and seen her having sex with one of those men. He had not told his father, but from that time on had tried to cut himself off emotionally from his mother.

In the third case, too, the husband was convinced that his faithful wife was having affairs. Once again it came out that when he was fourteen, he had returned home one day after having been sent shopping by his mother, and had found her having sex with a strange man.

From Freud's perspective, it's obvious why a mother's sexual infidelity would have such a traumatic effect, especially when it happens in early adolescence—a period characterized by an Oedipal resurgence. As the mother has demonstrated that she can be sexually available to someone other than the father, the adolescent experiences a marked intensification of Oedipal fantasies and drive toward their fulfillment. However, while the mother appears to be more sexually available to the boy, she is not. Her promiscuity constitutes, in effect, a tease.

The trauma can also explain the aggression that at times accompanies jealousy in these cases. Docherty and Ellis explain: "The rage that the son feels for being second best in the Oedipal situation is exacerbated in a more serious, profound, and damaging way. Now he is not only second best to his father but to a strange man who has no valid claim on his mother at all. By cuckolding the father, the mother makes him second best. Thus the son is unable to use identification with the father to achieve preeminence. He is doomed unalterably to second-rate status."[9] It is significant that all three men described their fathers as passive, hardworking, and long-suffering. We can add to the list Sam's description of his father as passive, weak, and impotent.

It is not necessary for the adolescent boy actually to witness his mother engaged in sexual intercourse for the trauma to occur. Finding out about her infidelity (the way Sam did) or seeing her acting openly flirtatious with other men can be enough.

The rage the boy experiences upon discovering his mother's infidelity is enormous, and so is his need to undo the trauma. How does he accomplish this? One way is to marry someone who will never be unfaithful, and then continuously harass her with groundless accusations of infidelity.

For each of these men, the faithful wife represents his mother, the way she should have been in their childhood fantasies. He accuses the wife of being unfaithful, the way his mother was in reality. The accusations enable him to replay his childhood trauma, but this time with a different ending. His wife's repeated assurances of her fidelity are supposed to help undo the terrible reality of his mother's betrayal. Yet no reassurance is quite enough because the trauma was so enormous, the wife is not the mother, and the situation is not really the same.

This helps explain why people with delusional jealousy avoid situations that might provide positive proof of their suspicions. They don't *really* want to believe that their mates have been unfaithful. On the contrary, they want to be convinced that unlike their fathers, and unlike the childhood situation, this time they are "number one" with their faithful mates.

Choosing a faithful wife and harassing her with groundless accusations is one way a man tries to overcome a trauma of his mother's betrayal. Another way is to choose an unfaithful mate who will provide ample opportunities to master the childhood trauma. In this case the jealousy is not delusional; it derives from an actual situation. Yet it is still not under complete control of the conscious ego. It represents a "repetition compulsion," an irrational need to replicate a traumatic experience. In such a case the adult seeks situations in which he or she can seem to master repressed conflicts and traumas of childhood, even while the true conflicts remain repressed.

Not all people suffering from delusional jealousy have a parent who was sexually unfaithful during their adolescence. Another cause reported in the scientific literature is either undergratification or overgratification by parents during the earliest stages of life—both of which leave the person in chronic need of self-aggrandizing love from others, and suspicious of rivals. (The clinical term for this is *narcissism*.) Such people enter romantic relationships to bolster their self-esteem. When doing so they unconsciously relive their childhoods.[10]

Another cause of delusional jealousy, discovered during treatment of five women, is identification with the husband's greater freedom and opportunity. The identification led to vivid fantasies of their husband seducing others, or of themselves acting as their husbands in the act of seduction.[11] According to their therapist, the women's need to identify with their husbands was caused by low self-esteem, which may be related to women's lower status in our male-dominated society.

In men, another cause of delusional jealousy related to self-esteem is real or imagined smallness of the penis. Clinical work with men who suffer from this problem suggests that they feel at a disadvantage to other men in the struggle to obtain and hold a mate. Their feelings of inadequacy—which are also common among impotent husbands, frigid wives, elderly husbands married to young wives, and plain spouses wedded to handsome ones—pave the way for the advent of delusional jealousy.[12]

Alcoholism can also contribute to delusional jealousy.[13] According to some psychotherapists, jealousy delusions that appear in alcoholism and paranoia are triggered by chemical changes in the brain and have little to do with events in the person's environment, whether in childhood or in the current situation. Consequently, their treatment of choice is pharmacological, i.e., drug therapy.[14] Other therapists believe that the best way to treat delusional jealousy is with a combination of drug therapy and psychotherapy.[15] The majority of psychodynamically oriented therapists, however, agree with Freud that delusional jealousy is a defense, or the result of a defense, against repressed memories and thus should be treated with individual psychotherapy.[16]

Having explored some of the theories about the unconscious roots of jealousy, we can return to Sam and Amalya.

BACK TO SAM AND AMALYA

After falling in love with a woman like his mother (both promiscuous and attractive) and experiencing the powerful jealousy such a relationship can generate, Sam chose to marry a woman he did not love and who, because of her dependence on him, was sure to be faithful. It worked. Throughout the years of his marriage Sam never felt the pangs of jealousy. The price was that he didn't feel the ecstasy of love, either—just a comforting sense of security. For a while this was enough.

Things were sure to be different with Amalya, an attractive woman who had had many sexual liaisons with other men, just as his mother had done. A relationship with her had to be both more passionate and more emotionally risky.

Sam's jealousy of Amalya was not entirely delusional—he was not harassing her about imaginary affairs with other men. His jealousy was of men she had indeed had affairs with and, for all he knew, could have affairs with again. Yet Sam's jealousy wasn't rational, either; it wasn't congruent with reality. Sam knew Amalya loved him and was faithful, yet he couldn't stop imagining her with other men, men she no longer cared about.

Why would anyone imagine things that cause him pain?

One of the factors contributing to Sam's jealousy was an unconscious mechanism called "split-off projection." The "split-off" part is a disavowed part of ourselves that we project on to another person. We do this because it is easier to deal with negative features in another person than it is to deal with these features in ourselves. If we think we are lascivious and immoral, we can try to cope with these difficult feelings. We can also do something much easier: choose someone appropriate and project these qualities onto that person. We can then deal with the feelings without having to acknowledge that they are within us.

In Sam's case, the "split-off" was the part of him that was like his mother: immoral, lascivious, unfaithful. Sam could not accept that he was like his mother. He could not accept that maybe, just maybe, he too did the unthinkable (for example, desired his own mother). Once he split off that part of himself and suppressed it, he could convince himself that he was pure and moral.

But the split-off part continued pushing to be expressed, and it was expressed in Sam's relationship with Amalya. Sam projected on to Amalya his own forbidden desires and the internalized image of his unfaithful mother.

While Sam was helpless to do anything when he witnessed his mother's unfaithfulness as a child, as an adult he had some control over a similar situation. He could punish Amalya (who represented his mother) for her involvement with other men by withdrawing from her sexually and by refusing to marry her. It is telling, however, that Sam started doing this only after he was sure that Amalya loved him and would not be unfaithful.

In addition to reenacting the childhood trauma of his mother's betrayal, the jealousy served two important functions for Sam. First, it gave him a "legitimate" excuse to postpone his divorce from his wife and his marriage to Amalya. Second, it enabled him to entertain sexual fantasies that, given his self-perception as pure, moral, and innocent, he had difficulty admitting even to himself. The jealousy gave him an excuse to both imagine and interrogate Amalya about the details of her sexual relations with other men.

If you are concerned about the intensity of your (or your mate's) jealousy—the "crazy" things you feel, think, and do when jealous— you need to examine two questions. First, is it possible that your jealousy is not only a response to your mate's behavior, but also a reenactment of an early childhood trauma? In other words, what are the roots of your jealousy? Have you seen your mother or father be unfaithful? Has either parent shown unusual jealousy? Have you ever witnessed a violent jealous outburst between your parents?

The second question is, What hidden payoffs do you get from being jealous? What function does the jealousy serve for you? Do you get affirmation of your mate's love and loyalty? Does it force your mate to behave in a more reserved, "considerate" way when you are together in public? Does it enable you to project your own impulses toward infidelity? Is it a way to punish yourself? Is it your way to indulge in sexual fantasies?

AN EVALUATION OF THE PSYCHODYNAMIC APPROACH

The psychodynamic approach contributes to our understanding of jealousy by making us aware of unconscious forces. These forces explain behaviors that are otherwise difficult to understand, such as jealous people's choice of an unfaithful mate, their efforts to seek out confirmation of their worst fears, their drive to push their mate toward their rival, or their tendency to become obsessed with painful images of the mate in a passionate embrace with the rival. Such thoughts and behaviors increase the jealous person's pain. But as we've seen, they also provide a defense against even more troubling feelings and thoughts.

Another contribution of the psychodynamic approach is its description of the roots of adult jealousy in childhood experiences. According to Freud, these emotional experiences are associated with the Oedipal stage. Since Freud saw these experiences as universal, he was sure that reexperiencing them as jealousy in adulthood was inevitable and universal.

Other psychodynamic writers believe that the origin of jealousy may be even earlier than the Oedipal stage. When a hungry baby cries and its mother doesn't appear, the baby experiences tremendous anxiety, helplessness, and fear of abandonment. These fears are universal; consequently jealousy, which is their manifestation in adult life, is also universal.[17]

In every one of us there is a child that at some point felt abandoned and scared, a child that cried in pain and raged with frustration. In all of us there is a longing for the complete security we felt in our first weeks of life. We all felt resentment for the love we had to share with a sibling or a parent. We may not remember those feelings, but we carry them with us. They often cause us to respond in exaggerated and inappropriate ways to jealousy triggers.

Because psychodynamically oriented therapists believe that jealousy both expresses and disguises some of our deepest fears and desires, they treat jealousy primarily as a psychological problem in the mind of the jealous individual. Other approaches question both the psychodynamic approach's assumptions and its methods.

While reading this chapter, you may have thought that jealousy couldn't result entirely from events in our childhood that are reenacted through our unconscious. What about the influence of real events that threaten our relationship and trigger our jealousy? Indeed, one of the major criticisms of the psychodynamic approach is directed against its tendency not to consider the reality that may have prompted the jealousy, and to assume that *all* jealousy is to some extent delusional—a product of our own mind, unrelated to reality. Little attention is paid to literal infidelity, except sometimes to show how we provoked, or in some sense desired, the very betrayal that aroused our jealousy.[18]

A related criticism is directed at the psychodynamic tendency to blame the individual for choosing or creating the circumstances that give rise to the jealousy problem. Psychodynamically oriented therapists tend to ignore what jealousy suggests about anyone other than the jealous individual.

The psychodynamic approach is also criticized by the advocates of other approaches for putting too much emphasis on the role of the unconscious, and not enough on conscious expectations and real events that create a jealousy problem and help maintain it.

Yet another criticism is directed at the tendency to put too much emphasis on the role of childhood experiences in creating a jealousy problem and not enough emphasis on present forces, especially the dynamics of the relationship.

In the next chapter we will examine the systems approach, which provides an alternative to the psychodynamic approach.

Treating the Couple, Not the Jealous Mate

Quarrels would not last if the fault were only on one side.

—LA ROCHEFOUCAULD, REFLECTIONS, 1675

The Systems Approach to Jealousy

According to the systems approach, jealousy is a result of the dynamics within a particular relationship and is best treated as a problem the couple shares.[1]

In psychological terms, a system is "a complex of interacting elements and the relationships which organize them."[2] Emotions, actions, and thoughts are the interacting elements of a system we call a person. The person is a subsystem of a more complex system involving an intimate relationship, which at times is called marriage. This relationship is a subsystem of a more complex system of an extended family, which itself is a subsystem of a particular culture.[3]

Unlike the psychodynamic emphasis on events in our past, the systems approach considers the past mostly irrelevant to the treatment of jealousy. The unconscious roots of the jealousy problem also do not matter. What matters instead are the forces that elicit and maintain the problem. The focus is no longer the mind of the jealous individual, but the higher-order system, the whole, of which the individual is a part. The whole involves first and foremost the couple, but can also include the jealousy triangle, the couple's family of origin (both parents and grandparents), and in theory even the culture in which the couple lives.

Higher-order systems (such as the couple) both influence and are influenced by lower-order systems (such as the actions, thoughts, and emotions of the jealous person). This reciprocal influence can cause negative-feedback loops that maintain the jealousy problem, or positive-feedback loops that promote change. Disrupting a negative-feedback loop in a higher-order system (a relationship) may involve or lead to change in a lower-order system (the jealous person).

With the passage of time, patterns of behavior become rules, or habits that are difficult to change. A couple's relationship functions according to these rules. (One of the most important rules dictates who makes the rules in that relationship.) Once rules are established, the couple system tends to resist change. Yet a healthy system can exhibit both stability and change simultaneously.

Instead of asking "Why?"—i.e., why is the individual jealous?—systems therapists ask "What?" What is the cause of the jealousy problem? And, more important, what can be done to bring about change? Psychodynamic therapists give interpretations aimed at helping the troubled individuals gain new insights into their jealousy problem. By contrast, systems therapists give couples concrete recommendations designed to disrupt the destructive patterns that cause the jealousy problem, and to help maintain the positive change. Disrupting those destructive patterns, instead of unearthing their cause, is the primary goal of systems therapy.

To bring about change in the person suffering from a jealousy problem, that person's marital system must change. The focus of the therapeutic intervention is the behavior of both mates that maintains the problem. Because the goal is to disrupt a destructive feedback loop, the therapist tries to find the point that is easiest to change. This can involve a change in behavior that produces a change in the rules of the system, or a change of rules which produces a change in behavior. The case of Dave and Lillian, presented later in this chapter, provides an example of a system change.

While the focus of the specific intervention can vary, the general focus of systems therapy is always the system and the circular processes (feedback loops) that take place in it. Systems therapists assume that a change in one part of the system (for example, one mate) always causes change in the other parts of the system (for example, the other mate), and therefore changes the whole system. When the husband withdraws, the wife responds with an attempt to get closer. When the wife tries to get closer, the husband responds by withdrawing. The response of one mate provides the stimulus to the other: Does he withdraw because she gets too close, or does she get closer because he withdraws?

In a marital system, according to systems approach, it is impossible for one mate to be totally passive. Even when you don't respond to something your mate did, such as blaming you unjustly for being unfaithful, your lack of response gives your mate a powerful message.

Roles such as victim and victimizer are seen as a result of an arbitrary decision in which both mates take part. For example, if a husband plays the role of the unfaithful villain, the therapist is likely to assume that the wife is either contributing to or getting something from the role of the betrayed victim. One goal of therapy is to change such arbitrary definitions. A change in the way a couple perceives a chain of events (for example, what preceded the affair that can help explain it) can change the couple's dynamic.

Systems therapists see jealousy as caused by destructive, self-reinforcing patterns of interaction and not by events in the individual's past. When a couple comes to therapy and describes the "crazy things" the wife does because of "her pathological jealousy," the therapist is likely to ask what in the husband's behavior caused her to behave in this way. Another question the therapist might ask concerns the husband's response, which may reinforce his wife's jealous behavior. When the wife identifies the husband's affair as the central problem, the therapist is likely to ask her what she might have done to cause her husband to have an affair, and what she did in response to the affair.

Even though only one person in the couple may experience jealousy, systems therapists believe that jealousy serves a function in the couple system. Symptoms such as affairs or jealousy are viewed as forms of communication. Dave and Lillian's story demonstrates how an affair can be a form of communication.

DAVE AND LILLIAN: AN AFFAIR AS A FORM OF COMMUNICATION

When Dave and Lillian first met, Lillian was insecure and impoverished.[4] She was attracted to Dave's stability and self-confidence. Dave, for his part, was attracted to Lillian's high energy and intense emotions. During the first years of their marriage Dave was a stable breadwinner, which enabled Lillian to go back to school and get a degree. Both were happy in the marriage.

After about six years, however, Dave decided he needed a change and took a job in real estate, a field that Lillian considered "gambling" instead of a "real job." Dave's income in this new job was unstable; in addition, the real-estate field went into a slump shortly after he entered it, making even his unstable income rather meager. During that time they had to rely on Lillian's salary, which she said was "all right," but in fact was not all right with her. Lillian explains:

> Dave's career has not been successful. For the past four years I have been the steady breadwinner while Dave has tried to break into commercial real estate. Although he did have one fairly good year, he brought in a total of about $40,000 during a four-year period. Even when he made some money, neither of us felt it could be freely spent because there was no way to know when or if he would make the next deal and another commission. Sales, especially during these hard times for real estate, can be very stressful work. Dave has put out a lot of effort, undergone a lot of stress, and gotten very little back for it.

Lillian understood that what she saw as Dave's "failure" was the result of bad luck rather than a symptom of inherent failure tendencies or inadequacies in Dave. Still, she felt "emotionally impacted by a sense of his 'failure.' " It triggered childhood fears and insecurities that were related in part to the fact that she saw her father as "a total and complete failure in the business world." Dave's lack of success threatened her feelings of security in Dave and in the marriage, and the experience affected her sexual feelings:

> The sexist woman in me expects a man to be stronger and steadier and more financially successful than I am. Someone inside me wants to be a delicate, charming little girl . . . with a big, powerful, successful man to take care of her and overwhelm her with his forcefulness, his sureness, his surefooted success. I must admit that I expect a husband to be successful, and Dave is not successful. Although I don't consciously make his career success a condition of my love, I am sure that on an emotional level I am experiencing deep disappointment in him. I have wondered if this disappointment is behind my lack of sexual attraction. . . . Dave's financial dependency is the crux of my anger and disappointment. . . . The whole failure issue—men should succeed; my father was a failure—has a lot of emotional energy around it and generates its own dynamic.

The effect of Dave's perceived career failure on Lillian's sexual feelings had a concrete manifestation:

> Dave is relatively short for a man. He is also very slender. I am fairly slender but more solid than he is. I never used to think about it at all, but lately I have been craving largeness in a man. Dave is wonderfully

endowed sexually, and fills me up as no other man has ever done quite so well. But in terms of body size and weight I have lately found him lacking. I crave bigness and power on top of me when we make love these days. I feel cheated because my arms wrap so easily around his slender body. I feel like a protecting mother/companion/comfort-giver . . . when I want to feel like a nymphet overwhelmed by a large, powerful, and passionate man who is driven to frenzy by my loveliness.

Lillian has not always been disappointed with Dave's size. As a matter of fact, the opposite is true.

I wonder why, after over a decade of marriage, I am suddenly disappointed and turned off by Dave's slenderness and shortness. I used to love the way he seemed on my level, my size. I liked the fact that he was not overwhelming. I was trying to express myself and achieve confidence and power in the world in my own right. I was sick of being overwhelmed by egocentric men. Dave was, and is, the most caring, loving, giving, wonderful man I have ever met. And I used to love his body. It hasn't changed a pound or an inch. Where have I changed, and why?

Is this body-disappointment based upon the failure-disappointment that I feel on an emotional level? Have I got his smallness of body mixed up with his smallness of income? Will this body-disappointment go away when Dave gets a new career under way and has success? And will sexual excitement ignite between us then?

Despite the intensity of her disappointment and rage, Lillian was unable to discuss her feelings openly with Dave. She valued the security her marriage provided, and was afraid that if she expressed her true feelings openly, Dave might get so upset and angry that he would leave her. So she blocked out her negative feelings. It is impossible, however, to block emotions selectively; once you put on an emotional shield, it inhibits all emotions. Consequently, when Lillian repressed her anger she also repressed her feelings of love and passion.

Although he did not admit his failure in real estate, Dave was worried about his financial future. He wanted to protect Lillian from his fears, and his feelings of insecurity and inadequacy—feelings that were caused by his "unmasculine" dependency on Lillian's earnings. Dave couldn't admit those feelings even to himself. So he blocked them out, blocking with them his passion.

Lillian describes the results:

> As must be typical, the symptoms of the problem come up most glaringly in the bedroom. I no longer feel sexually attracted to or excited by Dave. Dave says he is still attracted to me—and that the lack of enthusiasm comes from me rather than from him—but the predictability and low-key style of his lovemaking cause me to think that perhaps our lack of enthusiasm is shared. I have no complaints about his willingness, frequency, sweetness, or consideration and giving during lovemaking. It is the lack of creativity, of genuine excitement, of passion that I refer to. And I do nothing to introduce these elements myself, since I no longer feel any passion or strong attraction. I do not find myself motivated to exhibit feelings I am not having—although some pretense on my part might get the ball rolling, perhaps. It's just not something I want to force myself to do.

Just then, passionate sex became very important to Lillian:

Maybe I am no longer the same person who fell in love more than ten years ago? Certainly I have very different needs today than I did when I met Dave a decade ago. As a thirty-five-year-old woman (no children, successful career) I find that passionate sex (or the lack of it) is far more important to me than ever before. I am no longer working to build a career. I enjoy my work and feel successful. I think this is the age when a woman is supposed to reach her sexual peak . . . perhaps that is why I crave passionate sex in a way that I did not use to.

According to Lillian, it was boredom with marital sex that precipitated her illicit affair. But, clearly, boredom was only a small part of the story. It all started during a party at which Dave pointed out to Lillian a grubby-looking bearded man wearing a dirty, torn T-shirt, and said, "Isn't that the most disgusting-looking man you have ever seen?" Earlier, Dave had heard the man talk about his teenage daughter in lascivious terms that just added to the negative impression made by his appearance. Soon afterward, Lillian chose to have an affair with this man.

About six months ago I became involved with a man who elicited passion in me that I did not know I was capable of feeling. For years I had just figured that I was not a very sexually oriented person. Though Dave and I had had much more exciting sex before we were married and during the early years, we had not had passionate sex for at least three years prior to my affair with this other man.

Although my affair was with a strange and crazy man whom I no longer have any interest in or desire to see, it elicited some powerful feelings at the time— so much so that it was impossible for me to hide the fact that I was having an affair.

Lillian's behavior could have made it easy for Dave, who claimed to be "not the slightest bit jealous," to discover the affair. But he simply refused to notice the hints she was dropping all around him. So she started to make those hints bigger and more obvious until he finally understood and responded, for the first time ever in their relationship, with tremendous jealousy. His interrogations enabled Lillian to tell him about the affair—something she secretly wanted very much to do. In fact, letting him know and making him jealous were the main reasons she had started the affair in the first place.

> Indiscretions on my part aroused Dave's suspicions, and I ended up telling him (in stages) the full extent of my extramarital involvement.
>
> Dave was wounded to the core. His infinite trust in me dissolved, and he said he lost the capacity to trust completely. It would do him no good to divorce me and try to find another woman he could trust, since he had lost the capacity for complete trust in another person. If I—whom he loved and trusted so completely—could betray him that way, then anyone could, at any time. He had never felt such jealousy before, and never wanted to feel it again.

Once Dave discovered the affair and was appropriately jealous, Lillian suddenly lost interest in the other man.

> When I came so close to losing Dave, my emotions swung back powerfully toward him. I no longer cared about the other man or the affair, but only about repairing the damage I had done to the man I love— my husband. I felt that I would kiss his feet for the next ten years if that were necessary to win back his love and trust . . . to restore the bond and comfort that I had ruptured.
>
> It was mostly my intense desire to right the wrong

and stay on the good-wife path in the future (as well
as his love and need for me, and his perception of my
love for him) that convinced Dave to give me another
chance.

Coming to therapy was part of Lillian and Dave's attempt to "right
the wrong" and give their marriage another chance. Their work as a
couple was fueled by Lillian's "passionate desire to heal Dave's jealousy
and pain and repair the damage I had done . . . and not lose the man
I had loved all these years and still love so much."

As is often the case when an affair is explored openly and nondefen-
sively, Lillian and Dave realized that the affair was, more than anything
else, a form of communication. The affair enabled Lillian to communicate feelings toward Dave that she was too embarrassed to admit even
to herself, and too scared to communicate directly to Dave.

Clearly the affair had more to do with what I was
feeling toward Dave than what I was feeling toward
the other man, especially given that the other man is
of absolutely no interest to me anymore. Now that I
am not acting out affair-type behavior, feelings about
Dave are surfacing that I was not allowing myself to
experience before.

Perhaps the affair was a way of doing something
to prevent myself from knowing what I was feeling
toward Dave, since these are threatening feelings. I
experienced anger, resentment, disappointment, concern, fear. I am beginning to see the affair as a way
of not having to experience these feelings.

In a tearful and highly emotional session, after much encouragement
and with great effort, Lillian and Dave were finally able to open up
to each other. They discussed all their feelings, negative and embar-

rassing as they were. The result was a tremendous relief. Lillian was able to tell Dave about her anger and resentment. She said she was afraid that if she expressed her anger and disappointment (she envisioned these emotions as a monster she was keeping in the closet), something terrible would happen and her whole world would collapse. Dave was able to admit his jealousy, despite his belief that it was a negative and shameful response.

Lillian discovered that despite her "terrible feelings" Dave still loved her, and actually was delighted to find out what had been troubling her all along. After learning that jealousy is a protective response to a perceived threat to a valued relationship, Dave was able to share his jealousy and his financial insecurities with Lillian and discover that her feelings toward him were not altered because of this. With the emotional relief they experienced during this mutual exploration came a powerful surge of the old passion. And, as both reported, "sex has never been better."

Open discussion also enabled Dave and Lillian to confront directly the sensitive issue of money, and to come up with a solution that suited them both. Dave continued in real estate while training for a new career with a much better potential for providing a stable and secure income. In the meantime they decided to rent a part of the house, which helped ease some of their financial stress.

Lillian and Dave's case demonstrates that an affair can be a form of communication to the mate. As Lillian said:

> The affair needed to be looked at as communication to Dave, rather than as an inability to restrain my impulses. I needed to look at what I was feeling toward Dave, and trying to communicate to him by having an affair—and by being so obvious about it.

The case also demonstrates several key points of the systems approach. Dave and Lillian, in their years of marriage, created a system in which the unspoken rule was that Dave was the stable provider. When Dave changed this established pattern he broke the rule. Lillian punished him by having the affair, breaking the fidelity rule. Dave's jealousy, an unusual experience for him, and Lillian's fear that he might leave brought them to therapy.

The focus of the therapy was not on the unconscious roots of Dave's jealousy or Lillian's infidelity, but instead on the rules governing the marriage. As a result of this exploration, Lillian and Dave were able to compromise and accept a change of rules with which they both felt comfortable.

Throughout therapy, the affair and the jealousy it triggered were treated as a couple issue. The therapy made it clear that Dave and Lillian each played an active role in the process that led to the affair, and played an equally active role in trying to save their marriage when they perceived a threat to it. Treating the affair and the jealousy it triggered as a couple issue enabled Lillian and Dave to reestablish trust and turn the traumatic event into a growth experience.

JANE AND DAN: AN AFFAIR AS A FORM OF ESCAPE

The most common trigger of extreme jealousy is an illicit love affair. You may recall from the disscussion in chapter two that virtually all the people who were asked about it said they would feel "very jealous" if they discovered their mate was having an illicit affair. How should such jealousy be treated in a constructive and growth-enhancing way? While the jealous response seems justified, it not only causes excruciating pain for the individual, but also can be destructive to the relationship and, in extreme cases, even lead to violence.

Systems therapists look at the affair in the context of the relationship as a whole. The affair is not "something that just happened" to the unfaithful mate, but a statement about something important that happened to and involves both mates.

In a recent book dealing with treatment of marital conflict, Philip Guerin, Leo Fay, Susan Burden, and Judith Gilbert Kautto note that affairs "almost always represent externalization of a dysfunctional process going on within the family."[5] Their approach to the treatment of affairs, which is shared by many systems therapists, focuses on three goals:

1. bringing out the part each spouse played in the process

2. changing the behavior of both spouses

3. reestablishing trust in the marital relationship

The following case, mentioned in chapter two, illustrates this systems approach. The case involves a woman called Jane, who found out that her husband of thirty-five years, Dan, had had an affair.

The discovery of an affair is painful for both mates. It sets off a crisis in which ordinary daily functioning suffers severely. The first thing Jane needed to do was learn to take a day at a time and make priorities in her daily responsibilities so she could manage what was most essential. Then, to minimize the emotional impact of the affair, both Jane and Dan needed to understand the parts each of them had played in the affair, the function the affair served in the marriage, and the process that had led up to it. Understanding these things does not mean that people are not accountable for their behavior. Dan had an affair, Jane did not. Yet both were responsible for the state of their marriage. Since an affair often is seen as an unforgivable sin, it is important for both mates to put the affair in the larger context of their marriage.

Many times an affair is a refuge from a relationship problem or from pain in one's personal life. To understand the function of Dan's affair, it is necessary to understand the state of things prior to the affair. Two problems seem particularly relevant: an operation for cancer of the prostate that Dan had before the affair, and Jane's overinvolvement with their daughter.

The prostate-cancer operation was traumatic for Dan. Not only did it make him confront his own mortality, it made him question his sexual adequacy—something he had never questioned before. He desperately needed Jane's support, but Jane was too involved with their daughter's recent divorce to notice. She stayed with their daughter for weeks at a time, and when she was home they spent hours on the phone. In fact, when Jane first sought therapy it was to discuss her daughter's marital problems and how she could best help her resolve them.

Over the course of the months following the operation, an emotional distance grew between Jane and Dan. Each felt distressed, yet was unable to share feelings with the other. Dan's affair with an attractive woman, ten years younger than he, helped him get the emotional and sexual reassurance he needed. It started when Jane was out of town. Dan had a business dinner to attend and didn't like the thought of going alone. It was natural for him to invite a woman who was working in a nearby office to join him.

After the dinner she invited him for a drink at her apartment, and Dan rediscovered how wonderful it was to talk to someone who was totally attentive and focused on him, the way Jane had been during most of their married life. The fact that a young, sexy woman still found him attractive and desirable was exhilarating. With her he felt more alive sexually than he had in a long time—more manly, more interesting.

As long as the affair remained secret, Dan had his sexual and emotional needs met, and Jane was free to continue her intense involvement with their daughter. When an anonymous phone call from a watchful secretary in Dan's office informed Jane of the affair, Dan stopped it right away. He told Jane he was sorry for what he had done, and for the pain he had caused her. What he wanted more than anything else was to forget the whole thing. But Jane was inconsolable in her jealousy and couldn't let go. She barraged Dan with questions about the affair, searched through his drawers and office files, couldn't stop thinking about it, and vacillated between rage, humiliation, and despair. Her jealousy brought her back to therapy.

At the beginning of my work with Dan and Jane, I encouraged Jane to talk about the feelings she had experienced since the discovery of the affair. It was important to validate the emotional turmoil she was in, without making Dan the villain. Pursuing Dan for details added to her emotional turmoil, and it was important that she stop the interrogations. She was able to do that by focusing on her own role in the marriage and the affair.

Once both Jane and Dan understood the function the affair had in their marriage and the roles both of them played in making it happen, and once they were able to talk about the affair openly, the arduous task of reestablishing trust in the marriage began. Many couples, relieved that the crisis is over, hope time will take care of old wounds, and drop out of therapy before achieving this difficult and important goal.[6]

JEALOUSY SERVES A FUNCTION

Whether an affair is a form of communication or a form of escape, the jealousy it triggers is always a relationship issue. It focuses attention on a threat to the relationship. According to the systems approach, jealousy always serves a function in the relationship. While it is experienced and expressed by one mate, it is part of a particular couple's relationship and reflects a particular family disturbance. A nice example of this point appears in Robert Barker's book *The Green-Eyed Marriage: Surviving Jealous Relationships*.[7] Dr. Barker is not a systems therapist, but rather a psychodynamic therapist who sees jealousy as "the result of long-standing and deep-seated psychological and behavioral problems within the jealous person." Despite this clear allocation of blame, the case is a wonderful example of the systems notion of the function that jealousy plays for both mates—exactly the opposite conclusion from the one Dr. Barker drew.

Darryl and Lucy were married ten years and fought constantly throughout this time. In a typical interaction leading to a fight, Darryl would start making overtures signaling that he wanted to have sex, and Lucy would appear enthusiastic. Then she would casually mention something that would arouse his jealousy. The argument would culminate with one of them sleeping on the living room couch.

While Darryl may have been the jealous mate, it is clear that Lucy played an equal part in having the jealous scenes continue. Dr. Barker notes correctly that "both had something important to gain by keeping it going."

Both Darryl and Lucy had long histories of sexual disturbances. Darryl was often troubled by premature ejaculation and was anxious about his sexual performance. Lucy suffered from a chronic, painful sensitivity to touch and pressure in the genital area, which caused an aversion to sexual intercourse.

Lucy used Darryl's jealousy to minimize sexual contact with him. When he made overtures, she simply stirred his jealousy. His typical response made the outcome predictable—they'd fight and forget about sex. "Guilt-free absolution from sex" was Lucy's payoff: *she* didn't refuse him. *She* was willing until he started acting jealous again. Darryl, too, wanted an excuse to avoid sex and the performance anxiety associated with it. The jealousy-related arguments provided an acceptable way to avoid it.

Darryl and Lucy illustrate the degree to which jealousy is a couple issue. Even when one mate appears "abnormally jealous," it is legitimate to ask what benefits the non-jealous mate is gaining from the jealousy problem. The question is especially relevant when jealousy has been a problem in the relationship for a long time.

One of the most common discoveries in working with couples with an "abnormally jealous" spouse is that the "non-jealous" spouse has a good reason, psychologically speaking, to stay in the relationship. As Darryl and Lucy's case demonstrates, at times that reason is so important that the "non-jealous" mate actually fuels the jealousy.

Lucy provoked Darryl's jealousy in an attempt to conceal a sexual problem. In other cases, jealousy-based arguments may be used to divert attention from other problems in the spouses, in the relationship, or in both.

In addition to concealing other problems, jealousy can serve a positive function as well; in small amounts it can add excitement to the relationship. As we will see in the chapter on jealousy in open relationships, for example, swingers like to watch their mates having sex with someone else. The jealous flash they feel fuels their sexual interest in their mate.

Other couples enjoy the drama jealousy produces. Both mates identify drama with passion, and they keep passion alive in the relationship by co-producing the jealousy scenes. In one such case, the jealous lover is a successful businessman who makes frequent trips abroad. Since he can't stand the thought of his girlfriend staying home alone, he takes her along on most of his trips. On those rare occasions when that's impossible, he makes frequent overseas calls to her house, to friends and even to restaurants, to check on her.

The girlfriend, who is a plain-looking woman, grew up in a poor family. She loves the trips abroad and the attention her lover's jealousy produces. To fuel his jealousy, she drops little hints about men she saw during his absence. Yet when he makes surprise visits to check on her, he always finds her chatting innocently with a group of friends or a woman friend. When that happens, and it happens often, she accuses him of being pathologically jealous. They have a "terrible fight" and then make passionate love. This pattern has been going on for eight years, with no end in sight for either the jealousy or the passion. A couple like this may appear furious at each other, but they actually love the drama their jealousy creates. They rarely seek therapy for the jealousy, and when they find themselves with a mate who is not jealous or unfaithful, they find that mate "boring." Jealousy keeps the sexual spark in their relationship alive.

Jealousy indeed produces excitement, and can make life more interesting. In addition, it can make your mate look more desirable. If the businessman I just described saw his girlfriend not through his jealousy-struck eyes but the way the rest of the world saw her, she would doubtless lose much of her appeal.

Some people fuel their mate's jealousy when they feel taken for granted. Some do it because it gives them a sense of power over their jealous mate. Others do it as a form of revenge, using their jealous mate to heal an ego that was injured by this relationship or a previous one.

In all these cases, it is not enough for one mate to want to create a jealousy problem. Both mates have to collude in keeping a jealousy problem alive in the relationship. This is why, according to the systems approach, jealousy is best treated as the couple's joint problem, even when one mate is "abnormally" jealous.

Working on jealousy as a couple issue tends to bring about faster change, because it involves both mates. In Lucy and Darryl's case, for example, what would have happened if Darryl went for individual therapy to deal with his "abnormal jealousy"? The focus of therapy would undoubtedly have been on Darryl's feelings of sexual inadequacy, which were the cause of his jealousy. Changing those is a long and slow process. Changing the destructive pattern in the relationship that contributes to a jealousy problem can alleviate the problem much faster.

If you are in a relationship with a mate who is "abnormally" jealous, you probably have trouble accepting the idea that you, too, play an active role in keeping the jealousy problem alive. It is much easier to blame your mate than to take responsibility for your own part in shaping the relationship you share. Yet, in the long run, blaming your mate is not the best approach. Taking responsibility—which is not the same as taking blame—means that you have some control over the problem. If you accept that you played a part in creating the problem, you can draw comfort from the knowledge that you can also play an active part in solving it.

THE SYSTEMS APPROACH TO THE TREATMENT OF "ABNORMAL JEALOUSY"

Mark suffered from what was described by his psychoanalyst as "delusional jealousy."[8] This diagnosis was based on a whole set of symptoms: Mark could not stop tormenting himself about affairs his wife might be having. He said his jealousy was "like a poisonous gas that permeated everything." Every time he came home from work, Mark checked the mileage on his wife's car to make sure she hadn't taken trips out of town to see her imagined lovers. He checked her underpants for stains that would indicate she had had sex with those "lovers." He checked the contents of her wallet for any clues she might have left to an illicit affair. To find out whether she talked to her "lovers" on the phone while he was out of the house, he would put a hair on the receiver. If the hair was not there when he returned, it would be a clear sign that she had talked with some lover. But whenever he returned and the hair wasn't on the receiver, he could never be sure whether it was his wife or the wind that had blown it away.

Most significant in the diagnosis of delusional jealousy, however, was that Mark's jealousy was groundless. His wife has always been faithful to him. Since Mark's therapist was psychodynamically oriented, his therapy centered on the function that the jealousy served in the dynamics of Mark's inner life.

Although this was a case of "abnormal" jealousy, Mark already had a jealousy problem when his wife first met him, fell in love with him, and decided to marry him. What was it that attracted her to him at the early stages of their relationship? Could it have had something to do with his jealousy?

In similar cases I have worked with, I have discovered that non-jealous mates actually enjoy the jealousy at the beginning. The reason, in most cases, is that they perceive the jealousy as a sign of love and commitment to the relationship.

Unfortunately, we don't know what attracted Mark's wife at the beginning of the relationship, because Mark's wife was never seen in therapy. Since Mark, his wife, and his therapist defined the problem as "Mark's pathological jealousy," this was also the focus of his individual psychotherapy.

As you may recall from the discussion of jealousy as the shadow of love, the traits and behaviors that attract us most when we first meet our mate often cause us the most distress later in the relationship. This, as we saw, is also true for jealousy. If you have a jealous mate, one of the important and interesting questions for you to explore is what attracted you to your mate when you first met. Understanding the attraction helps us understand the jealousy. Ann and Leonard are an example.

JEALOUSY AT THE BEGINNING OF A RELATIONSHIP

Ann and Leonard met when Ann was seventeen. Leonard, twenty-four at the time, seemed not only older but wiser and more impressive than the boys her age. She loved the way he made her the center of his world and took care of all her needs. But now, after twenty-two years of marriage, she wants a divorce. The reason: "Leonard's pathological jealousy." "I feel suffocated," says Ann. "Leonard is so jealous, he doesn't let me breathe. I feel imprisoned. He can't stand the fact that I have my own interests. He doesn't let me go out on my own. He follows me everywhere I go. I've had it with him." Leonard, on the other hand, says he still loves Ann as much as he did when they were first married. "I am worried about her going out on her own at night," he says. "That's the only reason I follow her and why I want to know where she's going and with whom. I think my concern is normal and perfectly justified. Every man you'll ask will agree with me."

From the time they met through the first years of their marriage, Ann loved being the center of Leonard's world. She saw a sign of love in his protectiveness and concern. It made her feel secure. He was the loving father she never had. Now she sees his protectiveness as possessiveness, and his concern as pathological jealousy. Being the center of his world no longer makes her feel secure, because that world has shrunk into a cage. Ann and Leonard created a destructive cycle in which Ann responded to Leonard's jealousy by withdrawing, and he responded to her growing withdrawal with increasing jealousy.

DEAN AND MELANIE: SHIFTING FROM THE JEALOUS MATE TO THE COUPLE

Dean and Melanie came to therapy because of what Dean called Melanie's "pathological jealousy." He said that I had to "fix" her because he simply "can't take it anymore." Melanie agreed with the label and appreciated Dean's support in coming to therapy with her.

During our exploration of the problem, it became evident that Melanie had a reason to be jealous. When they first met, Dean was engaged to marry another woman while at the same time having an affair with that woman's sister. He told Melanie about all of his wheelings and dealings in trying to manage these two relationships— while starting a third one with her. You may ask, of course, why Melanie would get involved with a man she knew was engaged and cheating on his fiancée. But as I noted earlier, such a question is irrelevant for a systems therapist.

Several years after they married, Dean and Melanie had a fight and separated for a brief time. Melanie later discovered that during the separation Dean had had an affair with his secretary. Dean used all his "old cover-up tricks" to keep Melanie from finding out about the affair. This affair, on top of Dean's "history of deceit," made Melanie suspicious of anything that could possibly be a clue to a new affair. Her suspicions made Dean, who according to his own testimony was now "innocent as a lamb," furious. He didn't understand why Melanie needed to drag out things that were "old history." She was, he concluded, "simply pathologically jealous."

While Melanie agreed with Dean that she had a problem with jealousy, she observed, in her own defense, that she had never before been jealous, neither with any of her boyfriends nor with her former husband.

As is almost always the case, Dean and Melanie's jealousy problem was related to what they found most attractive about each other when they first met. Melanie was attracted to Dean's charm and charisma: "He was then, and still is now, a very attractive man." Dean was attracted to Melanie's sensitivity and attentiveness: "I felt from the very beginning that she was someone who could create a home for me." Now Dean's attractiveness to other women has become a major source of stress for Melanie, while Melanie's excessive sensitivity has become equally stressful for Dean.

To Dean it seemed that every interaction he had with another woman was a jealousy-trigger for Melanie. He argued fervently that all the things he had done in the past were "insignificant and trivial" compared to his "honesty and truthfulness in the relationship now."

To Melanie, however, it seemed that her suspicions were adequately justified by Dean's behavior in the past. The triggers of her jealousy were well defined; they included all situations involving women when there was even a slight chance that Dean was dishonest with her. Seeing Dean interact with an attractive woman and thinking that he might be attracted to the woman or even have an affair with her and lie about it, were enough to make Melanie wild with jealousy.

When Dean and Melanie walked down the street, Dean occasionally would bump into a woman he knew and exchange a few words with her. He knew that this was enough to raise Melanie's suspicions. She would start asking questions about the woman and his acquaintance with her. Her interrogations made Dean more and more angry. Finally he refused to answer her questions. "I know the way her mind works," he said, "and it drives me nuts."

The "scratches incident" was the final straw. Melanie noticed that Dean had scratches on his back, which he didn't remember getting; Melanie felt he couldn't possibly have caused the scratches himself. When she started to question him about the scratches, Dean felt "something explode" in his head. He says he didn't know what he was doing. He started to hit Melanie. The violence shocked and scared both of them, and was the real reason they came for therapy.

In trying to figure out how both of them contributed to the dynamic of their jealousy problem, Melanie claimed that her main problem was lack of trust in Dean. If Dean would swear to tell her the truth—even if he was attracted to another woman, even if he had a fling—she was sure she could handle it. But Dean refused to give his word. He saw Melanie's suspicions as groundless, and found her interrogations intolerable. "I've had enough of this madness," he said. "Melanie has a problem, and she is the one who has to solve it." Since Dean and Melanie seemed stuck in their positions, I asked them to reverse roles, and explain to me each other's positions.[9]

Both had difficulty with the task. Melanie had a great deal of trouble expressing the extent of Dean's resentment and anger at her suspicion. Dean had problems expressing the extent of Melanie's hurt and distrust of him. It was as though Dean and Melanie had supersensitive antennae, he to signs of her jealousy, she to signs of his possible unfaithfulness. Once they both realized the extent of each other's sensitivity, they were able to focus their effort on "reducing the volume" of their respective responses.

Dean agreed to tell Melanie the truth about his romantic involvements, actual or possible, with other women. In exchange, Melanie promised to trust him, to stop being suspicious of every woman he interacted with, and to cease her interrogations of him. Though this solution may sound too simple to work, in this particular case it did. Melanie stopped being "a jealous person." When I last spoke to Dean and Melanie, two years after they made their agreement, they no longer had problems with jealousy. One reason the agreement worked was that they attempted to solve the problem together. Another reason was Melanie's willingness to put complete faith in Dean's word. Once he gave it, she was convinced he'd never lie to her.

This does not mean that every "jealous person" will stop being jealous the minute his or her mate promises to be honest about involvement with others. Other couples may need different solutions. The challenge in each case is to discover the solution that works.

Systems theorists Paul Watzlawick, John Weakland, and Richard Fisch give an example of the way a jealous system is activated, maintained, and perpetuated. A wife feels excluded from her husband's life, so she starts questioning him. The husband feels her questioning is an intrusion, so he withdraws. His withdrawal increases her anxiety and suspiciousness, so her efforts to "find out" become more persistent and more desperate. Her jealousy and suspicion increase his resentment and cause him to withdraw and withhold even more. The husband and wife are caught in a no-win situation. The wife (in this case the jealous mate) realizes that questioning her husband will probably lead to angry withholding or forced reassurance that ultimately does not reassure her. The husband (in this case the non-jealous mate) realizes that withholding leads to further distrust and jealousy, yet is afraid that disclosing any information may exacerbate the problem.[10] In other cases the husband may be the jealous mate and the wife the non-jealous mate. Nevertheless, the jealous system is activated, maintained, and perpetuated in a similar way.

Systems therapists Won-Gi Im, Stefanie Wilner, and Miranda Breit suggest a technique that can help a couple with such a problem break out of this "double bind." They term the technique "Scrupulous Honesty."[11] The non-jealous mate is instructed to be unwaveringly honest about every detail of the day's experiences and to flood the jealous mate with information. The flood of information helps dispel anxiety in the jealous mate, who had felt excluded and suspicious about clandestine events supposedly taking place.

In another technique, called "Turning the Tables," the non-jealous mate is instructed to act the part of the jealous mate. The attentiveness and newfound interest enable the jealous mate to regain lost self-confidence, and allows the non-jealous mate to rediscover the partner's more positive qualities.

SYSTEMS APPROACH TECHNIQUES YOU CAN USE FOR COPING WITH JEALOUSY

The role-reversal technique I used with Dean and Melanie, in which each mate takes a turn describing the other's point of view, is a good place to start in exploring the systems approach to your jealousy problem. It can help you and your mate understand each other better, and realize how both of you contribute to the creation and maintenance of the jealousy problem.

Another technique, used throughout this book, is called *reframing*.[12] This involves changing the perception of a symptom, a problem, or an action by casting it in a new light. This may be accomplished by reframing the meaning or the function of the behavior. Rather than treating Lillian's affair as a terrible betrayal, the couple learned to see it as a form of communication. Similarly, Darryl's jealousy was described as serving a function in the marriage. This kind of reframing casts the problem, be it unfaithfulness or jealousy, in a less problematic light. Pejorative language used to describe jealousy often prolongs the problem. Instead of using words such as "pathological" or "irrational," you can describe jealousy as a protective response to a perceived threat to a valued relationship. You can further reframe the jealousy problem by describing it as a relationship issue, rather than as the jealous mate's problem. The next step is to figure out what function the jealousy serves for each of you in the relationship, and what you are doing to keep the problem alive.

Your shared awareness of what you are doing to foster the jealousy problem, and what is likely to trigger the undesired response from your mate, often helps to break the circular pattern. As family therapist Gayla Margolin notes, "In general, the more spouses know about how their own problems escalate, the more capable they are of handling them. All it takes is for one spouse to refrain from engaging in his or her prescribed role, and the cycle cannot proceed."[13]

Dr. Margolin cautions, however, that just because the couple has succeeded in disrupting a pattern does not mean the pattern will not reappear. She recommends the establishment of rituals that serve as cues for the new, preferred behavioral sequence—for example, weekly "dates" to assess how the marriage is doing. The development of new communication skills can also help circumvent the old patterns. The language of the systems approach, which emphasizes interpersonal processes rather than individual pathology, offers new ways of communicating.

Carlos E. Sluzki, one of the leading systems theorists, notes that jealousy is "an interpersonal scenario directed and acted by two players." "Characters involved in the scenarios of jealousy usually experience themselves as totally trapped by the plot, though they are, without knowing it, also its coauthors," Sluzki says. The goal of systems therapy is "to help them discover alternative plots, different scenarios that make them aware that they are the owners of their own lives."[14]

AN EVALUATION OF THE SYSTEMS APPROACH

In viewing jealousy as a problem that is best treated at the relationship level, the systems approach makes major contributions to our understanding of jealousy. Although the focus is on the relationship, the assumption is that treating the couple involves or leads to individual change as well. As people view their mates and relationships in a more positive and realistic way, they also begin to feel better about themselves. When both partners try to disrupt the destructive pattern in a relationship, positive change happens faster, is more visible for both mates, and is more likely to endure the test of time.

One of the major criticisms of the systems approach is directed at its disregard of the contributions of childhood experiences and unconscious processes to the origin of jealousy. According to critics (most of them psychodynamically oriented), a jealousy problem can never be cured entirely unless these "deeper" issues in the jealous individual are treated.

This brings me to a question some of you may have been asking yourselves throughout this chapter: Is jealousy a result of a particular dynamic in the relationship, or is it a product of unconscious forces in the mind of the jealous individual? My strong belief is that jealousy is both—and much more.

MEN GET ANGRY, WOMEN GET DEPRESSED

> *Jealousy is the rage of man: therefore he will not spare in the day of vengeance.*
>
> ——PROVERBS
>
> *The jealous are readiest of all to forgive, and all women know it.*
>
> ——DOSTOYEVSKI, THE BROTHERS KARAMAZOV

RON AND CAROL

When Carol met Ron, he'd been divorced and a swinger for several years, "trying to make up for all the good time" he'd lost being married for twenty-six years. Soon after they started dating, it became clear to both of them that there was something special about their relationship. Carol told Ron that she was not interested in being just another member of his harem. "If he wanted a relationship with me," she said, "it had to be with me alone." Ron agreed, and has remained sexually faithful to Carol. This, however, did not prevent him from keeping in touch with his former girlfriends. Carol describes the growing problems it caused:

> His girlfriends call him day and night, paying abso-
> lutely no attention to the fact that Ron is living with

me now. When I dare say anything about their phone calls or about his going to visit one of them, he attacks me for being jealous, demanding, and unreasonable. He has promised not to have sex with anyone else but me, and he says he has kept his promise. What else do I want? The main reason we decided to come to this workshop was that we both felt a need to work on this problem—which Ron keeps referring to as *my* jealousy problem. The other reason was to spend a week together at Esalen. [The Esalen Institute at Big Sur, California, became famous during the days of the encounter movement, and is still active as a site for a variety of workshops.] Ron has been here before and told me it was one of the most beautiful places he has ever been. With *that*, at least, I can agree.

When we arrived here yesterday, the first thing we did was go down to the office to register. All of a sudden, a woman called Wendy whom Ron knew from one of his previous visits here leaped at him and gave him this very big welcome hug. Then she proceeded to massage his chest with a circular motion and I saw the circles growing bigger and bigger, and her hand getting lower and lower down his chest, and I was standing there wondering how low her hand would get.

While all this touchy-feely stuff was going on, I continued standing there like a fool. He never even bothered to introduce me. I don't think he necessarily had to say, "Wendy, this is Carol, the woman I love and am living with now." He could have just put his arm around me to indicate that we are a couple, that he is no longer the swinging bachelor he was when they first met. But he just stood there, clearly enjoying himself, letting her give him a sensuous chest massage.

When we were alone in our room, I told him how

I felt, but I said it calmly. He said he was so excited about seeing Wendy, whom he hadn't seen for a long time, and whom he liked very much, that he behaved rudely, and he was sorry. I accepted his apology and thought this would be the end of it. I should have known better.

This afternoon, right after lunch, he disappeared. I looked for him everywhere. Finally, after about two hours, he appeared in our room and told me that he'd had "an interview" with Wendy.

I felt the blood rush to my head. What, exactly, is "an interview"? Why not call it "a date," which is what it was? And why is he having a date with Wendy on the week we took to be together and work on our relationship?"

Ron had a different perspective on these events:

I'd been married for many years, in a very unhappy marriage. My wife and I were high school sweethearts, so neither of us had experience with anyone else before our marriage. Even though we had practically no sex life for the last few years of our marriage, I was always faithful to my wife. I guess I'm just not the cheating type.

After the divorce, which, by the way, wasn't initiated by me, I discovered women. I also discovered that I love women. I had several girlfriends. Every one of them knew I was seeing others too, and accepted it. They understood that I wasn't ready for a monogamous relationship. Besides, each one of them knew that when I was with her I was with her totally. I know how to give to a woman, and I love giving. So they accepted what I had to give. We all had a *great* time.

Then Carol came into my life. Soon after we started

dating, it became clear to me that this was going to be a very different story. When Carol demanded that I stop seeing other women, I agreed. It was a tremendous sacrifice for me. I was willing to do it for Carol, only because I care about her a great deal. But there were all these women that during my years as a bachelor had become close, intimate friends. Was I supposed to just dump them because I was now living with someone? I've explained this to Carol a hundred times, but she refuses to understand. I've given her no reason to be jealous, but it makes no difference. She simply is a jealous person, and nothing I say or do can change that.

I feel that I have made a far greater sacrifice for the relationship than Carol has made, and I've proved to her that I care. I think her demand that I not see other women at all is unfair and unreasonable. Wendy is a dear friend of mine, whom I haven't seen for a long time. There was nothing wrong in my seeing her. We sat in her room talking, and the door was open the whole time. I feel that I did nothing wrong. So I called it an "interview"—does that justify the scene Carol is making?

It was clear that this discussion was familiar to Ron and Carol— so familiar, in fact, that they weren't really listening to each other. "I think we understand the way both of you are seeing the situation," I said. "But I'm not sure you two see each other's perspective that clearly. Maybe hearing it from someone else might help." I turned to the group and asked whether anyone felt familiar enough with the issue Ron and Carol were discussing to be able to present it.

Jim and Susan, who are not a couple, volunteered. I asked them to sit in the middle of the room facing each other, and to present Ron and Carol's positions to the best of their ability.

Without a moment's hesitation, Jim and Susan continued the

heated discussion. For the rest of us it seemed as though Ron and Carol's argument was never interrupted. "If you cared about me and about the relationship, you wouldn't go and spend time with another woman. Especially not here and not this week. The fact that you didn't go to bed with her on this particular occasion doesn't change that fact," Susan said.

"I've given you more than I've given any other woman in my life, but it's not enough. Nothing is enough for you. You are jealous, demanding, and unreasonable. Next you'll ask me to get rid of my bicycle, because it makes me spend time away from you," Jim responded.

Ron and Carol were listening, dumbfounded. "Does that sound like something you two could have said to each other?" I asked. "This is unbelievable," said Ron. "It's as if Jim were talking straight from my head." "Susan is saying it even better than I can," added Carol. "It's because I am speaking from my own experience," said Jim. "I can't tell you how many times I've had this very conversation myself," agreed Susan.

"Let's see if anyone else in the group has had a similar experience. If you feel that you can speak for either Carol or Ron, please come and join Jim and Susan."

In a few minutes every one of the twenty-two participants in the jealousy workshop was sitting in the middle of the room. The women sat next to Susan. The men (except for one who kept changing his place and position during the argument) sat next to Jim. The argument continued with raised voices and emotions. The women: "If you want to have a truly intimate relationship, you give up a little freedom. It's more than worth it!" The men: "Who are you to say that it's worth it? If you give up your freedom, you are a prisoner. In a good relationship, you trust each other. You don't imprison each other. You women are simply jealous!" The women: "You think we are jealous because we want to protect the relationship. Let's see you guys when you think there is a threat to the relationship. You'd be as jealous as we are, if not more. All we ask is for some safeguards. If we let you guys have your way, there'd be no relationship, or else there'd be a relationship not worth having!"

* * *

It became clear to Ron and Carol that they were not alone in their "jealousy problem." Like so many of us, Carol and Ron falsely assumed that their problem was caused by some innate personality deficiency— in the other. Ron blamed Carol's jealousy. Carol blamed Ron's womanizing. Hearing the men and the women in the group helped break Ron and Carol's "fallacy of uniqueness"—the false assumption that whatever is happening to us is unique, that no one else experiences it in quite the same way. The issue no longer was "*You* are not being considerate," but rather, "Men and women look at relationships differently and that can cause problems."

Men's and Women's Different Approaches to Relationships

What became clear to the group was that the problem had less to do with Carol's or any other woman's jealousy than with a basic difference in the way men and women view intimate relationships. Psychologist Bernie Zilbergeld describes one aspect of this difference: "No matter what else she's doing, no matter how successful she is in her career, it's usually the woman who takes the relationship more seriously and notices how it's doing. She's the one who wants clarification about where it is and where it's heading. She's the one who notices problems and brings them up."[1] Similarly, psychiatrist Jean Baker Miller notes that women's sense of self and of worth is grounded in the ability to make and maintain relationships.[2]

Not all men respond like Ron, and not all women respond like Carol. Sometimes the man wants a committed relationship while the woman wants the freedom to see other men. In such a case, the man is the one labeled "jealous." But in general the difference between men and women tends to be similar to the way it came out in the group discussed here. It is related to a difference in the way men and women view sex and intimacy. Analysis of many studies that investigate differences between men and women suggests that the difference in the meaning attached to sex may be the strongest of all gender differences. It can be summarized as follows: Women generally connect sex with affection, closeness, intimacy. Men generally connect sex with achievement, adventure, control, or pure physical release.[3]

She says: "After a whole day in which we didn't as much as say a word to each other, how can you expect me to want to make love?" He says: "Making love is a way to get close. After we break the tension by making love and feel close, we can talk." For women, notes sociologist Lillian Rubin, satisfactory sex almost always is in the context of an emotional connection. For men, the two are more easily separable. For her, the emotional connection generally must precede the sexual encounter. For him, emotional closeness can be born of the sexual contact. When she speaks of connection she usually means intimacy that's born of verbal expression, sharing of thought and feeling. For him, physical contact is the essence of intimacy.[4]

It's important to know about these differences because, as we saw in Ron and Carol's case, they affect the way all of us deal with jealousy.

In my clinical work I have discovered again and again the value of telling couples that their jealousy problem is shared by most men and women. Like Ron and Carol, when couples discover that their problem is commonly experienced by others, they stop looking for defects in each other. When it becomes clear that like most men and women they have different ways of being intimate, much of the energy that was spent in blaming the other and in protecting themselves from attack is freed and can be used for better coping.

Another important interaction between Carol and Ron in the workshop demonstrated a point made first in chapter one: the connection between our original attraction to our mate and the primary cause of our subsequent stress or jealousy in the relationship.

"What attracted you to Carol when you first met?" I asked Ron.

"Well, she's obviously a very beautiful, sexy woman," answered Ron. "She's also warm and intelligent. But what was most important to me was that she's a strong, independent woman who has a mind of her own. I don't like weak, dependent women."

"And what attracted you to Ron when you first met?" I asked Carol.

"First, I was attracted to his looks. I love thin, tall men and I love gray hair; Ron is skinny, very tall, and has wonderful gray hair. But I was attracted to his warmth and gentleness even more than to his looks. He really knows how to make a woman feel special, like no other man I've ever known."

"So you were attracted to him because he is good looking and knows how to relate to a woman, and now you are distressed because he is attractive to other women and knows how to relate to women," I said. "A bit unfair, isn't it? And you Ron, were attracted to Carol because she is strong and independent and has a mind of her own, but now you're distressed because she wants the relationship to be the way she believes a good relationship ought to be. Women who are strong and have a mind of their own tend to have their own ideas about relationships, too."

When I first observed that we tend to be most distressed by an aspect of our mate's character or behavior that we initially found most attractive, I related it to the notion of our romantic image. The person we are attracted to—the person we choose to fall in love with, and make a commitment to—fits our internalized romantic image in some significant way.

That romantic image is most influenced by our parents, who are our first models of love. It is also influenced to a lesser degree by our culture's definition of who is an attractive man or woman. According to the sociobiological approach, which this chapter will discuss in some detail, this definition of attractiveness is related to our evolutionary history, in which the men and women we have considered attractive were the ones who had a better chance to breed and provide for their offspring, and thus had a better chance to pass on their genes to future generations. In other words, the cultural stereotypes for attractiveness that influence all of us are based on qualifications for breeding.[5] Examples are big breasts in women and a tall, muscular body in men. (Indeed, Ron described Carol, who is big-breasted, as "a very sexy woman"; Carol, like many other women, said she liked tall men.) Why are big breasts attractive in a woman? Because, say the sociobiologists, they suggest that the woman has the attributes needed to nurse a baby. Why are height and a muscular body attractive in a man? Because, say the sociobiologists, they suggest that the man has the attributes needed to be a good provider and protector.

WHICH IS THE MORE JEALOUS SEX?

The answer to this question depends on our definition of jealousy. If we compare the frequency of the experience of jealousy, its symptoms, and its intensity, men and women are very similar. Actually, a consistent finding in my research has been the relative lack of differences between the sexes.[6] Similar findings were reported in other studies of jealousy.[7]

When asked how jealous they were, and how jealous they had been during earlier periods of their life, there was no difference between men and women. There was no gender difference in either frequency or duration of the most intense experience of jealousy, and no difference in either the emotional or the physical components of the experience. There was also no difference between men and women in the number of other people who considered them jealous, either among people who knew them well, or among people with whom they had an intimate relationship. There were few gender differences concerning people or situations that elicit jealousy, all related to women's greater belief in monogamy.

Women and men showed almost no differences in the components of the experience of jealousy, its intensity or its frequency, and showed few differences in the triggers of jealousy. There were major differences, however, in the ways men and women *responded* to jealousy.

HOW DO MEN AND WOMEN RESPOND TO JEALOUSY?

When you are jealous, how do you usually respond? Do you . . .

- talk about it with your mate?

- try to ignore the whole thing?

- let your mate understand that you are hurt?

- scream and shout?

- get away?

- respond with violence?

- respond in some other way?

After you answer this question for yourself, answer it the way you think your mate would. Then, if you care to know and are able to ask, let your mate answer it twice too (once for him- or herself and once for you). The four-way comparison of your responses is sure to be interesting and possibly even surprising. If jealousy is a problem in your relationship, this may open it up for discussion.

When the question was presented to 285 men and 283 women in one of my studies, there were several differences between the responses of men and women, although there were many more similarities than differences.[8] For both men and women, the most frequent response to jealousy was to "talk about it" (38 percent of the men and 30 percent of the women). Talking is obviously the best response. The finding that men report talking more often than women contradicts the stereotype of the silent man and the talkative woman. Yet it confirms the findings of many studies that show that men actually talk more than women do.[9]

For women, the second most frequent response (26 percent) was "try to ignore the whole thing." This was a far less frequent response for men (18 percent). It seems that when her mate is arousing her jealousy, a woman is able, or willing, to ignore it much more than a man can. The sociobiological approach, presented in the next section, provides one explanation as to why this is so.

While men and women are similar in their likelihood to let their mate know that they are hurt (25 percent of men and 24 percent of women), they tend to do it in different ways. For women, responses tend to include crying, sulking, and looking hurt. A man is more likely to express his feelings by lashing out, telling his mate straight out that she's hurt him, and demanding that she stop.

For most men and women, these three responses—talking, ignoring, and expressing hurt—accounted for the majority of the total responses mentioned (81 percent for the men and 80 percent for the women). Only a small percentage of both men and women described themselves as either shouting, getting away, or resorting to violence because of jealousy. Despite the small percentages, it's worth noting that women reported using more verbal abuse than men did, while men reported responding with physical violence three times more than women did. This too confirms the findings of others' studies.[10] A recent study, investigating the reasons for dating violence, found that jealousy caused men to become violent during a date more often than women.[11]

Men and women respond differently to the discovery that their mates have had an affair. Men tend to lash out in anger, which in extreme cases is expressed violently, and to leave the situation or the relationship. Women, on the other hand, tend to respond with depression, self-blame, and attempts to bring the man back. Such attempts might include an effort to make themselves more attractive, or to make the man jealous.[12]

One interpretation of the differences between male and female responses to jealousy is that men are more likely to protect and maintain their self-esteem, while women make a greater effort to maintain the relationship.[13]

When discussing affairs their mates have had, men and women have different concerns. Most men seem interested in the sexual and more "technical" details of the experience, and in comparing themselves to their rival: "How big was his penis?" "How many times did he make you come?" "Was he better or worse than me in bed?" Women, on the other hand, tend to be more interested in the significance of the experience for the future of the relationship: "Do you love her?" "Do you feel closer to her than to me?" Women also tend to be more concerned with the damage the affair could have caused to the intimacy of the relationship. They are often obsessed with such questions as, "What did you tell her about me?" "Did you share with her any intimate details about us?" Women feel tremendous betrayal in discovering that a mate has disclosed such intimate information.

One explanation of these different reactions to jealousy has to do with men's and women's different sex roles. Women are more likely than men to see the relationship as central to their identity and look to find a sense of meaning in it for their entire life. Because women tend to value relationships more than men do, and to have better interpersonal skills, they are more likely to take on the roles of a relationship monitor (the guardian of the relationship), and of an emotional specialist who understands feelings and helps take care of them.[14]

While women tend to be more relationship-oriented, men are more likely to identify with their professional roles. Lillian Rubin notes that when you ask a woman "Who are you?" she most likely will mention her roles as a mother and a wife first, even if she is successful professionally, and only afterward (if at all) will mention her professional role. When you ask a man the same question he is likely to start by telling you what he does for a living, and only afterward (if at all) mention his roles as a husband or a father.[15]

This difference in the level of involvement of men and women in their relationships helps explain why women are more likely to try to improve the relationship after an affair, while men are more likely either to use denial or to leave. A man may choose to deny or refuse to acknowledge the threat instead of consciously ignoring and minimizing it, which women are more likely to do. The reason: If he notices a problem, he will have to do something about it, and he's simply too busy for that.

Another difference between men and women, related to their different levels of involvement in their relationships, is women's greater likelihood to induce jealousy.[16] Psychologist Greg White studied people who admitted to inducing jealousy intentionally with their romantic partners. He discovered five motives for inducing jealousy: to get a specific reward, such as attention; to test the strength of the relationship; to inflict revenge because the partner was seeing someone else; to bolster self-esteem; and to punish the partner. The most popular method of inducing jealousy was to discuss or exaggerate attraction to someone else, followed by flirting, dating others, fabricating rivals, and talking about former romantic partners. Women were more likely to report intentionally inducing jealousy than were men, and were more likely to induce jealousy if they were relatively more involved in the relationship. White's explanation is that women tend to use power that is indirect (manipulative) and personal (based on interaction rather than on concrete resources, such as money).[17]

White's explanation focuses on the power difference between men and women. It assumes that women induce jealousy because they have less power than men in our patriarchal society. The sociobiological approach, on the other hand, assumes that all the differences between men and women, including the differences in their response to jealousy, are innate—the results of evolution through natural selection. Although the differences between men and women are a secondary issue in the psychodynamic and systems approaches, these differences are a primary issue in sociobiology.

THE SOCIOBIOLOGICAL APPROACH

The evolution of sex differences was one of the central themes in Charles Darwin's theory.[18] According to the theory, as males and females ascend the evolutionary scale the differences between them become more distinct—both biologically and behaviorally. Males become more aggressive and more intelligent. Females become more nurturing. The growing differences between the sexes are the result of natural selection.

An organism able to survive and to outreproduce others is an evolutionary "superior" organism. In fighting against each other for possession of the females, the most aggressive and intelligent males won and thus passed on their characteristics to the next generation. Such men were also the better hunters, and so were better able to protect and provide for their women and offspring. For similar reasons, the children of the more nurturing mothers had a better chance of surviving, and passed on these women's characteristics to the next generation.

Darwin also saw an evolutionary reason for jealousy. According to his reasoning, jealousy was an instinctual defense (or, according to the definition I offered earlier, "a protective response") of the pair bond. The feelings and behaviors associated with jealousy served to increase the likelihood that the pair would stay together and replicate their genes. The fact that jealousy appears among animals too, was seen by Darwin as a proof that jealousy is inherited.

Modern sociobiologists also describe jealousy as having an important function for genetic survival.[19] Males who guard at all times against sexual rivals are more likely to raise their own offspring rather than their rivals'. Thus the likelihood is greater that they will pass on their own genes.

A man whose wife has committed adultery is called a cuckold. The term is derived from *cuckoo*—the bird that lays its egg in another's nest. It is never used to describe a woman whose husband has committed adultery. Why? Because a woman cannot be cheated the way a man can in wasting her "parental investment" on a parasite. "Parental investment" is a key concept in sociobiology; it refers to the energy expended by parents to produce and raise offspring.

The sociobiological risk men face of being cuckolded explains why, in the majority of human societies, there is an asymmetry in chastity laws: while adultery is forbidden for both sexes, commonly the woman is more severely penalized for it than the man. A pre-reservation Apache husband, for example, could beat his adulterous wife, kill her and her lover, or cut off the end of her nose so that she was too ugly for anyone to want her again. An Apache wife whose husband committed adultery, on the other hand, could only withdraw from the relationship, attempt to get her husband back, or, in the most extreme of circumstances, divorce him.[20] In most known cultures a husband can punish his wife more severely and dissolve the marriage more easily than a wife can. Homicide statistics also show that men don't take being cuckolded lightly.

Because women are rarely at risk of misidentifying their offspring, a different process applies to them. For women it's not necessarily a faithful man but rather a stable pair bond—a man who is attached and willing to provide and protect—that has survival value. Thus, females who are better able to maintain a pair bond are more likely to have their genes pass on. Because of their different evolutionary risks, male jealousy focuses on sexual threats while female jealousy centers on relationship maintenance and enhancement.

As we can see, sociobiologists view jealousy as an understandable response, irrational only if attention is focused on the individual who experiences it. From the perspective of that individual's genes, jealousy is extremely rational.

Consider, for example, why a man should care about sharing his mate with others if he is convinced that it will in no way affect the satisfaction of his own needs. From this purely "rational" perspective there is absolutely no reason for jealousy scenes and jealousy-triggered murders. But when you view the situation from the perspective of the man's genetic survival, there is a perfectly good reason for his jealousy. It is a response to the threat that his genes may not be passed on to future generations. For a woman, who is always sure that the baby she carries has her genes, the focus of jealousy is on another kind of threat—that she won't have a man to provide for her and her baby.

Why should a man care if the lovely, loving, faithful children he is raising are not his? The reason is that genetic selection follows the rule of "inclusive fitness." All of us have been born because our parents and our parents' parents behaved in a way that guaranteed the passage of their genes to us.

From the perspective of sociobiology, jealousy is not only a component of sex, but also of the investment in offspring. In both men and women, jealousy results from a need for exclusivity: in men a need for sexual exclusivity, in women a need for exclusivity in caring, providing, and commitment.[21]

According to sociobiologists, it matters less to a woman that the man she is married to will spread around his sperm by having casual sex. It matters much more if he spreads around his commitment. In order to prove this point, sociobiologist David Buss asked men and women how upset they would be if they discovered that their romantic partner either had sex with or had a deep emotional attachment to someone else. His results show that 60 percent of the men were most upset at the thought of a sexual liaison, while 84 percent of the women were most upset at the thought of a deep emotional connection.[22]

Sociobiologist Ada Lumpart, as part of a study on vulnerability (defined in the study as fear of being abandoned and willingness to accept hurtful behavior from one's mate) asked men and women: What would you do if you discovered that your mate is unfaithful?

Lumpart discovered that women who had the highest scores of vulnerability said such things as, "I would accept it. What other choice do I have?" Women who had an average vulnerability score said such things as, "I would give him an ultimatum—it's either me or her." Women who had low vulnerability scores said, "I would leave."[23]

According to the study's findings women's vulnerability was not an innate personality characteristic, but instead a result of life circumstances. Vulnerability was low when the woman had no children, highest when she had young children, and low again after the children left home. Men's vulnerability was similar to women's vulnerability before the children were born, but went down with the birth of the children, and up again after investing time and energy in them. After the children left home, the vulnerability of men and women became similar again.

Jealousy is not symmetrical, argue the sociobiologists. In women it is directed at the man's ability to provide and take care of the mother and her infants. In men it is directed at the woman's ability to get pregnant and give birth.

During the reconciliation talk after the discovery of an affair, a man is likely to say—in an attempt to belittle the threat it posed to the relationship—"It was only a physical thing. I didn't feel anything toward her." (In other words, "I didn't make a commitment.") The woman, on the other hand, is likely to say, "It was a platonic friendship. He never touched me."

These explanations (chosen consciously or unconsciously) reflect the different sources of anxiety that the affair raises for men and for women. The opposite explanation—a man's excusing an affair as being a platonic friendship, and a woman excusing it as being only a physical thing—is far less common.[24]

In a survey of types of marriage around the world it was discovered that out of 554 societies in which some kind of marriage exists, only 135 practice monogamy. The majority of societies practice polygamy. The husbands in these societies can have two or more wives at the same time; there are almost no known cases in which two men willingly share the same woman. Polyandry, the practice of a wife having two or more husbands, exists only in four out of the 554 societies.[25]

In cultures that practice polygamy, such as that of Indonesia, many women are willing to share a wealthy husband with other women rather than have an exclusive relationship with a poor man. For such a situation to occur, the society must have a low poverty threshold and wide economic gaps, so that a rich man can compensate for lack of exclusivity.

In the Himalayas and in northern India, both difficult areas to live in, polygamy is practiced at times among brothers and cousins. When it is impossible to define paternity in confidence, males make their sisters' sons their heirs, thus investing in a known kin that will pass on their genes.

In addition to anthropological reports about different forms of marriage around the world, sociobiologists use evidence from a variety of other sources, some of them mentioned earlier. These include analogies to the animal world (with the assumption that if animals' jealousy is genetically controlled, so is human jealousy); the existence of differences between men and women in the ways they respond to jealousy; the fact that male jealousy often leads to conflict and violence; anthropological evidence, such as nearly universal male constraint of female sexuality; and anthropological and psychological reports of men's concerns about their paternity.[26]

From everything said so far, it is clear why sociobiologists think men and women should respond differently to the discovery that their mate has had an affair. For a man, such responses as rage, lashing out, taking revenge, or leaving the woman who betrayed him are all reasonable from an evolutionary perspective. The betrayal affects not only the situation at hand but also future generations. If a cuckolded man doesn't leave, he may be providing for someone else's offspring and genes. From an evolutionary perspective, the woman who has been betrayed faces a far less serious threat. The fact that her husband is spreading his sperm around is not a threat to her own offspring and genes—as long as he stays around and continues to provide for them. Thus her motivation (conscious or unconscious) is to get him away from the other woman and keep him attached to herself and to the family.

Although sociobiologists see jealousy as innate, their approach has an implication for coping, in that it helps break the fallacy of uniqueness, the false assumption that every jealousy problem is unique.

One of the workshop exercises I use to illustrate this is a jealousy sociodrama. I start by drawing an imaginary line across the room. On one end of it is the position that an intimate relationship has to be monogamous: "You can't truly love more than one person. Jealousy is normal and natural when your mate shows an interest in another person." On the other end is the position that loving more than one person is not only possible, but also natural: "Jealousy is not natural, but learned, and thus can be unlearned. If you truly love someone, you want to see him or her happy, even with someone else." I ask two volunteers from the group to argue for each of these two extreme positions. After that I invite the rest of the group to join in and find a spot that fits each of their positions along the continuum. What inevitably happens is similar to what happened to Ron and Carol in the role play described earlier. Most of the women in the group cluster around the "monogamy" side of the jealousy line, while most men cluster around the "love should be free" side—thus demonstrating the basic sociobiological argument. When couples discover that their conflict about jealousy is experienced by most other men and women in a similar way, and that it actually makes sense from an evolutionary perspective, they are able to stop blaming each other, stop feeling guilty, and devote their energy to coping.

A POWER PERSPECTIVE

According to the critics of sociobiology, the differences between men and women do not result from an evolutionary process; they are caused primarily by social processes and existing conditions in the society that affect all couples and all individuals. One such social condition with special relevance for the issue of jealousy is the power difference between men and women. Power, for the purpose of this discussion, is the difference between your dependency on your mate and your mate's dependency on you. The dependency can be emotional, financial, or of some other type.

Women tend to respond to jealousy in the typically "feminine" way, not because they are women but because they have less power in most relationships. Critics of sociobiology argue that one's response to jealousy has more to do with one's power in the relationship than with one's gender.

The more powerful person in the relationship, whether a man or a woman, tends to respond to the jealousy-triggering situation in the "masculine" way—lashing out in anger, leaving, and so on. The weaker person typically behaves in the "feminine" way: crying, trying to become more attractive, trying to make the mate jealous, and so on. Sadly, in most cases it is the person who cares less, and has more alternatives outside the relationship, that has more power in the relationship.[27]

This brings us back to the difference between men's and women's degrees of involvement in the relationship. Women are socialized to care more about relationships and to desire commitment more than men. The result is their loss of power to men. These power differences are not innate, but are primarily a result of power differences in the society, which are reflected in power differences within the couple.

A woman in her fifties who has spent most of her adult life rearing children and supporting her husband's career has far fewer alternatives outside the marriage than does her successful husband. When she discovers that her husband is having an affair with his young secretary, her jealousy is not only a response to a perceived threat to a valued love relationship; it is also a response to a threat to a marriage that defines her entire life.

A wife who creates alternatives for herself outside the marriage and is less dependent on her husband emotionally, socially, and financially is less likely to take on the role of the jealous mate. One couple in their early fifties is an example of this kind of role reversal.

The wife, Laura, had been a homemaker from the time her oldest child was born until the youngest finished high school. At that time she felt that she could afford to do something for herself, so she went back to school and got a degree in management.

With the help of her high grades and excellent recommendations from her teachers, she was able to get a good job in a large pharmaceutical company. There her enthusiasm and hard work earned Laura one promotion after another. Soon she was managing the state office of the company, traveling often, meeting interesting people, and coming home late.

Her husband, Adam, was an engineering manager in a small industrial company, and hadn't advanced much in his career during those years. At about the time Laura started flying up the career ladder, he started feeling bored with his work, frustrated, and angry. Just when she was finding great significance in everything she was doing, he started asking himself, "What's the meaning of it all?" While neither one of them acknowledged the change, Adam was now more needy of Laura than she was of him, and felt very threatened by the people she interacted with at work. Whenever Laura came home late, which was often, Adam demanded to know where she had been, with whom, what they had done, and what they had talked about.

At first Laura tried to be patient and understanding. Whenever possible, she called Adam if she was going to be late, and explained in detail what she did during her absence. She also tried hard to ignore his hostile tone when he interrogated her. But after a while she started to lose her patience and resent his jealousy. She was having a wonderful time at work and was doing nothing to justify his jealousy and rudeness.

The happier Laura was with her world outside the marriage, and the more unhappy Adam was with his own world, the more jealous he became. He didn't trust Laura's explanations, and continued to feel hurt and excluded even when he knew she had spent an evening with her women friends. Indeed, he *was* excluded from her world, just when he needed her most.

According to sociobiology, there was absolutely no reason for Adam to be jealous. First, Laura was spending time with women friends, so there was no chance of his being cuckolded. Second, Laura had already gone through menopause, so there was no chance she could become pregnant and carry someone else's genes. Furthermore, they had finished rearing their children, and he was as assured of his genetic survival as anyone can be.

From the power perspective, however, there was a good reason for Adam to be jealous. Throughout their life together he had been "the man" in the family and, as such, had had more power than Laura. Now suddenly their roles were reversed and he was the one with less power in the relationship.

Adam, who is a handsome, masculine, successful man, responded to the perceived threat to the quality of his relationship with Laura in a traditionally "feminine" way. He became depressed, sulked, bought himself new clothes (hoping Laura would notice), and tried to make her jealous by seeing friends without her. The only problem was that Laura didn't mind at all, and even encouraged him to see his friends more often.

Adam had to realize that as long as he was doing things to get a response from Laura, he was still dependent on her. He also had to realize that at the base of his jealousy were feelings of powerlessness and dependency.

In order to overcome his dependency, Adam renewed contacts with people he liked but with whom he hadn't kept in touch. Because Laura had been responsible for maintaining social contacts in their marriage, when she didn't like some of Adam's friends and colleagues she had arranged to avoid seeing them socially. Now that Laura had her own social world, Adam could choose the people he wanted to have as friends, independent of those he and Laura were seeing as a couple.

The task was not an easy one for Adam, who had relied on Laura throughout their marriage to do the social talking for him. In fact, Laura's social skills and high energy were the things Adam had found most attractive when they first met. Each time he called someone, he was afraid he would discover that the person was surprised and not happy to hear from him after all this time. This never happened.

When Adam became more involved with his own friends, interests, and activities—he loved hiking, for example, so he joined the Sierra Club and started mountain hiking regularly—he stopped perceiving Laura's work as a threat. His increased satisfaction with his own life and an increased sense of power in the relationship led to a decrease in jealousy.

WHY DISCUSS SEX DIFFERENCES IN JEALOUSY?

We've seen that men can respond to jealousy in a way that is typically female, and women can respond in a way that is typically male. Yet research shows that couples like Adam and Laura are exceptions, especially during the child rearing years. Most men and women tend to respond to jealousy in the way that is characteristic of their sex. As Ron and Carol's case demonstrated, knowing about these differences can help couples break their own fallacy of uniqueness and work toward resolving their jealousy problem.

The fact that there are exceptions, however, suggests that the differences between "male" and "female" responses to jealousy are not purely innate, as the sociobiologists claim. Genetic programming is not all-powerful, especially in a creature as sophisticated as a human being. Instead, these differences result from evolutionary forces in combination with a variety of other forces in society, in the relationship, and in the individual.

This brings us back to the notion of jealousy as a result of an interaction between a certain disposition and a certain trigger. Genetic programming and power differences prescribed by society each influence men's and women's differing predispositions to jealousy.

Whether or not these predispositions manifest themselves depends on the dynamics of the particular relationship and internal processes in the mind of the individual.

AN EVALUATION OF THE SOCIOBIOLOGICAL APPROACH

The sociobiological approach helps us focus attention on the different ways men and women express jealousy. When couples are told that other men and women experience jealousy conflicts in a similar way, they are vastly relieved. As a result they are often able to confront their own and their mate's jealousy with more understanding and less blame.

Unlike the sociobiological focus on the differences between men and women in jealousy, the psychodynamic approach, the systems approach, and the behavioral approach (presented in chapter nine) view gender differences as mostly irrelevant to the treatment of jealousy. The psychodynamic approach recognizes that the childhood experiences of boys and girls are different, but the process of unearthing the unconscious trauma at the base of a jealousy problem is the same for men and for women. In the systems approach, though men and women may play different roles in a romantic relationship, the goal of disrupting negative interaction patterns does not depend on who plays what role. In the behavioral approach, it doesn't matter whether a man or a woman responds inappropriately to a jealousy trigger; the goal of therapy is to unlearn that inappropriate response and replace it with a more appropriate one.

The sociobiological approach has received a great deal of criticism, for using circular reasoning and explanations that can never be empirically substantiated or refuted. It looks at existing phenomena, such as differences between the sexes in their responses to jealousy, and argues that there must be an evolutionary reason for their existence. Sociobiologists are convinced that if there were no evolutionary reason for the survival of a certain trait, it would not have been passed on until today. But proving a phenomenon by its existence is not a valid proof.

Another criticism has been directed at sociobiologists' attempt to link human jealousy to animal jealousy, both supposedly a result of genetic programming. In fact, the critics argue, there is no empirical research that directly links jealousy with a particular gene.[28]

Furthermore, the sociobiological notion that jealousy is "natural" and reflects some kind of biological imperative is dangerous. It can justify unacceptable responses to jealousy, such as violence.[29] As we will see in chapter eight, there is a long tradition of tolerance toward men who kill their lovers and rivals because of the belief that these men cannot help themselves. This biological imperative is far less likely to be evoked in defense of jealous women.

The notion that men and women are genetically "wired" to respond to jealousy in particular ways can also be used as an excuse not to work on a jealousy problem.

INTEGRATING THE SOCIOBIOLOGICAL AND POWER PERSPECTIVES

After reviewing the two explanations for the sex differences in jealousy—the sociobiological and the power perspectives—you may wonder which explanation is the "correct" one. Are the differences between men and women in jealousy the result of evolutionary processes, or are they the result of a certain social reality?

Scholars in each of these fields believe that they have the only possible answer to this question. It is possible, however, to integrate the two perspectives. Jealousy is, at least in part, a result of an interaction between evolutionary forces and current social forces. As we saw in the preceeding two chapters, it is also the result of certain processes in the mind of the jealous individual and of destructive patterns within the couple's relationship.

The picture of jealousy that emerges from the last three chapters is of a circle within a circle within a circle. The first circle is the individual. The second is the couple. The third is the culture in which the couple lives. Jealousy is experienced by the individual, is played out in the couple relationship, and is shaped by evolution and by social forces.

Now we can move on to examine the social forces that define when jealousy is experienced and how it is expressed.

ROMANTIC JEALOUSY IN DIFFERENT CULTURES

From the moment of his birth, the customs into which [an individual] is born shape his experience and behavior. By the time he can talk, he is the little creature of his culture.
—RUTH BENEDICT, PATTERNS OF CULTURE

Jealousy [has] a human face.
—WILLIAM BLAKE, SONGS OF EXPERIENCE

A comparison of the ways people in different cultures experience and express jealousy shows that social forces exert a major influence on people's responses to it.[1] A situation that provokes jealousy in one culture at a particular time in history does not necessarily provoke jealousy in another culture or time. A response considered normal and acceptable in one culture may be considered abnormal and unacceptable in another. The comforting conclusion is that everything you have done or imagined doing, no matter how strange your own culture would consider it, is probably normal somewhere else. In this chapter we will explore the social-psychological approach, which views jealousy as a social phenomenon rooted in the culture we live in.

Let us start with an example of the ways men in different cultures respond to being cuckolded. A turn-of-the-century Bakongo African husband who discovered that his wife had an affair demanded a large sum of money from her lover.[2] A Samoan husband cut out the eyes of the lover or bit off his nose and ears.[3] A "liberated" American husband, living at the end of the twentieth century, has been taught that jealousy is evidence of low self-esteem and tries hard to overcome it.[4]

Can you imagine a situation in which a newlywed bridegroom would actually ask another man to have sexual intercourse with his bride? This, too, happened at times among the Bakongo. Upon completion of the marriage ceremony, it was customary for the village elders to enter the house of the newlywed couple to make sure that everything was in order and, most important, that the bridegroom was able to consummate the marriage. If he was unable to do it, the marriage was dissolved. Sometimes, to avoid shame and humiliation, an impotent husband would find a suitable young man and permit him to have sex with his wife. If a child was born out of their union, the husband treated it as his own. A similar custom was practiced by the Plateau tribes of northern Zimbabwe. A sterile or impotent husband would at times ask his brother to have sex in secret with his wife, so the couple could have a child.[5] Similar choices are being made in modern Western society; infertile women have eggs donated by their sisters or mothers rather than have a surrogate ovum donor.

According to cross-cultural psychologist Ralph Hupka, cultures affect our response to jealousy in two primary ways:

1. By defining or not defining a particular event as a threat, which includes (a) designating the events that make us jealous; (b) specifying when are we allowed to perceive a threat; and (c) creating the conditions that dispose us to jealousy.

2. By giving us certain options for responding when an event is defined as a threat.[6]

EVENTS THAT MAKE US JEALOUS

Our culture defines for us the events that will make us perceive a threat to our marriage. These events vary widely, and don't always include an interloper having sex with our mate. For example, a husband among the Yurok tribe of California or the Pawnee of the American plains saw another man's request for a cup of water from his wife as a clear signal that the other man was after her.[7]

An Eskimo husband, on the other hand, offered his wife to a guest in a ceremony of "putting out the lamp." A good host was expected, after turning out the lamp at night, to invite the guest to have sexual intercourse with his wife. A husband who did not give his wife to his guest was considered stingy, inhospitable, and mean. Therefore, a husband upbraided his wife if she was slow to respond to the guest. Yet the same husband would become intensely jealous if his wife had sexual intercourse with that same guest in circumstances other than the lamp ceremony. It was not unusual for the Eskimo husband to kill such an interloper.[8]

The examples of the Yurok and the Eskimo demonstrate that the culture, far more than the individual, determines when it is appropriate to perceive a threat to the marriage. Anthropologist Margaret Mead describes another example of this in the marriage customs of the Banaro of New Guinea. These customs are full of occasions that in modern Western culture would give rise to tremendous jealousy.[9]

A young Banaro man who eloped with the woman he loved did not approach her sexually during the elopement. Instead of submitting to their mutual passion, he brought her, still a virgin, to his father's house where he knew she would be submitted to a cruel public defloration ceremony. Then the young bridegroom had to allow another man to enjoy his wife sexually for a whole year after their marriage, before he himself could approach her.

Each Banaro man had a ceremonial friend. It was the duty of this friend to initiate his friend's son's future wife into sex. This was done very formally in the "Goblin House," in front of the sacred pipes upon which no woman was allowed to look. After the ceremony the young bride was returned to her father-in-law's care. The ceremonial friend had sex with her, always ritually, until a child was born. The child was known as the "goblin child." Only then was the husband allowed to take his wife.

Meanwhile, the young bridegroom was initiated sexually by the wife of his father's ceremonial friend. The initiation started with the young man being sent to look for the older woman in the forest. Later, on ceremonial occasions, the young bridegroom and his ceremonial friend would exchange wives. Their wives could even bear children to their husband's friends, instead of their husbands. Clearly, what would be an obvious jealousy trigger for us had a different meaning for the Banaro.

WHEN ARE WE ALLOWED TO PERCEIVE A THREAT?

Cultures vary widely in what is considered acceptable evidence for people to conclude that there is a serious threat to their marriage. The Saora of India required the husband to see his wife in the act of sexual intercourse with her lover before he could accuse her of adultery.[10] For the Dobu of equatorial Africa, personal suspicion was legitimate enough cause to make an individual perceive a threat to the marriage.[11] Among the Plateau tribes of northern Zimbabwe, the proof of the wife's infidelity was the birth of a stillborn child or her own death in childbirth. The woman who lay dying or mourning the death of her baby was asked to name her lover, whether or not she actually had one. The man she named was considered guilty without a need for further proof.[12]

In chapter two, I mentioned that for the 728 Americans I questioned, the most serious perceived threat was a sexual liaison their mate had with someone else.[13] A Zuñi wife, on the other hand, did not perceive her husband's sexual liaisons as a threat to her marriage; instead, it was the gossip of the village people about her husband that caused her to perceive a threat and confront him.[14]

Another example of what our culture would consider a legitimate reason for jealousy can be found in polygamous societies. In such societies, marrying several women is the rule for rich and influential men, and women don't perceive their husbands' marriage to other women as a threat.[15]

Actually, it seems that when a woman is the first wife, she may even favor this arrangement for the help with household chores, friendship, and prestige that it provides for her husband and for herself. Margaret Mead describes a case of a woman in a polygamous culture who hauled her husband into court on the charge that she had been married to him three years and borne him two children, yet he had not taken another wife. The native court allowed the husband six months in which to take a second wife. A second wife would add to this woman's prestige by conferring upon her the rank of "first wife." In addition, the second wife would provide the household with another laborer and childbearer. Because the addition of other women to the household enhanced the first wife's status and self-esteem, there was no occasion for jealousy—*unless* one of those secondary wives became the favorite. The usurpation of the first wife's dignities provided both the occasion and the justification for jealousy.[16]

Similarly, in most polyandrous societies, the multiple husbands tend to show little jealousy as long as status differences are observed.

All of these examples demonstrate how cultures define the rules for verifying the existence of a threat to a marriage. Members of a culture will not support someone's jealous behavior unless that person provides the appropriate justification.

How Cultures Create the Conditions that Dispose Us to Jealousy

According to the social-psychological approach, jealousy is not simply a psychological phenomenon that takes place in the mind of an individual. It's a social phenomenon as well—a product of growing up in a certain culture, anchored in the basic decisions made in that culture about such fundamental issues as physical survival and mating. These decisions become integrated into the customs, morals, and laws of the culture. They define for the individual what is valued and must therefore be protected from possible loss. Thus, each culture also defines for the individual the situations that trigger jealousy. If we consider what is valued in our society, we discover that it is related to the most common triggers of jealousy.

Societies differ greatly in the conditions that make their members susceptible to jealousy. The more members of a society depend on their mate to fulfill different needs or help face threats to survival, the greater the potential for jealousy.[17]

The Ammasalik Eskimo, for example, was dependent on a competent mate to survive the long, harsh winter. Consequently an interloper presented not only a threat to the Eskimo's marriage, but to his actual survival. One cultural solution was a custom of wife-stealing. A man who lost his mate to another was allowed, among other solutions, to steal the wife of another husband. A man who dared to carry away the wife in the presence of her husband was considered a powerful person, and his status in the community increased.[18]

The Dobuan of the D'Entrecastreaux Islands, east of New Guinea, lived in tiny hostile kin groups on limited and unfruitful lands. A Dobuan man would stay up half the night uttering magic spells and incantations to protect his crop of yams and seduce the yams of his neighbor's field into his own. But no amount of spells and hard work produced a really fine crop. The Samoans, on the other hand, lived in large villages united by formal ceremonies on abundant fertile land. This difference is one of the conditions that, according to Margaret Mead, help explain why jealousy was a widespread phenomenon among the Dobuan, while among the Samoans jealousy was rare.[19]

Marriage happened at a young age for the Dobuan, and not always by mutual consent. It came after a period of great sexual freedom, and imposed strict fidelity on both mates. As a result, during the engagement both mates were tortured by the suspicion that the other was returning to those recently abandoned sexual adventures. The suspicions only increased after marriage. A Dobuan husband followed his wife everywhere. He sat nearby, watching while she did her work, and counted her footsteps if she left for the bush. A Dobuan wife was never allowed to go to another village alone.

The punishment for adultery among the Dobuan was as harsh as their jealousy. A man who was discovered having sex with another man's wife was likely to have a spear thrust in his back. When that option was not available, the betrayed spouse could try to commit suicide by taking fish poison.

OPTIONS FOR RESPONDING TO JEALOUSY

Culturally sanctioned responses to jealousy are as varied as the cultures on earth. They range from doing nothing to killing both the unfaithful mate and the interloper. The first option is most often given to women, the latter to men. You may recall the discussion in the last chapter of the difference between men and women in "paternity confidence"—the fact that while women always know that their offspring are theirs, men have no such assurance. This difference, according to sociobiology, explains why the majority of human societies penalize women more severely than men for adultery.

As an example of a woman's comparatively mild response to jealousy, we can look again at the Zuñi wife, who at first said nothing to her unfaithful husband. But when his sexual liaison became the source of tribal gossip, forcing her to respond, she refused to wash his laundry. This made it clear to him that the affair was common knowledge, and that he'd better stop it. Among the Murngin of Australia, a wife had only one culturally sanctioned way to respond to her husband's infidelity: to assault him verbally in public. If she ran away, her father and brothers would search for her and return her to her husband, who would then beat her as a punishment and a warning.[20] Physical aggression is allowed among women only when directed toward a rival. Among the Toba Indians of Bolivia, a wife was allowed either to leave her unfaithful husband or fight her rival. Such fights could go on for hours, the two women beating each other with their hands and scratching each other either with their fingernails or with cactus thorns.[21]

Culturally acceptable male responses to a wife's unfaithfulness tend to be on the more extreme pole in severity. In cases of jealousy-related "justifiable homicide," the justified party, almost without exception, is a man.[22] An Antakerrinya husband in South Australia who discovered that his wife had been unfaithful, was allowed to cut her across her thighs and buttocks, or burn her.[23] A Marquesan husband, under similar circumstances, could punish his wife either by whipping or by killing her.[24] Nineteenth-century Apache husbands would cut all the hair from the heads of their unfaithful wives, and sometimes cut their noses.[25]

A nineteenth-century husband of an aborigine tribe of New Zealand had several culturally accepted options for responding to his wife's unfaithfulness: he could beat, divorce, or kill her. He could also demand either compensation or a duel from her lover. In the duel, both men were armed with spears. The husband could try to pierce his rival's chest with his spear—while his rival was allowed only to ward off the thrust. After the rival warded off the third thrust, the debt was considered paid and both men continued to fight on even terms.[26]

In all the cases cited above, the options for response available to the jealous individual were related to the culture's evaluation of the offense and the threat it implied. In addition, cultures make responses available according to the assignment of responsibility for the jealousy-producing event.

For example, among the Maori of New Zealand, when a wife was unfaithful, her family was required to compensate her husband with a land settlement. But if she ran away with her lover, the husband was held accountable; in the interest of the community, he should have been aware of what was going on and prevented the escape. Because the husband was held responsible, his property was taken away as punishment.[27]

Since jealousy is a protective response to a perceived threat to the marriage, and since the stability of the marriage is important to the society as well as to the individual—it ensures that children will be born and taken care of by both parents—most societies accept jealous behavior as legitimate. According to sociologist Kingsley Davis, the jealousy situation is not a triangle but a quadrangle, because the public or the community at large is always an interested party. By failing to acknowledge the public or community, we fail to grasp the social character of jealousy. To understand jealousy we must understand the social function it serves.[28]

Most cultures support the betrayed mate, and condemn the transgressing mate and the interloper; the example of the Maori is an exception. Yet the punishments prescribed by the social norms of different cultures, and even the person designated to deliver the punishment, can vary greatly. Among the Plateau tribes of northern Zimbabwe, for example, when the adultery took place between individuals of equal rank, it was the duty of the chief to flog the male lover. Punishment was much more severe when the husband caught his wife and her lover "in the act." In such cases the husband was expected to kill both wife and lover. If he chose not to punish them, and the wife was caught again with a lover, the villagers took the responsibility for punishment. They impaled the unfaithful wife and her lover on sharp stakes, and then taunted them until they died.[29]

The punishments delivered by the husband, the villagers, and the chief were all prescribed according to a social code and designed to serve as deterrents. They demonstrate the relationship between the individual's response to jealousy and prohibition against adultery, aimed at protecting the institution of marriage.

Among the Hidatsa Indians of North America a husband had several options if his wife ran away with another man. One option was to kill his wife and seize the property that belonged to her lover and his friends. This custom encouraged men not to get involved with married women for fear their friends might have to pay for their transgression. But the most praiseworthy alternative was to treat the whole affair as good riddance from the wife by inviting the runaways to his lodge and formally presenting his wife to her new lover.[30]

Everything said so far indicates that the ways in which we experience and express jealousy reflect the norms and social structure of the society. What social forces encourage or discourage jealousy? Following the lead of Ralph Hupka, in the following section we will examine this question through a comparison of two cultures, the Toda and the Apache.

THE TODA AND THE APACHE

Two of the most extreme examples of the ways different cultures relate to jealousy are the turn-of-the-century Toda of Southern India[31] and the pre-reservation Apache Indians of North America.[32] The Toda tended to minimize the experience and display of jealous behavior. The Apache, on the other hand, expressed jealousy frequently. A close look at the two cultures can help explain this major difference in predisposition toward jealousy.

For the Toda, jealousy was akin to selfishness, and was therefore considered a minor sin. According to the Toda religion, people who died traveled across a river on a bridge made of spiderwebs before they reached the heavenlike home of their god. Individuals who were jealous during life had heavy hearts that tore the thin bridge, so they fell into the river, where they were bitten by leeches. Swamp-dwellers would then detain them for a period of time proportionate to the severity of their jealousy and selfishness. Only after they paid in this way for their sins were they allowed to reach the home of their god.

For the Apache, on the other hand, jealousy was a culturally acceptable emotion. One did not need to apologize for behaving in a jealous manner or repent for experiencing jealousy.

The Toda were primarily polyandrous. When a woman married a man, she automatically became the wife of his brothers as well, even of those not yet born. She had sexual relations with the brothers as well as with the husband who married her. The woman and her "husbands" lived together as one family. Marriage was not a requirement or a reward for anything. Physical needs for food and shelter were provided by the joint effort of all the men in the family. Emotional needs for companionship were also easily satisfied. Marriage had to be its own reward.

The Apache Indians, on the other hand, were monogamous. Marriage for an Apache was the key to recognition as a mature adult and to economic self-sufficiency. Adults without mates were rare and considered abnormal. Both husband and wife were expected to contribute to the economy of the family. Men hunted; women gathered wild fruits and vegetables.

For the Apache, marriage was also a prerequisite to sexual gratification. Only after marriage to her was an Apache man allowed to touch a woman's abdomen, thighs, shoulders, or legs. Before the marriage, sexual gratification was not freely available to the Apache. Virginity in both sexes was associated with purity, and premarital sex was discouraged. For the Apache, sexual pleasure was a reward earned after a long period of deprivation—a reward to be jealously guarded against the threat posed by an interloper.

The Toda, by contrast, had few sexual restrictions, and sex was easily obtained both before and after marriage. Both husbands and wives were allowed to have lovers. When a man wanted someone else's wife as a lover, he sought the consent of the wife and her husband or husbands. If consent was given by all, the men negotiated for an annual fee to be received by the husband(s). The man then visited the woman at the house of her husband(s), or in some cases had her live with him as if she were his wife. Since the wife's lover was not perceived as a threat to the marriage, her relationship with him was not likely to trigger much jealousy in her husband(s).

Among the Toda, the clan collectively owned the most valuable property: the sacred buffaloes and the land. Each family had its own non-sacred buffaloes, whose milk was a major source of food, and its own house. Material possessions were few and not highly valued. People had almost no personal property, and even things that belonged to individuals (such as dishes and jewelry) were shared by the whole family.

The Apache owned most property individually, and such property was not used by anyone else, even a sibling or a parent, without permission. A child given a horse by his father could kill it if he wished; his father was not likely to interfere. Handling someone else's belongings implied a special and intimate relationship. A husband's clothes, for example, could be washed only by his wife, mother, or daughter. Any other woman who did his laundry was assumed to be having an affair with him.

The Toda had a casual approach not only to personal property, but to personal descendants as well. Men took little interest in knowing whether a child they were rearing was their own; fatherhood was a legal relation established through a ceremony in which the man gave a bow and arrow to the mother. At times that man had no physical contact with the mother prior to the ceremony. The oldest husband in the family usually performed the ceremony when the wife was about seven months pregnant, yet all the husbands were regarded equally as the father of the child.

To the Apache, children were a great asset that provided not only status and prestige, but also a form of social security, since children fed and cared for their parents in old age. Daughters attracted sizable marriage gifts. After their marriage, their parents had access to free labor from their husbands and to portions of the game the husbands brought home. In addition, family and children were the major vehicle for attaining high status in the tribe, because family size was a reflection of wealth. The ability to support a large family indicated that a man was a good hunter. Because the Apache placed such great importance on personal lineage, "paternity confidence" was extremely important to them, and any possible threat to it provided an occasion for jealousy. When an Apache husband was away for any length of time, he instructed a close blood relative to spy on his wife to make sure she was not seeing other men.

· Another difference between the Toda and the Apache had to do with the importance of women's economic contribution. Toda women contributed little; the men did virtually everything, including the cooking. Women fetched water, embroidered clothes, pounded grain, and cleaned the house. They were not allowed to approach the buffaloes or handle the milk. They were also excluded from all political and religious activities. What compensated women for their low economic and political status was the great personal freedom they enjoyed.

The Apache husband and wife were economically self-sufficient and both contributed significantly to the economy of the family— men by hunting, women by gathering and preparing the food.

The Toda and the Apache had different options for responding to situations likely to trigger jealousy, which correspond to the level of threat presented by the situation. As mentioned earlier (see page 110), an Apache man whose wife had been unfaithful was allowed to kill her and her lover, or else mutilate her face. For the Toda man, the discovery that his wife had had sex with another man implied a far less serious threat. In fact, there was a positive side, in that an appropriate fee would be arranged for the borrowing of his wife. Consequently, the husband was not expected to show any jealousy at all.

The comparison between the Toda and the Apache suggests that the most important difference between a culture that maximizes jealousy and a culture that minimizes it is not in the social norms for or against *expressing* jealousy, but instead in the social organization that determines the likelihood that people will *perceive* threats to their intimate relationships.

Differences in the social organization of the Toda and the Apache can explain, far better than the individual characteristics of a particular Apache or Toda, why the Apache were so much more likely than the Toda to feel threatened and respond with jealousy.

According to Ralph Hupka, the comparison between the Apache and the Toda indicates that cultures that encourage jealousy have four major characteristics:

- emphasis on property rights
- social codes that make sex hard to get
- emphasis on personal descendants
- emphasis on marriage for economic survival and social status

Consider how twentieth-century North Americans compare to the Toda and the Apache, both in social organization and in jealousy. Is the social organization of North American society the kind that encourages or discourages jealousy? Furthermore, is your own jealousy strictly a personal matter or are you also responding to cultural norms, attitudes, and values?

JEALOUSY IN AMERICAN CULTURE

I think most readers would agree that except for extreme and "abnormal" cases, such as can be found in any culture, North Americans are much more likely to experience and display jealousy than the Toda, yet less likely to feel threatened in a jealousy-provoking situation than the Apache.

The reason for that can be found in certain characteristics of our culture that predispose us to respond to jealousy triggers in a particular way. Let us examine twentieth-century American culture according to the characteristics of cultures that encourage jealousy.

How are we socialized to relate to jealousy? Are we taught that it is a negative emotion akin to selfishness, or is it a culturally acceptable emotion?

Analysis of articles in popular magazines reveals that the experience, expression, interpretation, and treatment of jealousy in the United States have changed substantially in the last twenty years as compared to the twenty-five years following the end of World War II. Before about 1970, jealousy was seen primarily as a positive emotion and a proof of love. Since 1970 it has been seen primarily as a negative emotion that reflects a personal defect rooted in low self-esteem.

In a survey of popular magazine articles on jealousy over a forty-five-year period, sociologist Gordon Clanton discovered that from the end of World War II until the late 1960s, virtually all said that a certain amount of jealousy was natural, a proof of love, and good for the marriage. The reader (typically a woman) was advised to keep her jealous feelings under control and to avoid unreasonable jealousy marked by suspicion, hostility, accusations, and threats. The woman was told to avoid situations that might make her husband jealous, but to interpret *his* expressions of jealousy as evidence of love. Only when jealousy threatened the stability of the marriage was professional help recommended.

Around 1970, a new view of jealousy started to take root. Magazine articles began to question the appropriateness of jealous feelings in intimate relationships. They no longer assumed that jealousy was evidence of love. For the first time, *guilt* about jealousy became a problem for large numbers of people. According to this emerging view, jealousy was not natural; it was learned. "Jealousy was no longer seen as a proof of love," Clanton observed; "it was, rather, evidence of a defect such as low self-esteem or the inability to trust. Thus, jealousy was no longer seen as good for relationships; it was bad for them. From this it followed that one could and should seek to eradicate every trace of jealousy from one's personality. Various prescriptions for achieving this were offered by therapists, gurus, and advice-givers."[33]

American society is far larger, more complex, and more varied than the primitive cultures described throughout this chapter. Different subcultures relate to jealousy differently. If you are a member of an Italian, Japanese, or Mexican subculture, for example, chances are that your cultural heritage has a major influence on your predisposition to jealousy.

As we know by now, the most important difference between a culture that encourages jealousy and a culture that discourages its lies not in the norms for or against expressing jealousy, but rather in the social organization that determines the likelihood that jealousy will be provoked. Have the relevant aspects in the social organization of the United States changed in the last forty-five years? And today, do they maximize or minimize jealousy? Let's examine the evidence.

. Americans tend to be monogamous. When a marriage doesn't work, they divorce and remarry, a practice termed by family therapists "serial monogamy." Marriage may not be the key to recognition as a mature adult and to economic self-sufficiency, but it is nonetheless important. The vast majority of Americans marry at some point; remaining single throughout life is rare and considered not altogether normal.

Despite this testimony to the importance of marriage, in recent decades people have been getting married later, and more couples have been living together out of wedlock. According to the 1990 *Statistical Abstracts of the United States*, 2,588,000 heterosexual unmarried couples are living together. This is more than three times the number in 1970, and more than four times the number in 1960. According to sociologist Jessie Bernard, the importance of marriage is reflected in the attitudes toward jealousy.[34]

Another change that has taken place since World War II is the growing contribution of married women to the family income. Labor statistics indicate that women's participation in the labor force has increased steadily since 1950. According to 1988 census data, 65 percent of all mothers and 57 percent of all wives are employed outside the home. Societal attitudes toward married women's work have also changed. In the 1990s, more people accept a career as a life choice for women than have ever done so in the past. A nationwide survey discovered that three-quarters of the Americans surveyed approved of employed wives. A similar survey conducted forty years earlier showed that three-quarters of the Americans surveyed disapproved of a wife working if she had a husband who could support her.[35] Financially independent working wives are less dependent on their husbands and on the marriage than are housewives. When such career women do not find their marriages fulfilling, they are far more likely than housewives to leave their husbands.[36]

Other survey studies show that the American view of women's roles has become increasingly more liberated in the last decades in terms of such qualities as independence and assertiveness.[37]

One of the results of women's growing economic and psychological independence is a decrease in their dependence on their husbands and marriages. Losing her husband is less likely to threaten a career woman's financial and social position, and consequently her jealousy is less likely to focus on this kind of threat.

Over the last forty-five years, American society has also become more permissive, especially toward premarital sex. A Harris poll taken in the mid-1980s found that 70 percent of the women and 79 percent of the men aged eighteen to twenty-nine thought it was all right for regularly dating couples to have sex. On the other hand, only 40 percent of the women and 55 percent of the men aged fifty to sixty-four thought this was acceptable behavior.[38] This change in attitude is manifested in behavior as well. A survey among married couples indicates that of the couples who were eighteen to twenty-four years of age, 95 percent of the men and 81 percent of the women had had premarital sex.[39]

According to Kingsley Davis, jealousy is a culturally sanctioned response to a violation of sexual property rights.[40] As sexual norms regarding such issues as premarital sex and virginity become more liberal, we can expect that the norms supporting the expression of jealousy will weaken.

There has, indeed, been a change in attitude toward virginity in the United States. The same Harris poll mentioned earlier showed that 22 percent of men and 27 percent of women aged eighteen to twenty-nine thought it was important for a woman to be a virgin when she married, as compared to 41 percent of men and 64 percent of women aged fifty to sixty-four. Clearly, virginity is no longer considered necessary to marriage for young women, and therefore few feel compelled to retain it or to say that they have retained it. As a matter of fact, Lillian Rubin argues that the sexual revolution which freed women to say yes, actually went too far in making it difficult for them to say no.[41]

For most Americans, sexual pleasure is not a reward earned after a long period of deprivation, the way it was for the Apache. Yet before marriage, and even more so after marriage, Americans have far more sexual restrictions than the Toda. Norms restricting free sexuality give legitimacy to jealousy. Monogamy remains a strongly held moral idea, even when couples don't always adhere to it. The results of eleven large surveys of extramarital sex conducted in the 1980s indicate that about 50 percent of married men engaged in intercourse with outside partners. The figure for married women is rapidly approaching that level.[42] Despite this high rate of infidelity, most people still continue to say that they believe in monogamy.[43] Sociologist Robert Whitehurst argues that the importance of viewing the American society as a paired and family-oriented society cannot be overestimated. Strong pairing norms make for a heightened sense of ownership ("my wife," "my husband") and exclusivity. They encourage overprotectiveness and vigilance, and increase our predisposition toward jealousy.[44]

Social organization of personal property in American society also falls somewhere between the Apache and the Toda. Material possessions are many and highly valued. Our concepts of ownership and private property tend to make us protective of people as well as things, Whitehurst argues. Even a spouse may come to be seen as a possession.

Growing up in America, young men and women also are taught to take a serious approach to personal decendants. This can explain the growing popularity of such solutions to infertility as implanting a husband's sperm artificially in his wife's uterus, or paying another woman to be artificially impregnated, carry the husband's baby for nine months, and deliver it. Fatherhood is a legal relation that, once established by blood and tissue tests, defines certain financial obligations toward the child. While children are important in North American culture, they don't provide the kind of status and prestige or the kind of social security for old age that they did among the Apache.

Despite women's economic contribution in housework, child care, and actual income, they still don't participate equally with men in political and religious leadership. As we saw in the discussion of sex differences in jealousy, this lack of power influences both their likelihood to perceive threats to their relationships and their likelihood to respond to those threats with jealousy.

The results of a study I conducted recently suggest that attitudes toward jealousy may be changing again in America. The study involved 120 people (55 men and 65 women) who responded to 24 different jealousy scenarios. In addition, they were asked to respond to the question, "How jealous are you?" I compared the responses these people gave in 1991 to the responses of 103 people who were asked the same question in 1980. People today report significantly higher levels of jealousy. One reason for this may be that in the 1990s people are more committed to monogamous relationships, either as a result of the threat posed by AIDS and other sexually transmitted diseases, or in backlash against the sexual promiscuity of previous decades. With the greater commitment to monogamy comes a greater acceptance of jealousy.

IS JEALOUSY UNIVERSAL?

No known culture, including those in which jealousy is considered shameful and undesirable, is completely free from jealousy. This seems the most reasonable conclusion to our review of the way jealousy is experienced and expressed in different cultures. Even among the Toda, despite the societal sanction against jealousy, their belief that they would be punished in the afterlife for being jealous indicates that the sanction did not eliminate it altogether. If there is punishment, there must be offenders. A culture can socialize us against expressing jealousy, but it cannot keep us from feeling jealous when we perceive a threat to a valued relationship.

The conclusion that jealousy is universal is supported by some recent research as well. In one study, Dutch and English children were compared to children living in an isolated Himalayan village. Both groups were found to be knowledgeable of situations that provoke various emotions, among them jealousy.[45] In another study, students from Hungary, Ireland, Mexico, the Netherlands, Russia, the United States, and Yugoslavia were asked about certain situations likely to elicit their jealousy. Results indicate that for nearly everyone, kissing, flirting, and sexual involvement between their mate and a third person evoked a jealous response. Far less jealousy was provoked by the partner's dancing with others, hugging them, or having sexual fantasies about them. There were, however, some cultural differences related to particular responses.[46]

We have seen that Freud also believed jealousy was universal. Unlike cross-cultural psychologists who base their conclusion on wide-range evidence gathered in many different societies, Freud based his conclusion on evidence gathered from the unconscious depths of the human psyche. He believed that jealousy is universal because it is rooted in childhood experiences all of us share.

It may be worth noting, however, that while Freud believed that jealousy is the product of the mind of an isolated individual, he also believed that the culture contributes to its development. Jealousy, according to Freud, is aggravated in a culture that worships a monotheistic god who proclaims, "Thou shalt have no other gods before me . . . for I the Lord thy God am a jealous God."[47] Jealousy is also aggravated in a culture that upholds an ideal of monogamous marriage and of a rational and repressed self. Such a culture encourages us to expect exclusivity in love, which makes it difficult to accept both our own and another's infidelities, real or imagined. Though some cultures may mitigate the pains of jealousy, Freud could not imagine a civilization in which people would be wholly free of this "discontent."[48]

Sociobiology also supports the notion that jealousy is universal. You may recall that Darwin saw jealousy as an innate defense of the pair bond, which evolved through natural selection to increase the likelihood that the pair would stay together and reproduce.

WHAT DOES ALL THIS HAVE TO DO WITH YOUR JEALOUSY PROBLEM?

If you have a jealousy problem, you can take comfort in the knowledge that such widely differing sources as psychoanalysis, sociobiology, and cross-cultural psychology come to the same conclusion: your jealousy is universal. But is this kind of comfort enough to help us cope with jealousy?

As I was writing this chapter, Amalya (whose problem with her boyfriend's jealousy was described in chapter three) asked me what was I working on. I started telling her about the Apache and the Toda and the Eskimos. "But how can knowing about the Eskimos help me deal with Sam's insane jealousy?" she asked. "It can make you realize how much his jealousy is influenced by the culture we live in," I responded. "That doesn't help me," said Amalya. "I need to understand what makes *Sam* jealous and what *I* can do about it." Amalya noted a potential problem in the application of the social-psychological approach to the individual: Because the focus is on the culture, we may lose sight of the individual's jealousy problem.

Although drawing practical advice from the study of other cultures

142 • ROMANTIC JEALOUSY

may seem difficult or irrelevant at first, it is far from impossible. In fact, sociologists such as Gordon Clanton believe that a social perspective on jealousy can lead to better self-understanding and more effective therapy. Awareness of social forces, Clanton argues, can both enhance our understanding of our jealousy and provide a basis for a critique of misleading views.

According to Clanton, an example of such a misleading position is the view that jealousy is caused by low self-esteem, and that raising one's self-esteem can reduce or "cure" jealousy. Instead of accepting this assumption uncritically, Clanton believes that we should search for its social roots.[49]

His own search suggests that this view, which is taken for granted both by professionals and laypeople, is typical of a wide tendency to attribute a variety of personal failures and problems to low self-esteem. In fact, Clanton argues, one may have high self-esteem in general, but still feel uncertain and vulnerable in some situations. Someone with high self-esteem may still experience jealousy if a valued relationship is threatened. Furthermore, it is at least as plausible that the jealousy causes the low self-esteem and not the other way around. Clanton's position is supported by cross-cultural surveys that reveal that low self-esteem plays little or no role in explaining jealousy in various cultures.

In Sam and Amalya's case, it is possible that the powerful and disturbing experience of jealousy helped diminish Sam's good feelings about himself. His bad feelings were reinforced by the view of jealousy as a personal defect, a view reflected in Amalya's attitude toward his jealousy. Awareness of the culture's influence on our experience of jealousy makes us less likely to adopt erroneous and potentially damaging views.

In addition to making us more aware of the cultural influences on our jealousy, social psychology—which focuses on the interaction between individuals and their social environment—has another important implication for coping with jealousy. It can help individuals and couples see their jealousy problem in a new and more manageable way.

There are two kinds of explanations or attributions for events:

dispositional (related to stable personality traits of the person or people involved in the event) and *situational* (related to the special circumstances in which the event took place).[50]

People who describe themselves as "a jealous person" explain their jealousy in dispositional terms. When they have certain feelings, thoughts, and physical symptoms in response to a situation that triggered their jealousy, they say, "I am experiencing these symptoms because I am a jealous person." In other words, "that's the way I am and there's nothing that can be done to change that." Another person experiencing a similar set of symptoms in response to a similar situation may explain things in situational terms: "I am experiencing these symptoms of jealousy because the person I am married to has had an affair."

People who explain their jealousy in situational terms leave open the possibility that in a different situation they may respond in a different way. When they feel excluded because their mate is flirting with a good-looking stranger, they are likely to attribute their jealousy to that particular circumstance, and consequently focus their efforts on changing it. People who explain jealousy in dispositional terms are far less motivated to change, because for them change means the virtually impossible task of changing a "jealous person" to a "non-jealous person."

When an individual or a couple comes to therapy, most often the dispositional label "jealous person" is already in place. Their typical goal for therapy is to change the jealous person so that he or she will stop being jealous. To challenge this dispositional attribution, I ask the "jealous person" such questions as, "Have you been that jealous in *all* your relationships?" or, "Have you *always* been that jealous in this relationship?" The answer to these questions is almost always no. Even if the person can recall only one instance of atypical jealous behavior, it still means that the person is not "a jealous person" but someone whose jealousy is triggered more easily in some situations than in others. The challenge then becomes to identify what it is about this particular relationship or situation that makes the person jealous. As difficult as that task may seem, it is far easier than changing a "jealous person" to a "non-jealous person."

The task of shifting from a dispositional to a situational attribution of the jealousy problem is accomplished by addressing at length such questions as, What is it about this relationship or this particular situation that triggers your jealousy? In what other relationship or period of time in this relationship have you been least jealous? What was it about that other relationship or period of time that made you feel more secure and less likely to respond with jealousy? Another line of questions can address the couple's perception of norms related to fidelity and jealousy, to find out whether the jealousy problem is related to a difference in their understanding of these norms.

These kinds of questions are different from the questions "Why am I a jealous person?" or "How can I stop being so jealous?" By treating jealousy as a situational issue, the couple is motivated to work together to change the situation so that jealousy is less likely to be triggered.

If the person has in fact been extremely jealous in all previous intimate relationships, and during all stages of the current relationship, the label "jealous person" might seem appropriate. It is still unlikely that he or she has felt equal degrees of jealousy in all relationships and in all situations. The person can try to discover which situations increase the jealousy and which situations reduce it, then make an effort to avoiding the former and seek the latter.

AN EVALUATION OF THE SOCIAL-PSYCHOLOGICAL APPROACH

The major contribution of the social-psychological approach is the notion that jealousy is a social phenomenon as well as a psychological one. The different ways that people in different cultures respond to jealousy help to prove that jealousy is related to the values and norms of the culture in which we live.

The major criticism of this approach is that it underestimates the importance of processes operating in the mind of the jealous individual. Ralph Hupka's conclusion is an example of this extreme social position: "Jealousy is a function of a culturally defined event, not the cause of it. It is the situation which sets the occasion for jealousy. It is not the jealousy which creates the situation. Jealousy is a social phenomenon. It is not a product of the mind of an isolated individual."[51] Instead of this either/or proposition, I would like to suggest that jealousy is both a social phenomenon *and* a product of an individual's mind.

The psychodynamic, systems, and behavioral approaches are all part of clinical psychology and, as such, have elaborate recommendations for the treatment of jealousy. Unlike these clinical approaches, social psychology doesn't offer explicit suggestions for coping. Yet an awareness of the cultural influences on jealousy and the ability to shift from dispositional to situational attribution can help people cope with jealousy in a less emotionally loaded way.

ROMANTIC JEALOUSY IN OPEN RELATIONSHIPS

Erotic love is exclusive, but it loves in the other person all of mankind, all that is alive. . . . In essence, all human beings are identical. . . . This being so, it should not make any difference whom we love.

—ERICH FROMM, THE ART OF LOVING

Jealousy is a kind of fear related to a desire to preserve a possession.

—DESCARTES

uppose that your spouse admits to having sex "on the side" occasionally, but assures you that it is the result of a need for variety and is not caused by any lack of love for you, or by a problem in the relationship. The extramarital sex will in no way affect your relationship—but will go on—because your spouse feels there is nothing wrong with it. Assume further that the marriage has been happy and satisfying for you up to this point. Would you agree to this "arrangement"? Would you consider a divorce? Would you consider separation? Would you be jealous?

A study comparing one hundred "swingers" (husbands and wives who together engage in sexual mate exchange) and one hundred nonswingers indicates that swingers are far less likely to consider extramarital sex (which to them is not the same as an affair) a sufficient reason for divorce or separation. They also said they would be far less jealous in such a situation.[1]

Swingers are an example of people who manage to develop a relative immunity to jealousy.[2] Such people consider sexual variety and freedom important to a relationship. Some also subscribe to an ideology of universal love (of which Erich Fromm's quote above is an example), which makes combating jealousy an important philosophical issue as well as a practical one.

In their book *Open Marriage*, George and Nena O'Neill devote a whole chapter to love and sex without jealousy.[3] As can be expected, the O'Neills believe that the "dark shadow" of jealousy has no place in an "open marriage"—and is not necessary in a "closed marriage," either.

According to the O'Neills, jealousy is not natural, instinctive, or inevitable, but is a *learned* response, determined by cultural attitudes. And since it is a learned response, it can be unlearned. As evidence for their claim that jealousy is not "natural" in intimate relationships, the O'Neills mention societies around the world in which jealousy is minimal (such as the Eskimo and the Toda, described in the previous chapter).

Why is jealousy so prevalent in Western society? The O'Neills blame the "closed marriage" contract, which creates the impression that we "own" our mates. The idea of sexually exclusive monogamy breeds dependencies and insecurities. Contrary to the view expressed in the previous chapter, the O'Neills believe that "jealousy is never a function of love, but of insecurities and dependencies. It is the fear of a loss of love and it destroys that very love."

The O'Neills discuss several "misconceptions" that, in their view, cause jealousy to occur in closed marriages. They believe that by doing away with such misconceptions, an open marriage helps disassociate jealousy from love and sex.

One of these "misconceptions" is the idea that there is a limited quantity of love—that you cannot love more than one person at a time. The "truth," they argue, is that we can love different people, each one of them for the unique things that make him or her lovable.

Another "misconception" is the idea that jealousy proves the existence of romantic love. The "truth" is that jealousy proves the existence of insecurities and dependencies, not love. Monogamy, they say, "perverts" jealousy into a "good" (for example, some husbands and wives actually try to make their mates "a little jealous"). But jealousy is never good or constructive.

A third "misconception" is the idea that humans (especially women) are sexually monogamous. The "truth" is that humans of both sexes are not sexually monogamous by nature, evolution, or force of habit. The obvious proof, they say, is that most people fail to live up to a standard of monogamy. Indeed, monogamy does not mean having sex only with your marital partner. It simply means being married to one partner at a time.

Albert Ellis, the developer of rational-emotive therapy, has a similar criticism of monogamy, which, in his opinion, does not only "directly encourage the development of intense jealousy, but also by falsely assuming that men and women can love only one member of the other sex at a time, and can only be sexually attracted to that one person, indirectly sows the seeds for even more violent displays of jealousy."[4]

In my own work with people who have had open relationships, I discovered that the practice of nonmonogamy is far more complicated and difficult than the O'Neills and Ellis imply. First, it is difficult to unlearn the jealous response. Second, we do not live among the Eskimos or the Toda, but in a culture that encourages both possessiveness and jealousy. Because of these and other reasons, overcoming jealousy, while possible, requires tremendous work.

One couple, Kim and Larry, decided to open their marriage after seven years of monogamy. Both felt secure in the marriage and wanted to add variety to their sex life, which had lost some of its passion. They decided that on Tuesday and Thursday nights Larry could go to see his lovers, while Kim could bring her lovers home.

One of Kim's lovers recounted the strange experience to me:

You wake up in the morning naked under the
blankets after spending the night making love. Suddenly her husband comes into the bedroom, says good
morning to you, and then starts an argument with her
about who was supposed to take out the garbage last
night.

Kim described some of her own experiences:

I was the one who originally pushed to open the
marriage. I thought this would be the ideal arrangement—you get to have your cake and eat it too. At
times it really is like that. This happens when I have
an exciting lover, with whom I can spend the night
on Tuesday and Thursday, without having to deceive
Larry. The problem comes up when I don't have an
exciting lover, or when I don't have any lover at all.
In those times, the fact that Larry goes out and spends
a night with a woman that he finds exciting (possibly
more exciting than me) drives me absolutely nuts.

Studies of swingers suggest that unlike Kim and Larry's case,
swinging is usually initiated by the husband out of boredom or desire
for sexual variety, with the wife's reluctant consent.[5] Like Kim and
Larry, other couples in open marriages have rules that limit the
extramarital involvement: one couple is open only with other couples,
another is open only when one of them is out of town. For one
couple, the rule is "you can have sex, but not spend the night"; for
another, sex is allowed "only with strangers whom we are not likely
to meet socially." Contracts differ in degree of openness and are
rewritten whenever the mates see fit to do so.

Despite the rules, many couples discover that the effort to keep a
marriage strong while being open to involvement with other people
is simply too much effort: "You have to talk all the time in order to
make sure that your relationship will not suffer. The time and energy

involved in that are so enormous that little is left for anything else." Many of the couples I interviewed or worked with who had tried open marriage decided eventually to go back to monogamy. Studies of swingers suggest that despite the self-selection that screens out highly jealous people from swinging, jealousy remains a problem for swingers: up to a third of swingers soon drop out because of their own or their spouses' jealousy.[6]

Some people have made unusual attempts to combine the security of a good relationship with the sexual variety offered by other people.

A LIFE WITHOUT JEALOUSY?

Is it possible to eliminate jealously from your life? The answer, according to the members of an urban commune called Kerista, is "definitely yes!"

The Keristans describe themselves as an "egalitarian, nonmonogamous, utopian community." Kerista includes fifteen women, seventeen men, and two children living together in San Francisco. It was founded twenty years ago by two people of different ages and backgrounds: Jud, who was at that time forty-eight and who "left a fairly straight lifestyle in search of meaningful communal living"; and Eve, a high school graduate looking for a utopian community. They met after Eve responded to a small notice Jud had put in the Berkeley Free University catalog about his still-fictitious utopian community. Although they were the first two members of Kerista, Jud and Eve were never a twosome or a couple. At least two other people were always there with them, sharing their ideas about building a utopian community.[7]

Kerista is a "polyfidelitous family." "Polyfidelity," a coined word, is defined as a "group of best friends, highly compatible, who live together as a family unit, with sexual intimacy occurring equally between all members of the opposite sex, no sexual involvement outside the group, a current intention of lifetime involvement, and the intention to raise children together in multiple parenting."

A polyfidelitous family resembles a traditional marriage in that family members do not become sexually involved with each other until they have made a mutual commitment to a "current intention of a lifetime involvement," and in that once the commitment is made, they are totally faithful to each other. A polyfidelitous family differs markedly from a traditional family in its basic assumption that one can have many primary relationships simultaneously.[8]

Members of the commune describe a high degree of love and tenderness for each other. Each one of the men claims to be equally "in love" with each one of the women, and the women claim to love equally each one of the men. Women refer to other women affectionately as "starling sisters"; men refer to other men as "starling brothers." The terms connote the affection experienced and expressed by the commune members toward their same-sex partners. The members all have three-letter names (Jud, Eve, Geo, Ram) that are selected after an individual enters the commune.

Sexual relationships within the family are also nonpreferential and happen within a rotating sleeping pattern. The sleeping pattern, which follows a set formula, schedules nighttime to be spent in a twosome. The sleeping pattern does not schedule sexual intercourse; having sex or not having it depends on the feelings of the two partners spending the night together.

The economics in Kerista are managed according to a system of "surplus income sharing." In this system, members put all their surplus income above their own expenses into a common fund and set a personal wealth limitation of one thousand dollars. Policy decisions on how and where to spend this common fund, like all other decisions, are made by a majority vote.

Kerista is doing well financially. In 1990 its gross revenues came to fifteen million dollars. The common fund enables Keristans to purchase vehicles, equipment, and property—things that few of them could ever afford by themselves. One of the first major expenditures voted on after instituting the economic system was the purchase of two white-water river rafts.

In addition to river rafting, the community takes several ski trips every winter. The Keristans also like to bicycle, jog, backpack, swim, see movies, go dancing, walk in the park, play volleyball and basketball, and learn. "All of us read a lot, so we are able to get information on many more issues than we would alone," one member said.

Kerista has developed its own religion with its own holidays and rituals and is a legally recognized church. Members share a belief in "Divinity—a higher order of reality." In addition, they have a mythological deity called Sister Kerista, who is "an intermediary between you and Divinity, that the mind can more easily reach out to."

Interactions among members, including strong differences or personal problems, are settled through a round-the-clock communication process that the Keristans describe as "direct, honest, verbal expression of thoughts, feelings, fantasies, fears, and observations." There are no group leaders and no facilitators. All members are equal participants.

Even though some people, through the power of their personalities or insights, may exert more influence during a particular group discussion, the official power structure is one of absolute equality. All decisions are made democratically by majority vote: one vote per person. Issues are generally discussed at length, with all sides being represented before a vote is taken. On an important matter that concerns the whole community, discussions can go on for days. When the issue is minor, the decision can take only a few seconds, with a quick show of hands.

All of the important (and many of the not-so-important) matters of life are covered by a social contract that constitutes the community's code of living. The following are some examples:

- current intention of lifetime involvement with Kerista

- balanced, rotational sleeping cycle

- fidelity bond within the family cluster

- sex always in the context of loving, mutual reciprocity

- no overt display of affection between adults in public

- total honesty in all interactions and high verbal level

- mutual admiration, appreciation, and respect

HOW POLYFIDELITY COMBATS ROMANTIC JEALOUSY

The Keristans approached me twelve years ago when they discovered that I was going to lead a jealousy workshop. They volunteered to tell the workshop participants how they have managed to overcome their own jealousy. I found the things they said so interesting that I asked them to take part in my jealousy research, which they did. Since then we have kept in touch, and developed a friendship.

Before joining the commune, the Keristans say, they had all felt jealous at some point in life, but the alternative lifestyle of the commune enabled them to rid themselves of their jealousy. Following are some of the elements in their lifestyle that helped them overcome jealousy.

In Kerista, nonpereferentiality is an ideal and a norm. All one-on-one relationships are viewed as unique and are given equal importance. A member named Way explains:

> The nonpereferentiality doesn't mean limiting the depth of intimacy and caring for the sake of equality and variety. Because of the strength of each one-to-one bond, no one sees the strength of another relationship as a threat to the uniqueness of their intimacy bonds.
>
> What the Keristans have done is to extend the limits of the twosome to include up to thirty-six people in one family. Within a family unit of thirty-six people jealousy is ridiculous, just as it is within a traditional family structure.
>
> Furthermore, in a traditional marriage, all the emotional resources are invested in one person. When that person withdraws or leaves, the result is a serious trauma. In Kerista, the emotional investment is spread among many people. Consequently, when one person leaves, the trauma is much smaller.

The possibility of losing a partner is far less threatening in a polyfidelitous family than it is in a traditional marriage, for two main reasons: First, if a person leaves the family, the other members are not likely to see this as a personal rejection, and therefore can tolerate the loss more easily. Second, the pain of loss is shared by all members of the group, and therefore is likely to be less severe. Since the threat and the pain of loss are small, they are less likely to trigger jealousy.

In Kerista, jealousy is considered "a conditioned response that flashes whenever residual emotions from the past are triggered." It is not considered a response to a threat to the relationship's exclusiveness. On those rare occasions when someone feels jealous, everyone is expected to talk about it openly, assuring the person experiencing jealousy of his or her secure place in the community. In addition, there is no exclusive relationship to be guarded or threatened. Every intimate detail about the sexual habits of each member is well known to everyone and is the subject of open discussion. "Everyone knows if one of the men has a problem with premature ejaculation, or if one of the women has a problem reaching coital orgasm, and we all talk about it together," one member explained.

Here's an example: When Eve and Ram went together to an erotic film festival (on their scheduled night for being a twosome), Azo experienced a flash of jealousy. He didn't recognize it as jealousy at first; all he knew was that he felt somewhat depressed.

When he entered the kitchen, several people were there. Right away he said he was upset. This was a recognized invitation, and the others responded accordingly. They started to question him about his depression. Eventually they discovered that his depression was triggered by a fear that he might lose a measure of intimacy with Eve because he was not included in the erotic films evening and was not sharing the experience with her.

When his feelings were clarified, his partners assured him that both Eve and Ram were solid in their commitment to nonpreferential love, and that he was not likely to lose any intimacy with Eve. (As we will see later, when a person becomes "preferential" in his or her love for someone at Kerista, it is no longer considered appropriate for that person to be a part of the family.) Azo also had a chance, during the discussion, to examine his own wishes to have a preferential relationship with Eve, and to reaffirm his own commitment to a polyfidelitous lifestyle.

At Kerista, the sexual involvement between one's lover and another person, which for most people is the strongest elicitor of jealousy, is expected to increase one's sense of security instead. Keristans see sexual involvement between their male and female partners (they are heterosexual) as an affirmation that their polyfidelitous ideology works. They don't see it as a threat to their relationship with those partners or to their egos, so they are not likely to feel jealous.

The Keristans claim that their total trust in each other (and consequently their lack of jealousy) extends to people outside the community. In other words, outsiders are not viewed as a threat. For example, when Lee stayed out until the early-morning hours on a date with an old boyfriend, no one doubted her total fidelity, and therefore no one experienced jealousy.

A major component of jealousy, for most people, is suspicion or resentment of the rival. In Kerista, the relationship that every man has with the other men and every woman has with the other women elicits what they call "compersion" rather than jealousy. "Compersion," explains Way, "is the positive warm feeling you experience when you see two of your partners having fun with each other. It's the antonym of jealousy."

The Keristans disagree with the sociobiologists who claim that jealousy is a natural, instinctive reaction. They believe instead that "it is natural to be free of jealousy. The natural instinctive reaction is compersion." Like the O'Neills, the Keristans are convinced that because jealousy is culturally learned, it can, and should, be unlearned. Later I will describe in some detail how a new Kerista member learned to overcome his jealousy.

Since the Keristans see jealousy as a function of a particular social structure and sex-role socialization, they have put a great deal of effort into creating a new social structure and new sex roles within it.

In most marriages, romantic jealousy is seen as natural and to be expected when there is a perceived threat to the marriage. In Kerista, "compersion" is the sanctioned emotion, and jealousy is viewed as unwholesome and immature.

If jealousy is a response to a feeling of powerlessness in the relationship, as some psychologists have argued,[9] then a community like Kerista, in which members share equal power, is likely to minimize it.

If jealousy is a sanctioned response to a violation of sexual property rights, as some sociologists have argued,[10] it is less likely to occur in a social structure where sexual property rights include all the adults in the community rather than a single couple, and where intimacy is shared equally by all members of the family.

Likewise, if jealousy arises from a desire to preserve a possession,[11] a society that discourages possessions is less likely to elicit jealousy—especially in a group for whom sexual involvement of one's partner with others doesn't imply a threat of possible loss.

When I compared the responses of the Keristans to the Romantic Jealousy Questionnaire (see the appendix, page 247) with the responses of 103 people in conventional relationships, I discovered that the Keristans reported far less jealousy.[12] In fact, all the Keristans described themselves and their partners as "not at all jealous."

The Keristans said that they never experience jealousy, dislike jealousy, do not want their partners to be jealous, and do not consider their own jealousy a problem. All this is true only from the time they joined Kerista. During their childhood, adolescence, and young adulthood they were just as jealous as the other people surveyed.

The Keristans considered jealousy an undesirable personality characteristic and never thought it to be an appropriate response, even in the most extreme of situations. Unlike most of the other people surveyed, they believed that one can stop oneself from being jealous.

As can be expected, none of the Keristans believed in monogamy. All of them described themselves as being totally open with their partners about other sexual experiences, and all of them believed that their partners were totally open with them as well. They also believed that they were totally faithful to their partners (every single one of them) and that their partners were totally faithful to them.

Their responses were so similar that I wondered whether they discussed the questions, and decided on the "group answer." The Keristans assured me that they did nothing of the kind. They didn't have to. They talk about these issues with each other so often that they know each other's positions without having to talk about it. Actually, they claim to share a well-articulated and elaborate worldview, which they describe as a "group mind."

The preceding chapter noted that whether or not jealousy is expressed in response to a particular event depends on the culture in which the individual lives and on how that culture views the event. In Kerista, jealousy is an unlikely response because, within a polyfidelitous subculture, events that usually trigger jealousy (your mate going to bed with someone else, for example) are not likely to be appraised as threats.

In addition to the way the Keristans appraise jealousy-triggering situations, they also make every attempt to keep such triggers to a minimum. They avoid displays of physical affection in front of other partners; they are faithful to their partners; and they share a commitment to a life-long involvement with each other, thus ensuring that even if some of the group members leave, the "family unit" will remain and the individual will not be left alone.

As a result of all this effort, Keristans are not likely to encounter many situations that trigger jealousy. On those rare occasions when they do encounter such situations, they are not likely to appraise them as threatening. And when a situation is appraised as threatening, social norms that define jealousy as unwholesome and undesirable guarantee that the response to the threat will take the form of an open discussion.

Rif's story demonstrates how the Keristans deal with a jealousy problem. It shows how a person who joined the community managed to unlearn jealousy and learn "compersion."

Rif, twenty-four, received his Keristan name when he joined the commune in 1987. He describes what happened before and after:

> I was reading the Kerista literature for about a year.
> When I came for a visit I knew the stuff. I came to

see if it was true. I was attracted to the idea of polyfidelity. It was a gut-level reaction. I had a series of monogamous affairs that left me cold. I was especially attracted to the friendship aspect of it.

In the past I had experiences with jealousy. In high school, a woman I was seeing started seeing another guy. She said she wanted to see both of us. At first I agreed, but then it started really bothering me and I had to get out of the relationship. Later I had another girlfriend. We were basically friends and the sex was secondary. Then she met someone else. At the beginning I didn't mind at all. Then it started being difficult. Once they started kissing in my room, and I just got up and left. I started distancing, and the friendship ended. None of the three of us knew how to deal with what was going on.

For about two years after I joined Kerista, things were blissful. The group called me a "natural." I was in the center of things. Then I started to have strong feelings about Tye. I would hear her having sex in the other room and felt jealous. At first I tried to rationalize my feelings, say to myself that others can hear me having sex. Then it became clear that I felt it only toward Tye. I tried hard to push the thoughts out of my head. But instead came thoughts about having a special relationship with Tye. It was something that was happening to me, not something that I had control over. It became an all-consuming fear: Through no fault of mine I'm drawn to Tye and I can't control it, and I'm going to be thrown out of Kerista.

One night I was intoxicated, sleeping alone because the woman I was scheduled to sleep with was out of town. I could hear Tye and Eco in the other room. I realized I could watch them through a closet between the two rooms. I watched them having sex. I was comparing myself. Does she like him more than me?

Does she have more fun with him? Does she consider me number one? I felt I was acting like a nut. I knew I had to get this out of my head. I was sure everyone would be weirded out by it and want me out. I knew I had to get myself together. When they were finished, the closet doors shut. Eco noticed it. He came out and saw me. He asked whether I was watching them. I said "Oh, no!" and he accepted it.

Slight hints indicated to the other members that Rif had a problem. Sex with the other women became infrequent. The women compared notes and discovered that there was one notable exception—it was not happening with Tye.

In the group discussion that evening the consensus was that there was a problem, but everyone was trying to figure out the right perspective. During the whole discussion I was thinking to myself that what was going on was exactly what I was afraid of. I felt unmasked. I realized I had to leave. I told the group I really had to deal with those obsessive thoughts and I had to leave. I had practiced that scenario so often that it was a relief to finally say the words.

When he left, Rif was told that he would be in exile for three years. After that he could come back. The group felt that the break needed to be long enough for Rif to sort things out.

I went to live in one of the homes that Kerista owns in San Diego. It doesn't have polyfidelity, but has many of the other aspects of communal life. I stayed there for six months. At first I was dazed, confused, and depressed. I didn't know what the next step would be. I didn't know what the past events meant about me as a person. I missed all the women in Kerista, not only Tye. Everything was in a fog. After about a month of confusion I was able to verbalize some of the issues I was struggling with. I was single and available, but was alone much of the time.

I decided that I didn't like jealousy and I could stop myself from being jealous. That made me feel better about myself. I left San Diego, got a job, and started getting back my self-confidence. Communal living was looking attractive to me again, and I started thinking about returning to Kerista. I wanted to go back and rebuild my life there. I talked to people and said I missed everybody and really wanted to come back. The response was enthusiastic.

On the airplane to San Francisco I was concerned. What if the thoughts about Tye came back? They did not. And if they surface in the future, I am ready. I feel that I can talk about them in an open way. Now I have a perspective and a structure. It goes into the category of a "negative intrusive thought."

The Keristans weren't particularly interested in the unconscious roots of Rif's jealousy, or in what it was about Tye that triggered both his love and his jealousy. They assumed that he could unlearn his jealousy, and didn't want him to be a part of the community until he did so.

In case you've decided by now that the best way to conquer your jealousy is to join Kerista, or perhaps establish a similar commune in your own neighborhood, a word of caution is in order. Kerista represents a selective group of people who got together from all parts of the country because they strongly believed in a polyfidelitous lifestyle, and because they share a commitment to a utopian ideology whose ultimate goal is to make the world a better place. Despite their unusual practice of sleep rotation, the Keristans are quite conservative in their sexual attitudes. Few people today require a lifetime commitment before they get involved sexually, but the Keristans do. The Keristans don't practice open marriage. They are totally faithful, only in their case that means being faithful to seventeen partners instead of one.

It would be tempting to conclude that polyfidelity eliminates jealousy. This may be true, but there are problems with relying on what people say about themselves. People may be unaware of their own feelings, or they may be unwilling to be truthful if their responses put them in an "undesirable" light. It may be that since jealousy is not acceptable in the community, Keristans are reluctant to own up to it.

It also may be that when describing their experiences and filling out the questionnaire, Keristans simply reiterated their ideology, rather than reporting an actual change in their experience with jealousy. I am reluctant to accept these alternate explanations, however; in my twelve-year acquaintance with the Keristans, I learned to trust their honesty and willingness to explore difficult issues.

On the other hand, self-deception cannot be ruled out completely. It is possible that because of their enormous investment in the polyfidelitous lifestyle, Keristans can't accept the possibility of failure; therefore they distort their feelings unwittingly.

Still, the Keristans demonstrate that a selective group of people, living in a secure social milieu where jealousy-triggers have been reduced to a minimum, can succeed in overcoming jealousy. This can be seen as proof that jealousy can be conquered.

It can also provide testimony to the power of jealousy—if it requires so much effort to be conquered. After all, only a small and unusual group such as the Keristans, living in an unusual, self-created social structure, were able to overcome it. For those of us who have made the kind of monogamous commitment the Keristans outlawed, and who live in a less protected environment, some degree of jealousy seems almost inevitable.

The less protected the environment, the more likely is jealousy. A good example of this is another commune I visited. This was an urban commune like Kerista, comprising about twenty adults who shared living space and expenses. Unlike Kerista, this commune had many children, which meant that members had to put much more effort into parenting. More significant to the issue of jealousy, however, was that the commune's members had constantly shifting preferential relationships. At the time I visited the commune, for example, one of the men was living with two women, one of whom had previously lived with another man in the commune. The man himself had been married to one of the other member women, who was now living with another threesome, and so on. In addition to changing sexual liaisons within the group itself, members were open to outside relationships. The first man, for example, made an obvious pass at me during the interview—something unthinkable for the Keristans.

As a result, every woman in the group was perceived as a competitor for every other woman, and every man was a potential threat for every other man. This caused a serious problem with jealousy, which hours of conversation among members of the commune did little to help.

When I last visited the town where the commune lived, I discovered that internal conflicts around jealousy had overwhelmed the commune and caused it to fall apart. Though jealousy wasn't the only cause of these internal conflicts, it was definitely a major contributor.

A review of the literature about communes suggests that the role played by jealousy in this second commune is the rule and not the exception. Jealousy, it turns out, is a significant problem in communes in general and especially in group marriages.[13] A survey of thirty group marriages suggests that jealousy was a problem for 80 percent of the respondents. This percentage did not vary much as a function of the stability of the relationship or the age of the group members.[14] It seems that without the elaborate social structure that the Keristans have created, jealousy can unleash its destructive power.

As in Rif's case, when jealousy comes up in a commune or a group marriage, it is most often a result of men comparing themselves to other men. This is true even among swingers, the group we will discuss next.[15] A survey of 280 swingers indicates that men were far more likely than women to be involved in such social comparison and to feel threatened by it.[16] This is especially interesting since, as noted earlier, husbands are most often the ones who initiate swinging.

The comparison between the Keristans and members of other communes and group marriages suggests that low sensitivity to jealousy is an important selection factor for living within a sexually open relationship, but it is not enough. A social organization that minimizes threat, prescribes how to handle threat constructively, and provides members with a sense of security is essential in overcoming jealousy.

JEALOUSY AMONG SWINGERS

Most readers of this book, especially those who have a "jealousy problem," will probably find it inconceivable that people could allow their partners to have casual sex in their own home with a stranger or acquaintance. But to swingers this is considered an acceptable form of social recreation, according to family expert Brian Gilmartin.[17]

Gilmartin studied one hundred swingers and compared them to nonswingers living in the same California neighborhood. While the study was done in the 1970s, before the spread of such sexually transmitted diseases as herpes and AIDS, a 1990 *New England Journal of Medicine* article suggests that sexual practices have not changed much since then. "There has been little change in sexual practices (including number of partners) in response to new and serious epidemics of sexually transmitted diseases, with the exception of an increase in the use of condoms."[18]

Gilmartin's comparison between swingers and nonswingers indicates that, like the Keristans, swingers seldom experience jealousy when their mates have sex with someone else. Swingers believe that it is possible to engage in a great deal of extramarital sex without being unfaithful or untrue to your marriage partner. This is especially so, they say, when the sexual mate exchange happens "together," with both mates present at the particular social situation. Few nonswingers believe that this is possible.

Swingers are not likely to respond with jealousy, even to this common trigger of jealousy, because they don't perceive it as a threat. In their own system of beliefs, sex with another person doesn't mean being unfaithful or untrue; it simply means having harmless fun.

Three times as many nonswingers as swingers agree that when adultery occurs it is usually a sign that a marriage is not going well.

Gilmartin argues that with this association in their minds, and with this interpretation of the *meaning* of adultery, it is not surprising that most middle-class suburbanites view the mere thought of their spouses engaging in any kind of extramarital sex as a strong threat to their egos as well as to their security, masculinity or femininity, and self-esteem.

Swingers manage to differentiate (both ideologically and emotion-ally) romantic sex from physical sex, or, in Gilmartin's terminology, "person-centered sex" from "body-centered sex." Sexual intercourse at a swinger's party is viewed as a valuable and rewarding form of social recreation and convivial play. It has nothing to do with romantic or conjugal love and is very different from clandestine adultery. Therefore it doesn't pose a threat to the integrity and security of the marital bond.

For swingers, the analogy for a sexual mate exchange is a bridge party, in which it is quite common for participants to select someone else's spouse for a partner. This is rarely perceived as a threat by the men and women involved.

To keep triggers for jealousy to a minimum, swingers (like the Keristans) structure the context of the extramarital sex. They have extramarital sex only as a *shared* leisure activity. They make sure that the couples they "swing" with are committed to preserving a reason-ably happy marriage. Most swingers' groups don't permit single men to participate, although many welcome single women. Even married men rarely are allowed to attend without their wives. The reason is that men are perceived as a greater threat.

Almost all swingers' groups have strong norms prohibiting members from expressing romantic feelings (such as saying "I love you") and falling in love with one another. Swingers can and do express warmth and friendship toward their sex partners, but they forbid any sign of desire for sexual or emotional exclusivity, which is part of the romantic experience of falling in love. These rules are aimed at protecting the marital bond of all the couples involved.

Despite all these protections, swingers are not entirely free from jealousy. Most often, jealousy surfaces when one or more of the people participating in the sexual mate exchange has accepted the idea of swinging on an intellectual level, but not on the deeper and more significant emotional level.

At times, when people bored with marital sex hear about sexual mate exchange they get very excited and bring up the idea with their spouses. This, as noted earlier, tends to be the case for husbands more often than for wives. My research on marriage burnout also suggest that boredom is one of the greatest problems with conjugal sex for many men.[19] A man who is bored with sex at home feels the need for sexual variety. He has fantasies about the exciting sex he would enjoy as a swinger. In his zeal to persuade his wife, he often forgets to deal with the real implications of swinging—such as seeing his wife undress and have sexual intercourse with other men. If, as often happens, his wife first objects vehemently to the idea but ends up enjoying the experience, such a man typically feels tremendous jealousy.

One man who found himself in this situation describes it as the most intense experience of jealousy he has ever had. "I couldn't concentrate on the woman I was with. My ears were tuned to my wife, who seemed to be having a great time with the man she was with. It was horrible. I simply couldn't take it." This man decided that swinging was not for him, and instead found sexual variety in illicit affairs.

Experienced swingers also report occasional jealousy, but their experience tends to be milder than that of the novices and not necessarily negative. When jealousy happens, they typically don't mention it until they come home, and then share it as a tease and a sexual turn-on.

Seeing or imagining their mates with another person at times reactivates swingers' sexual interest in their mates. Even when they are physically depleted after spending several hours having sex, the emotional charge produced by their jealousy and by talking about it helps rejuvenate their sexual desire.

This positive aspect of jealousy happens so often among swingers that it has become a part of the swinging ideology. When swingers hear their friends talk enthusiastically about how they come home from a party even more erotically charged toward their spouses than when they left, they look for similar feelings in themselves. As is often the case, when we look for a particular emotional experience, we tend to find it.

Once again we see that the experience of jealousy is moderated by the interpretation we give it. For the swingers—members of a group whose ideology includes an interpretation of jealousy as a sexual turn-on—it is likely to become that, even if at some other period in their lives it was a response to a perceived threat.

The technique the swingers use, as you may remember from chapter four, is called "reframing," and you can try it too. Next time you are at a party and you see your partner flirting with someone attractive, say to yourself, "This pang of pain I'm feeling is actually a sexual turn-on." Imagine all the wonderful, sexy things you can do with your partner when you finally get home—instead of having a jealousy scene.

Adopting new beliefs about the meaning of extramarital sex is only the first step in the complex process of overcoming jealousy. Even among people who manage to reduce their jealousy, chances are that not many will take the next step and agree to multiple extramarital relationships. In that respect, swingers are indeed an unusual group.

Certainly, one of the characteristics of swingers is that they are more interested in sex than are nonswingers. Swingers not only engage in extramarital sex more often than nonswingers of roughly the same age; they also engage in more sexual intercourse with their own spouses. Gilmartin asked husbands and wives separately about sex with each other. The discrepancies between their responses were small. The data showed that, among the swingers, 23 percent of the couples had sexual intercourse an average of six or more times per week, compared to only 2 percent of the nonswingers. Similarly, 32 percent of the swingers, as compared to only 14 percent of the nonswingers, had intercourse an average of four or five times per week. On the other hand, only 11 percent of the swingers, as compared to 48 percent of the nonswingers, had intercourse an average of once (or even less than once) per week.[20]

While nonswingers didn't engage openly in extramarital sex, many did so secretly. In 34 percent of the couples, one of the mates had at one time or another been involved in an extramarital affair. In 5 percent of the couples, both the husband and wife had affairs.

Among the nonswingers, those people who had affairs had the lowest ratings of marital happiness. People who remained sexually faithful were far more likely to describe their marriages as happy and satisfying.[21] One can conclude either that having a poor marriage pushes people into extramarital affairs, or that having extramarital affairs destroys marital happiness.

Yet the swinging couples who engaged in far more extramarital sex than the unfaithful nonswingers were even more likely than the faithful nonswingers to describe their marriages as "very happy." Because the swingers don't associate extramarital sex with unfaithfullness, disloyalty, or betrayal, it doesn't reflect problems in the marriage and doesn't generate the same jealousy that it generates among nonswingers.

In addition to having more sex with each other, swinging couples also tended to express more love and affection toward each other, spent more time in informal conversation, and showed greater interest in each other than did the nonswingers. This suggests that the swingers derived the love, security, and emotional nurturance they needed from their marital partners. This is why the "strictly physical" extramarital sex didn't trigger jealousy. On those rare occasions when the extramarital relationship became a threat to the marriage, it evoked jealousy.

LESSONS FOR NONSWINGERS

Throughout this chapter I have described three groups of people who have managed to reduce jealousy to a minimum: people in open marriages, the Keristans, and swingers. All three groups demonstrate that it is possible for people to be involved sexually with several people with little apparent jealousy.

Like the Keristans, swingers are quite conventional in some ways. The Keristans don't have sex unless there is a "current intention of a lifetime involvement," and afterward remain sexually faithful to each other. The swingers are likewise sexually faithful except for the mate exchange. Like people in open marriages, swingers believe in traditional marriage (and in what Brian Gilmartin calls "residential and psychological monogamy"). They want to improve their marriages by opening the possibility of nonthreatening extramarital relationships.

All three groups believe in "togetherness"—the sharing of activities and interests between mates within the context of a committed relationship. All three groups value honesty in their intimate relationships and derive a sense of security from them. At the same time, all three groups also believe in the value of sexual variety. The main difference among them, and between them and people in more conventional marriages, is the social structure they create to achieve what they do not perceive as conflicting goals: intimacy with their mates together with sexual variety with others.

Even if you are satisfied in a monogamous marriage and would never be a swinger, have an open marriage, or live in a commune such as Kerista, you can learn several lessons from these three unusual groups that may help reduce jealousy in your intimate relationship.

The first lesson has to do with trying to eliminate triggers for jealousy. Discuss with your mate the things that are most jealousy-provoking for each of you (in most cases you'll each have different triggers) and explore together ways that your mate can do his or her "thing" without evoking your jealousy. For example, your mate may love to dance. You're less interested in dancing, yet feel threatened when your mate spends the whole time during a party dancing with someone else. You may explore the suggestion that after every three or four dances with someone else, your mate will dance one dance with you.

To be able to discuss such things with your mate, you need to spend time together in informal conversation. This is one thing the Keristans, the swingers, and the open-marriage couples do frequently. They also express love and affection toward each other and show a great deal of interest (both sexual and nonsexual) in each other, which helps increase their sense of security in the relationship. While you may disagree with their method for keeping their interest in each other alive (that is, sexual involvement with other people), you can still apply the principle in a way that seems more appropriate to you.

The swingers, the open-marriage couples, and the Keristans share the conviction that jealousy is a learned response. They know it can be unlearned because they have done it. The notion that jealousy is learned, which is the major contribution of the behavioral approach (an approach we will look at in chapter nine), is more conducive for coping than the sociobiological notion that jealousy is inborn and natural. Even if you're sure that you—or your mate—were born jealous, explore the implications of the idea that your jealousy may be learned. What will you need to unlearn and what will you need to learn in order to reduce your jealousy? Think, for example, about the meaning of extramarital sex. For the three groups described here, it almost never means that "there's something wrong with the marriage." For most traditional couples it means exactly that. Still, the affair and the jealousy it triggers don't have to be the end of the marriage. If couples learn to see the outside involvement as a message or a distress signal, the marriage can evolve into a deeper, more honest sphere. We will return to this point in chapter ten.

The importance of feeling secure in our primary relationship as a way to avoid jealousy is one of the most important implications we can derive from the Keristans, the swingers, and the open marriage couples. Without a sense of security, these three groups could not possibly have maintained the quality of intimacy that they achieved in their different relationships.

Another valuable implication is the importance of social support and the power of social approval. Imagine a couples' support group. A woman describes the way her husband expresses appreciation of every attractive woman he sees on the street as "outrageous" behavior that "makes her wild with jealousy." If the rest of the women in the group tell her that there's nothing wrong with her husband's behavior, make a joke of it, and themselves start to express appreciation of attractive men they have noticed, chances are that this woman will reevaluate the threat implied by her husband's behavior and respond with less jealousy in the future.

Finally, it is important to remember that even among the swingers, the Keristans, and the open marriage couples, some jealousy occurs. It is difficult to eliminate jealousy entirely in a culture that emphasizes possessiveness and exclusivity to the extent that our culture does. Yet these three groups show that it is possible to reduce jealousy and minimize the role it plays in our lives.

While the three groups we have met in this chapter are unusual in their lack of jealousy, the group we are about to meet in the next chapter is unusual in its extreme response to jealousy. The groups in this chapter can teach us what to do to reduce jealousy; the group in the next chapter can teach us what *not* to do, so that jealousy doesn't lead to violence.

CRIMES OF PASSION

For love is strong as death, jealousy cruel as hell.
It blazes like blazing fire, fiercer than any flame.
—SONG OF SOLOMON 8:6

[Jealousy] is the hydra of calamities, the sevenfold
of death.
—EDWARD YOUNG, THE REVENGE

*J*ealousy has produced violence throughout history. "Crime
of passion" has become so familiar a term that we rarely consider
how paradoxical it is—passion and crime, love and death. It's the
cruel paradox in which one murders the person one loves most. "Love
is strong as death," says the poet in Song of Solomon, and Edward
Young, the eighteenth-century English playwright, calls jealousy "the
sevenfold of death." Shakespeare's Othello, the archetype of the jealous husband, strangles his beloved wife, Desdemona, because he
suspects her of infidelity. Discovering that his suspicions were groundless, he then kills himself.

Studies of spousal murder followed by suicide list jealousy as one
of the precipitating causes.[1] FBI statistics indicate that about a third
of all solved murders involve spouses, lovers, or rivals of the murderer
and a real or suspected infidelity as a major cause.[2] A wide range of
hostile and bitter events has been attributed to jealousy, including
suicide, destruction of property, aggression, and wife-battering.[3] Stories of murder and other violent acts triggered by jealousy often

appear in newspapers and magazines. The popular interest in such stories suggests that although stories about passion and stories about violence each have a certain attraction, those about passion combined with violence are particularly fascinating to most people.

Despite the interest they generate, however, crimes of passion may not seem relevant to your own jealousy problem. Indeed, when I asked 607 people how they usually cope with jealousy, only 1 percent said they respond with violence. When I asked another group of 103 people how they coped with their most extreme experience of jealousy, only 7 percent mentioned an act of violence.[4] While many violent acts are attributed to jealousy, relatively few people resort to violence to solve their jealousy problems.[5]

Violent responses to jealousy deserve a discussion, however, because of the great harm they can cause. Even flying dishes (or, in the case of one couple I worked with, a flying watermelon) can cause great physical and emotional damage—much more so flying fists and bullets. It's important to know how to defuse the potential for violence in a jealousy situation.

In this chapter I will describe the stories of several men who are serving time in prison for crimes related to jealousy. They were part of a group of inmates I worked with as a therapist in one of California's state prisons.[6] As is the case with other violent crimes, crimes of passion are most likely to be committed by young males from low socioeconomic classes and minority ethnic and racial groups, who are subject to economic and social deprivation.[7] Most of the men I worked with were no exception; each had a high predisposition for jealousy and for violence. More significant for the prevention of jealousy-related violence, however, is the dynamic of situations that provoked the violence.

STAN

On September 3, 1979, Stan, eighteen years old, shot and killed his girlfriend Kathy. Stan's background is different from that of most of the other men in the group I worked with. He is white and comes from a middle-class family. In high school he was the running back for the football team, and a member of the Block Club, the Service Club, the Spirit Club, the school newspaper, and the yearbook. Stan was active in the school government and was the class president during his sophomore and junior years. He maintained a 3.8 grade point average, and became a lifetime member of the state's scholarship federation. One year he received the Scholar/Athlete Award, presented to him by the High School Hall of Fame based on his excellence in studies and sports. He was also chosen as a Junior Republican delegate by one of the state's senators. He could not exercise his duties, however, because of his arrest.

At 8:00 P.M. on the night of September 3, Stan and Kathy had a date to meet on the university football practice field. They had a heated argument, one of many. The reason was always the same: Stan wanted a more serious and committed relationship than Kathy was ready for. Kathy told Stan she wanted to devote herself to her studies and be able to see other men. Stan was so emotionally dependent on Kathy that the thought of losing her was horrifying:

> I could never talk to my family. Kathy was the one
> person I was able to open up to. I felt I was losing
> her. . . . I was more involved with her than she was
> with me. It was very scary. I was trying to hold on.

Stan was caught cheating on his college application for an Ivy League school and got into serious trouble. This, combined with Kathy's withdrawal, made him panic. He needed Kathy desperately. The more he fought to hold on, the more Kathy struggled to get away. Their argument on the night of the murder became increasingly heated:

> She told me to stay away from her and her family.
> I felt rage . . . violence . . . I felt I was losing her. She
> hit me twice with her fist on my cheek. . . . She tried
> to pull the gun out of my hand. We struggled. . . . I
> heard a gunshot and saw Kathy fall to the ground. I

panicked and started running. I threw the gun into a
body of water nearby.

The "body of water" was never identified and the gun never found.
The .38-caliber handgun that killed Kathy was taken from her father's
store. Stan had stolen it while working for Kathy's father the summer
before. His reason for stealing the gun and having it with him on the
night of the murder, he said, was to be able to protect Kathy.

When Kathy fell to the ground she was severely injured, but still
alive. She was discovered some time later and was taken to a nearby
hospital, where she was pronounced dead on September 4. Hospital
records indicate that she died of a single gunshot wound.

I met Stan in prison, where he was serving a life sentence. He
looked like an all-American college kid with blond hair, blue eyes,
and an athletic build. He was working as an EKG technician, receiving
straight A's in his premed classes, exercising, and attending Catholic
services regularly.

I worked with Stan in group therapy and interviewed him individually about his jealousy as a precipitator of the murder. I discovered
that Stan had little emotional connection with his parents. His father
was a football coach and a "very dominant figure." Stan admired his
father, but perceived him as critical and demanding. Stan had worked
hard all his life to gain his father's approval, but nothing he did,
nothing he achieved had seemed enough. Although he had a somewhat
closer relationship with his mother, he had a great deal of difficulty
communicating with either of his parents. During the three years that
Stan had dated Kathy, he had spent so much time at her parents'
house that they started to treat him as a member of the family. He
had felt closer to them than to his own family.

Stan was in love with Kathy and could not imagine life without
her. "She was like a dream come true." Loving Kathy more than she
loved him made Stan feel weak and dependent. When I asked him
who had the control in their relationship, Stan said "Kathy!" and
explained, "She was like a crutch."

For all his athletic and academic successes, Stan "felt very dissatisfied" with himself. The standards he set for himself (the internalization of his father's severe standards) were so high that he couldn't help but fail: "I always wanted to improve myself. I wanted to be perfect." Unlike Stan, Kathy was sure of herself: "She wasn't afraid to voice her opinions. I was insecure because of my shyness." Kathy was Stan's connection to people.

Stan and Kathy met when both of them were fifteen. From the start, Kathy felt secure enough in the relationship to encourage Stan to go out with other people. At first he did it a few times. Sexual liaisons with other women were easy for Stan because of his involvement with football. But they were pale in comparison with the love he felt for Kathy. He was attracted to her physically and emotionally. Unfortunately, Kathy was much less attracted to him. Stan described himself as "extremely jealous," and explained, "It was a result of my loneliness, dependency on Kathy, and insecurity about her." Over time, Stan's jealousy became a growing problem in the relationship. He became possessive of Kathy, and was envious of anyone she spent time with:

> She would go away for the weekend with her family, and it really bothered me. I felt lonely. I felt emptiness in my heart. She was the only person I could express feelings to.
>
> I always had a need to have control, and I didn't have control over any decision she was making, whether to go away for a weekend with her family or which school to go to.

Stan's reaction to the jealousy he experienced was extreme, and at times it took a violent form:

> I was more emotional than Kathy. I just kept the pain in. When I got really frustrated, I'd get it out, the rage—physically—by hitting the wall or something. . . .

On the night of the murder, Stan was nervous and shaky, and felt close to a nervous breakdown. His heart was beating fast, blood was rushing to his head, and his hands were sweaty and trembling. He felt anxious, terrified at the thought of losing Kathy, possessive, enraged, confused, and frustrated. His self-esteem was low and his self-pity high. With Kathy he felt such extreme jealousy often, and when he did, it lasted for days. She gave his whole life a sense of meaning. If he lost her to another man, he felt his life would be empty and meaningless. He couldn't accept it. He couldn't let her go. The total rejection and disdain Kathy expressed during their fight caused Stan's frustration, pain, and rage to explode in violence.

A study of jealousy-related homicides has identified overt disdain or rejection expressed toward the jealous spouse as an important precipitant of the violent outburst.[8] The critical role played by a humiliating rejection is also evident in the published accounts of the case of Jean Harris, headmistress of a prestigious school for girls, who killed Dr. Herman Tarnower, creator of the Scarsdale Diet.[9]

The much-publicized details of the case are as follows: After a fourteen-year affair during which he refused to marry her and had affairs with other women (both very compromising of her values), the fifty-seven-year-old Jean found out she was going to be replaced by Herman's nurse, the much younger Lynn Tryforos. She drove from her home in Virginia to Scarsdale, New York, and shot him in his bed.

JEAN

The following analysis of the case is based on the written account of journalist Shana Alexander, who interviewed Jean Harris extensively.[10] When Harris met Herman Tarnower, she was divorced, working full time, and supporting her children. In her work as a headmistress and in her former marriage (to a man who was weaker and far less ambitious than herself) she was in charge. She was living up to her high standards—"integrity" was of paramount importance to her—and was impressing those standards on the girls under her supervision. In her work as well as in her personal relationships she was strong, authoritative, and proper. Herman Tarnower changed all that.

The affair with Herman brought new life into Jean's otherwise rather lonely existence. Unlike her former husband, he took charge and became the loving, accepting father she had never had. He allowed the dependent child in her to emerge, while at the same time treating her both as an equal and as a desirable woman. In his presence she felt more attractive and feminine than she had ever felt before, and had never quite believed to be true of herself. She also felt respected for her strength and capabilities.

Jean idolized Herman. He gave meaning to her life. If she were to lose him, her life would be empty. Her neediness gave Herman all the power in the relationship. He determined when she could see him and when she could not. She was in constant terror of losing him.

When she went to see Herman on the day of the murder, Jean felt that her life was ending. Not only was she going to be replaced by another woman, but she was also in the midst of a professional crisis that could have meant the end of her career. In addition, she was suffering withdrawal symptoms from the diet pills Herman had been prescribing for her for years.

When Jean arrived, Herman was in the bedroom. He wasn't compassionate or understanding. He responded to her despair with insensitivity and irritation. He was was not empathic to her desperate need for him. Jean had brought a gun with her, thinking she might persuade him to change his mind by showing him she was thinking about ending her own life. But Herman wasn't taking her seriously. He was kicking her out of his life at the time she needed him most. In her frustration, despair, and rage, she picked up the gun and shot him. As in Stan's case, Jean's violence seems to have been triggered by Herman's disdain and ultimate rejection during their last meeting.

Although Jean was a woman of fifty-seven at the time of the crime, and Stan was a man of eighteen, there were important similarities in their childhoods as well as in the circumstances leading to their crimes. Both Stan and Jean were raised by distant, critical, and demanding fathers whose high standards they internalized and tried to follow. Despite their desperate attempts to live up to those high standards, and despite their successes, both felt inadequate.

Throughout their lives, both Jean and Stan felt a need to be in control of themselves and of things around them. Being in control all the time made for a rather inhibited emotional existence. Until Stan met Kathy, and until Jean met Herman, they both had rather lonely lives. For both of them the relationships brought love, joy, and escape from loneliness.

Both fell in love in ways they never let themselves love before. The relationships gave meaning to their lives and made them feel complete. Both became dependent on their lovers. Both wanted to get married and both were refused. Both felt powerless and needy in their relationships. They were willing to accept the asymmetry only because of their great dependency on their lovers. When they discovered—in a cruel and insensitive way—that they were going to be jilted, their despair, rage, and pain made them kill the person they loved more than themselves. In both cases there was a component of envy in the jealousy. It was expressed in the impulse to destroy the beloved who had the ability to make them happy, yet refused to do it.

This does not mean that Jean's and Stan's crimes are justified. It means that the way in which a jealousy crisis is handled plays a critical role in determining whether or not it will escalate to violence. Jean and Stan are not very different from other people who are completely dependent on a romantic relationship. Their crimes were the result of an escalation that could have been avoided.

NEIL

Unlike Stan and Jean, who are serving life sentences for killing their lovers, Neil was serving time for killing his ex-girlfriend's lover.

Like Stan, Neil was a shy and insecure young man. The only time he got into trouble was during his adolescence, when together with a group of boys he was caught shooting a BB gun at streetlamps. After finishing high school, Neil enlisted in the army and was sent to Vietnam.

When he was released from service, for the first time in his life Neil was able to afford an apartment of his own. It was also the first time in his life he had a girlfriend. Since he was very much in love with his girlfriend, and dependent on her emotionally, he invited her to move in with him. She agreed, and for a while it seemed as if his dreams were coming true. But only for a while.

After several months his girlfriend started an affair with a security officer and eventually broke up with Neil. Then she kicked Neil out of his own apartment. When Neil returned from a trip out of town, he discovered that his ex-girlfriend and her new lover had moved his belongings back to his parents' house. Neil went there and spent several hours turning the events over in his head. Then he took his father's old gun, went back to the apartment, and burst into the bedroom, where he found the girlfriend and her lover in bed.

During the trial, Neil claimed that he didn't mean to kill either his girlfriend or her lover; all he wanted was to scare them with his gun so they would get out of his place. But the security officer, seeing the pointed gun, came at him naked. During the struggle that followed, in which the officer tried to get the gun out of Neil's hand, a shot was fired by mistake and the officer was killed. Neil's first instinct was to flee. His girlfriend came with him and they drove for hours, both of them crying. Eventually she persuaded him to turn himself in to the police. At the trial, the girlfriend supported Neil's story. As a result of her testimony, the verdict he received was second-degree murder rather than first-degree.

Today, Neil is a free man. He is working as an engineer, is married, and has two children. Jealousy is not a problem in his marriage, and he is convinced that he will never again respond with violence either to jealousy or to any other problem.

While Stan, Jean, and Neil did something that most of us will never do—respond to a jealousy-trigger with violence—they are "normal" enough for their crimes not to be blamed on such things as mental illness, drugs, alcohol, poverty, or an abusive childhood. One of the most noteworthy things the three of them had in common, besides a predisposition toward jealousy and a jealousy-related crisis, was a gun. They are people who, if it weren't for the crimes they committed, would have been considered successful members of society. For the people I will present next, violence was not a one-time event, but a way of life.

MIKE

Mike, a thirty-year-old man, is serving a life sentence for rape and murder. He describes the events that led to his crime:

> I met Rosemary after getting out of a very painful relationship with Pat. I was extremely jealous of Pat. I could get killing mad about her. I didn't want people to even look at her.
>
> The worst jealousy I ever felt was when I came back after ten days, and I found out she got married. I knew the guy. She told me he was just a friend. . . . I know her, she was up to no good. I would never be comfortable with her seeing other men. There was a lot of insecurity on my part. If I had married Pat, I would have ended in prison much sooner.

While Mike wasn't in love with Rosemary the way he had been with Pat, he still became very emotionally dependent on her:

> Rosemary was there, and it helped in terms of Pat. I got married at seventeen. She was twenty-one. I thought I couldn't live without her. I was dependent on her emotionally. I felt she really cared about me.

Mike was totally unprepared for what he found out:

> Rosemary and I were living with Ann (a friend of Rosemary) before our marriage, and after that too. . . . It was comfortable for all of us. We were happy together.
>
> When I found out that Rosemary and Ann were lovers, I was really shocked. I just got into the car and split. I felt that she'd rejected me. I felt abandoned. I couldn't handle it.

Abandonment is a core issue for Mike:

> I felt abandoned by my mother. I don't remember my father. He commited suicide when I was three years old. He shot himself because of another woman. No one ever talked about him. I was the only child for a long time. But it was difficult for my mother— being single and a black woman—to make a living. When I was six she started dating. Until then we were together. I got very jealous. I attacked the men she was dating. I would steal from them. I would curse them. I tried to beat one of them up, but he moved out of the way, and I fell down the stairs. I still have a scar. . . . When I was eight, she took me to my grandmother, who used to beat me up regularly.

At the time of his father's death, Mike was in his Oedipal stage— experiencing the first stirrings of sexual feelings and in love with his mother. Most boys have to compete with their fathers for their mothers' love. Mike didn't need to do that. Mother was his. They were together, and close. He was her only one—a young boy's heaven. Things changed when his mother started dating. Suddenly he had competition for her love. Mike responded with tremendous jealousy.

He expressed his jealousy in violence—not toward himself, the way his father did, but toward his competitors. His violence caused the ultimate rejection: Mike was sent away to live with his abusive grandmother. These childhood experiences had a profound impact on his predisposition toward jealousy. As an adult, Mike tried to excuse his mother's betrayal, but the little boy in him still felt terribly abandoned. Mike sees the feelings of abandonment as the root cause of his jealousy:

> I have the gravest fear of abandonment. This is probably why I am so jealous. Mom, Pop, Coot [a friend]—in one way or another I lost all of them. Even the pets. Somebody poisoned my ducks, my dog was given away, another was taken. They gave my dolls to a cousin [a girl]. Everything I ever cared about, I ended up losing. When I love, I expect total fidelity. I know I don't handle infidelity very well, and I say it up front. A close, intimate relationship has to be monogamous. If not, it's like a betrayal to me. I could never be with someone who is open to have casual sex with others. That would hurt me too much. I couldn't live with that. To me sex isn't casual. If there's no emotional involvement, to me it's nothing.

Sounds reasonable, doesn't it? A man who has a fear of abandonment and a problem with jealousy makes sure the women he gets involved with don't make him feel abandoned and don't trigger his jealousy. Why is it, though, that Mike chose to fall in love with Pat, a woman he knew was "up to no good," a woman who caused him to feel insecure, and eventually abandoned him in a most cruel and inconsiderate way? Why is it that Pat triggered more jealousy in Mike than did Rosemary, his wife? ("I wasn't threatened by Rosemary's relationship with Ann, but could get killing mad about Pat.") The reason is that Pat fit Mike's negative romantic image better.

You may recall, from the discussion in chapter one about romantic images, that these images develop early in life and are particularly powerful because of it. They are based on the significant characteristics—positive and, even more so, negative—of the people who were most influential in our early childhood.[11] For most people, these are our parents. We internalize the image of the people who taught us the meaning of love by the way they gave us love, or withheld it from us. As adults, we look for a person who fits that internalized image. When we meet such a person, we project our romantic image onto him or her and experience it as falling in love.

Why do men like Mike, Stan, and Neil, who fear rejection and abandonment, choose to fall in love with women who reject and abandon them? The reason, as noted in chapter one, is that the women they choose represent a painful part of their romantic image, and thus provide them with an opportunity to heal a childhood injury. The relationship may seem like a living hell—and in extreme cases may even trigger violence—but it actually represents a hope to master a childhood trauma.[12]

Mike fell in love with Pat *because* he knew she wouldn't make him number one, just as he wasn't number one for his mother. If Pat had returned his love, it would have helped heal his childhood wound. Unfortunately for Mike, she did not.

Mike cared less about Rosemary, yet got a sense of security from her love. When she too betrayed him, he was devastated. Just then he thought he was failing in his work too. He knew he was going to destroy everything, the way he had as a child.

> My supervisor at work came and mentioned something about me being moved. I felt like a failure. I was very angry. That morning I put my gun in my lunchbox. [Mike is an electronics technician and was sent out to customers' homes to make repairs.] I knew I was going to kill someone. When I got into the house and saw it was a woman, I decided to rape her too.

She was very brave. I admired her. At a certain point I had second thoughts about killing her. But I knew I had to kill. I wanted to get it over with.

It was a cold-blooded murder. In a world where he felt he had lost everything, the only power Mike had left was the power to destroy.

JEALOUSY AS A TRIGGER OF MURDER

Mike was black. Stan and Jean were white. Mike belonged to a lower socioeconomic class than Stan and Jean. Yet there were several important similarities that brought all three of them to prison with a life sentence.

For all three, control was extremely important. The reason, as their childhood histories suggest, is that as children they felt powerless to get love and recognition from a parent they admired. Despite their need for control, all three actually felt rather insecure and inferior (none of Stan's and Jean's successes helped change that). They also frequently felt isolated and lonely. This made them emotionally dependent on the people they finally allowed themselves to fall in love with, and very susceptible to jealousy.

When the person they depended on to give their life a sense of meaning was leaving them for someone else, the feelings of pain and despair were overwhelming. Violence was their way to gain back some sense of control. When nothing was left to lose, the only thing left to do was to destroy everything. In Stan's case, that meant killing Kathy, in Jean's case it meant killing Herman, in Mike's case—killing anyone. In all three cases, the impulse to destroy represented the component of envy in the jealousy situation.

Chuck's crimes were rape and robbery. Yet the events that led to his crimes resemble those in Mike's story in many ways.

CHUCK

Chuck, a short, husky man, grew up in the South. He was the oldest of six children born to a religious Baptist family. When he married, Chuck expected his wife to be faithful. The reason, as he readily admits, is that he is "a very jealous man" and has been jealous throughout his whole life.

When Chuck's wife had an affair with another man, he became "violently jealous":

> I tried to push the picture of the two of them together from my head, I wanted to erase the picture from my mind, but I couldn't do it. I was very upset. I would ask her questions. . . . I wanted to know all the details. I started making threats of what I would do to her. Once I punched her.

His violent outbursts of jealousy were the cause of their subsequent separation:

> After that, everything went downhill. I made up my mind that the marriage wouldn't work. I got very depressed. I let the house and everything else go. I went back to the military. But I still loved her.

After the separation, things started falling apart in other areas of Chuck's life:

> After my wife and I split, I got into trouble for using dope and going AWOL, and had to leave the army. I had given up on the hope of getting back with my wife. I was living with my grandfather. It was a low period in my life. Nothing was going right. I tried to commit suicide, but the gun wouldn't fire. I didn't

want to do anything with anybody. I just gave up on life.

It was at this time that Chuck started breaking into houses:

> I started burglarizing. When I went in I didn't know someone was there. I came in through the window at 1:00 A.M. A woman was asleep in the bedroom. I got scared and tried to escape quietly. All of a sudden she woke up. When she saw me she had such a terrified look that I changed my mind. I raped her. I felt in control. I knew I could do to her anything I wanted. I stayed there through the whole night— raping her again and again and again. With her pants on, and with her pants off, in the bedroom and in the bathroom, in every position I could think of.
>
> I'm not trying to justify my crime, but it wasn't like I tried to hurt her. I told her I didn't want to hurt her. I was there for eight hours. We talked a lot.
>
> In the next burglaries I was already hoping someone would be there. It went on for three or four months. I was convicted of two rapes, but there were actually five. I contacted the first rape victim, and the phone was tapped. I called her to tell her I was sorry. I felt I loved her. I felt she understood me.

It may be worth noting that during the time of those rapes, Chuck (like many of the other rapists I talked to) had a girlfriend. Clearly, it wasn't sex alone he was after, but something else, something he had lost when he discovered his wife's affair—a sense of control, especially over a woman:

> I didn't have much control over the relationship with my wife. The lack of control was particularly

painful in terms of jealousy. During the rape I had
complete control. Having total control was one of the
most important things in the rape. I definitely don't
want to go back to it, but if those feelings are still
there when I get out, I'm afraid of my jealousy and
my need for control.

Like Mike, Chuck is black and comes from a low-income background. Like Mike, he was emotionally dependent on his wife, and
extremely susceptible to jealousy.

For Chuck, as for the others, the pain over losing a love relationship
was exacerbated by problems in other spheres of life: Chuck got into
trouble in the army, Stan got into trouble in school, Jean had a serious
crisis in her work, and Mike was convinced he was about to lose his
job.

For each of them, the relationship that was lost promised to heal
some painful childhood wounds that in all four cases were related to
problematic relationships with their fathers. Chuck had never lived
with his father; Jean and Stan had critical, demanding, and distant
fathers; Mike's father committed suicide when he was three. At the
beginning the relationship seemed to heal these childhood wounds.
Consequently, when the relationship ended, the loss was devastating.

Why is it that Chuck robbed and raped a series of random victims
in response to his jealousy, Mike murdered and raped another chance
victim, and Neil killed the interloper, while Jean and Stan killed their
lovers? Despite differences in their personalities and backgrounds, the
most significant reason seems to be the cruel and humiliating way
Jean and Stan were told the relationship was over. In Stan's case,
Kathy hit him in the face and told him to get away from her and her
family. In Jean's case, Herman responded to her despair with irritation,
insensitivity, and ridicule.

Once again we see that the way a jealousy crisis is handled can
determine whether it will escalate to violence.[13]

THREE RAPISTS

Besides Chuck, several other rapists committed their crimes as a result of jealousy. I will describe three of them. All three men were white, blue-collar workers in their early twenties. Ed had alcoholic parents, started college, but left after one year, and until his arrest worked as a carpenter. Ken grew up Baptist and worked in construction until his arrest. Al, a Mormon, had a father who had married six times, nineteen brothers and sisters, and worked as a driver until his arrest. All three men described themselves as "very jealous," and the events preceding the rape as starting with a betrayal by a woman they loved.

Ed lived with his girlfriend for over a year before the rape and his arrest. He describes the relationship:

> It was intense, both good and bad. Sometimes I had the control, and sometimes she. We both were very needy. I really loved her. I was always afraid it wouldn't last, based on relationships I'd had in the past. For the whole year and a half I was afraid that the relationship would crumble. I was insecure about myself and my identity. Several times I wanted to get married and was rejected.

The discovery of her betrayal was devastating:

> When the time was right she told me about being involved with my best friend. That really hurt me. As if I wasn't enough. There was an emptiness in my chest, a heavy lump. I couldn't handle hearing the details. I had nightmares about her leaving me— driving her car and going away. I felt a tremendous love for her. I was scared. Someone I cared about was slipping away. When you love someone and the love that they felt for you is gone, that's the greatest pain in the world. I saw no way of controlling the situation.

The discovery started a process of deterioration that eventually led to a rape of a woman on the beach:

> The reality was hard, and I started being more involved in fantasy than in the real world. I was involved with drugs and alcohol. Once I tried to commit suicide. I had a deep sense of helplessness. I was feeling passionate and needy, but I didn't feel she really loved me. The crime was intended to destroy the relationship. I felt inadequate as a man. I had a lot of anger toward women going back to my past. I was very scared during the rape, more than she was. It was scary to be out of control that way.

Ed is aware of his jealousy and his tendency to respond to it with violence. Even after his trial and imprisonment, jealousy continued to be a difficult issue in his relationship.

> I am a jealous person. I feel the emotion very intensely. I was always an emotional person. I punched a guy once, right in the throat. I have a lot of emotional involvement in the relationship. I can feel when she's with someone, and couldn't continue subjecting myself to this kind of pain. It's a cruel punishment. When I went to prison she started seeing other people, and I always know. Last week she told me she met someone else she wants to date. I gave her back all her pictures and letters. I couldn't handle my jealousy.

Ken was also living with a woman he loved, and experienced tremendous jealousy when she showed interest in other men:

> We were living together three and a half years and were going to get married. I was very attracted to her

physically and emotionally. I loved her. I wanted to spend all my time with her.

Everything was great until about a month before my arrest. In the last month my brother told me he saw her with two guys. It kind of hurt me. I didn't understand it. She told me she was pregnant, but she didn't want me next to her. She pulled away. I experienced pain. I couldn't fall asleep. I thought I was losing her.

Like Ed, and the other inmates described earlier, Ken felt he was losing control over the relationship at a time when other aspects of his life were falling apart too. It was a difficult and scary feeling:

I was eighteen at the time. I lost my job. I lost my car, my dad went to jail, my mother was kicked out to the street, and my girlfriend was withdrawing from me. I was on "crystal" about five or six days, driving my friend's car. I was mad at myself for letting everything happen. I lost control with my girlfriend. I was afraid I was losing her. She never believed my crime. She cried and cried and cried. I told her I didn't understand it myself. She told me she still loved me.

The events leading to Al's crime were similar to those that led Ken and Ed to violence. Al loved his girlfriend. ("I always felt that she was a very attractive woman and a great person.") They lived together four and a half years. Al hoped the relationship would last forever, yet felt extremely insecure about it:

Things went from terrible to excellent and back again. I never trusted her. She always flirted, flaunting herself. She's an exhibitionist.

The jealousy crisis that eventually led to rape started when Al discovered he had been cuckolded:

I found out at the hospital about her going to bed with this guy. That meant that the baby she had is probably not mine, because my sperm count is very low. After we talked, I went and got loaded on grass. I felt emptiness. I was afraid I was losing her. I started going out with different women and taking them to bed. The woman that called the police on me was one of these women. My crime was a revenge toward my old lady. I was telling her, "You can do it, I can do it." I didn't care during the trial. I thought about suicide. I still loved her.

Al had responded to jealousy with violence in the past:

I know that jealousy is a problem for me. I am extremely jealous. Too jealous. Almost all my relationships ended because of it. I was always jealous of this one dude. I kept my old lady away from him. I told him if he does something to my lady I'll fuck his. One time at a party she disappeared for a long time. At first I was worried, then I found out she was talking to this dude, so I kicked his ass and I got really mad at her. I was very jealous, very angry. If I thought she was having an affair, I'd try to catch them and hit her or split. After I found out, it would come to a stop. Either I would leave or she would.

All four of the rapists I mentioned described themselves as "extremely jealous." All four were desperate to feel in control, yet were extremely dependent on their wives or girlfriends. Each felt devastated by the discovery that "his" woman was involved with another man. Other crises made them feel that they were losing control over their lives. The use of drugs exacerbated the problem. The rape gave them a sense of control over a woman, control they felt they had lost in their own life and relationship.

This explanation is not an excuse for the crimes these men committed. It also does not mean that the women in their lives deserve blame for their crimes. Instead, it means that men who have an unusually high predisposition to jealousy and violence and are otherwise unstable emotionally, who are dependent on their intimate relationship and feel betrayed—especially when they are in a crisis and using drugs—are likely to respond to their jealousy with violence.

WHAT CAUSES CRIMES OF PASSION?

Mike, Chuck, Ken, Ed, and Al are typical of criminals who serve time in prison for violence related to jealousy. As noted earlier, such criminals tend to be male, young, and from a low socioeconomic class.[14] In virtually every case the crime was a result of an extreme predisposition to jealousy combined with an extreme jealousy trigger: withdrawal or actual betrayal by a woman they loved and depended on emotionally.

During group therapy and individual interviews with these men, we explored the roots of their jealous predisposition.[15] The exploration revealed two shared experiences in virtually all of their backgrounds. The first was *a traumatic experience of abandonment in early childhood*. At times the abandonment was by the mother, at times by the father, at times by both parents (in one case the boy arrived home from kindergarten to discover the house locked and both parents gone). In some cases the parent left the family; in others he died of illness, committed suicide, or withdrew emotionally. In all cases the boy experienced panic, rejection, loss, abandonment, and total helplessness. As adults these men tended to be especially dependent on their intimate relationships. When they felt that their lover was withdrawing—because of interest in another man, or because of problems in the relationship—the withdrawal triggered tremendous jealousy marked by emotions closely related to the traumatic childhood experience.

The second experience shared by most of the men had to do with *the lack of a positive masculine role model during childhood*, caused sometimes by the absence of a father altogether, and at other times by the presence of an abusive father, or one who was distant, cold, and critical.

The lack of a loving, "normal" father—strong sometimes, weak other times, supportive sometimes, angry other times—caused each of these men to internalize instead a sex-role stereotype of a man who was a macho caricature. Consequently, when his lover began to withdraw, the withdrawal was perceived as a serious threat to his masculinity. In his extreme jealousy, the man felt the need to do something that would prove to his lover, and even more so to himself, that he was a "real man." His feelings of powerlessness in his relationship and life in general made him desperate to feel powerful, and he regained his feeling by attacking his victim.

The crimes that the jealousy triggered had two characteristics: they gave the men a sense of control, and they "proved" their masculinity. Most of the men admitted that having control over their victim was the most exciting part of the crime. The crime itself—whether a murder, a robbery, or, most particularly, a rape—enabled the men to prove their masculinity to the women who made them doubt it. The crime often involved a high level of daring and risk; the "masculine" risk-taking was a great source of pride for these men.

WOMEN AND CRIMES OF PASSION

While women are less likely to commit violent crimes than men, on rare occasions women also respond to jealousy with violence. In a second study of jealousy and violence, I compared the responses to the romantic jealousy questionnaire of twelve women in prison who described themselves as having a jealousy problem to those of twelve women who were similar to the prisoners in age and socio-economic status but had not committed a crime.[16]

The results of the comparison indicated that the women in prison described themselves as jealous, and believed their intimate partners perceived them as jealous, to a much greater degree than the control group. When describing their most intense experiences of jealousy, the women in prison reported feeling more rage, aggression, anxiety, humiliation, frustration, depression, grief, and pain. They also felt more possessive and self-righteous, and closer to a nervous breakdown.

When asked how they coped with their jealousy, the women in prison were far more likely to say that they used violence. They also reported being more likely to suffer silently but visibly, or to leave their mates.

When asked about their childhoods, the women in prison described a more troubled home life; a relationship between the parents marked by violence; having a jealous mother; and being beaten while growing up. They were also likely to feel less secure in their current intimate relationships.[17]

We see that, like the men in prison for committing crimes of passion, these women had traumatic childhoods that contributed to their extreme jealousy and violence.

HIDDEN CRIMES OF PASSION

So far, the discussion of the relationship between jealousy and violence has focused on people who were serving time for committing crimes. However, not all people who act violently as a result of their jealousy end up in prison. How likely are people with a serious jealousy problem to act violently?

A study of 138 people referred for psychiatric assessment for a serious jealousy problem (none of the referrals came from the courts) revealed that while only 1 percent had ever been charged with a violent crime, a mere 19 percent had *not* acted aggressively toward their partners. Close to 57 percent had a history of committing acts of violence, including threats to kill or maim (24 percent), accompanying threats by brandishing knives (nine men and two women, together 6 percent), underlining threats by waving blunt instruments such as pokers, (nine men, or 7 percent), and holding a gun to the mate's head while issuing threats (one man).[18]

Fifty-six percent of the men and 53 percent of the women inflicted assaults on their partners. The seriousness of the attacks varied widely. Ten men throttled their wives with homicidal intent. Twelve people stabbed or slashed their partners with knives. Nine men and two women struck their partners with clubs or other blunt instruments on one or more occasions, causing multiple fractures in four instances. The most common pattern of violence was that of repeated attacks involving hitting, punching, and kicking the partner. This catalog of violence had never come to the notice of the police, despite the hospital treatment a number of the partners received for their injuries.[19]

WHAT'S IN ALL THIS FOR YOU?

By now you may be saying to yourself, "Okay, so I understand to a certain extent why these people did what they did, but *I* would never do it. I would never kill, rob, or rape because of my jealousy, and I wouldn't hit, punch, or kick my partner." But, as I noted at the beginning of this chapter, it is important to know how to defuse the potential for violence in an extreme jealousy-triggering situation—whether you are being jilted, are doing the jilting, or are a concerned observer.

Be aware of emotionally charged situations that could lead to violence. When you find yourself involved with an emotionally dependent partner and you have fallen out of love, don't just come home one day and say, "I've found someone else I love, and I'm leaving." Jilting a person who loves and is dependent on you without giving him or her an opportunity to discuss the matter is an invitation to violence.

Such a situation can unleash jealous rage with an enormous explosive potential. You can avoid this by treating your ex-lover with sensitivity and respecting the love you shared in the past. You might also consider the role you may have played in creating your mate's dependency on you. (What attracted you to your mate when you first met? Could it have been the intensity of his or her feelings for you, which made you the center of his or her world?)

If you are the jilted lover, and you feel that without your mate, your life will have no meaning, it's important to realize that your greatest danger is your own jealousy. You need to deal with the jealousy and forget, just for the time being, the person who triggered it. If at all possible, get away. Clinical experience suggests that a prolonged separation usually results in the amelioration or even the disappearance of jealousy, particularly if the jealous person can come to accept the separation as permanent and begin to disengage.[20] Separation is especially advisable for people with a history of extreme jealousy or violence.

It is also crucial for you to be able to discuss your jealousy openly and gain control over yourself and your life. There are workshops and books aimed at helping people deal with their jealousy, heal their broken hearts, and let go of destructive relationships.[21] Three of the most important things such workshops can do are to make you realize that (a) you are not alone in this predicament, (b) there's life even after a lover leaves you, and (c) it's possible to turn a jealousy trauma into a growth experience. All three may seem impossible in the midst of a jealousy crisis, but keep them in your mind. It's important to focus on the things in your life that are in your control (such as the decision to take a few days off and get away), on things that you enjoy, and on people you love aside from your mate (make a list of people you love, and who love you).

It's also important to figure out what role you played in creating the jealousy crisis in which you find yourself. Is your jealousy related in some way to an aspect of your mate's personality that attracted you when you first met? Could it have been the fact that all women seemed drawn to him? That she was sexy and flirtatious?

If you find yourself unable to deal with your jealousy, and are concerned that you may resort to violence, don't hesitate to ask for professional help. Otherwise you may find yourself in the kind of situation that the men and women described in this chapter found themselves.

Most important: If you have firearms in the house, get rid of them right away. If you really need your gun for your work or protection, you can get it back later. Police records indicate that when there's a gun in the house, the people living in the house are the ones most likely to be hurt by it.

All these recommendations apply to coping with situations in which the jealousy has a high violence potential. In the next chapter we will discuss coping with jealousy in all situations.

COPING WITH ROMANTIC JEALOUSY

There are palliatives [for jealousy]: the first is the recognition of the problem (disease) and the second is the wish to cure oneself.

——A. R. ORAGE, ON LOVE

One of the most common questions from people with a jealousy problem is, Can jealousy be overcome? The answer, as we've seen throughout this book, is yes, but with great effort. Like most other difficult emotional experiences, jealousy, if treated correctly, can be a trigger for growth. It can become the first step in increased self-awareness and greater understanding both of your mate and of the relationship.

People tormented by jealousy often find comfort even in the knowledge that their response is normal, universal, and motivated by a need to protect a valued relationship. Awareness alone, however, is not enough.

Since this chapter is devoted to coping, it seems appropriate to start with a clarification of what coping is and what it is not. Coping is not the same as treatment. There are many different methods for treating jealousy cited in the scientific literature, including hypnosis, the use of various drugs, rational-emotive therapy, behavior therapy, systems therapy, couples therapy, psychoanalysis, and a combination of couples and psychodynamically oriented therapy.[1] In these treatment approaches, the individual or couple suffering from jealousy goes to an expert and is treated for the problem. Going to an expert is just one form of coping.

WHAT IS COPING?

Richard Lazarus, a leading expert in the field of stress and coping, defines coping as "efforts to master conditions of harm, threat or challenge when an automatic response is not readily available."[2] Coping does not imply success in overcoming the harm, threat, or challenge, but only efforts to master it. When you take a sleeping pill for a temporary escape from unbearable pain caused by your mate's unfaithfulness, you are making an effort (even if an unsuccessful one) to cope.

Different coping strategies vary in their effectiveness. Some—such as talking about the problem with your mate in an open and honest way, or learning about yourself to understand your jealous response— are almost always useful. Others, such as acts of violence, are almost always disastrous. Still others fall somewhere in between, and merely serve to delay the inevitable. Taking sleeping pills, drinking alcohol, and using illegal drugs are some of the more negative examples of this last category.

Whether a particular coping strategy is useful or disastrous can be determined by its consequences. As a result of the actions you took in response to jealousy, do you have increased self-awareness? Do you have a greater understanding of your mate's perspective? Does the relationship as a whole seem more loving, harmonious, and satisfying for both of you? If the answer is no, the coping technique has not been useful.

In the remainder of this chapter I will present different strategies for coping with jealousy. Some of them you may already know and use. Others probably will be new to you, yet will seem appropriate.

Even if a certain technique or exercise does not seem right for you, don't reject it right away. The more strategies you have in your coping arsenal, the better you will be able to cope.

Effective coping always involves four parts or stages:[3]

1. being aware of the problem

2. taking responsibility for doing something about it

3. achieving some degree of clarity about what needs to and can be done

4. developing new tools for coping, and improving the range and quality of old tools.

Adequate coping is impossible without *awareness* that there is a problem. Some people hide from the problem and try to avoid thinking about it. When there is an illicit affair, the betrayed mate almost always knows about it at some level, but at times chooses "not to know."

Other people who are aware of their "jealousy problem" tend to think that the jealousy is all their own fault ("I'm simply a jealous person"). This reaction does not show true awareness of the problem, because it fails to put the jealousy in the context of the relationship and the particular situation that triggered it.

Awareness has two parts: one is the simple realization that a problem exists; the other is the ability to recognize that the problem is a function of certain dynamics in the relationship or the particular situation, rather than the fault of the "jealous person." Once we recognize this, the focus of the coping efforts shifts from "What's wrong with me as a person that makes me so jealous?" to "What can I do to change the situation so that my jealousy is not triggered so easily?"

To effect a change, we must be willing to *take responsibility* for changing the relationship or the situation. This is usually quite difficult. Yet taking responsibility for effecting a change in a difficult situation is therapeutic in and of itself, because it reduces the debilitating effects of feeling helpless.

When we are aware that a problem exists in a relationship, and take responsibility for trying to change it (instead of waiting for our mate to change), the third necessary step is to achieve *clarity* about what needs to be done and what can be done.

Most people in the midst of a jealousy crisis cannot easily discriminate between what they can change in the relationship or situation and what they cannot.

Some people assume that everything in themselves, their mates, and their relationships can be changed. When they discover the hard way that this is not always so, they feel hopeless and helpless and come to believe that nothing can be changed. There are also people who believe from the outset that nothing can be changed. These individuals never attempt to change anything. "That's life," they say. The slogan may reduce their stress to some extent, but it also prevents them from actively seeking positive change.

The truth is that some things in a relationship cannot be changed or would be extremely difficult to change—for example, the basic personalities of both mates. But many triggers in a jealousy-provoking relationship or situation—certain behaviors, for example—*can* be changed with varying degrees of effort. The most important advantage of achieving clarity is the ability to distinguish between those aspects of the relationship and the situation that can't be changed, and those that can. This allows us to channel our efforts where there will be the greatest likelihood of important progress.

Jealousy has been described as "the eruption of attachment that can be transcended only through awareness."[4] As we move with awareness into the core of our jealousy, we may discover such unpleasant things as ungrounded expectations, projections, fears, and insecurities. Awareness of their existence in ourselves is the first step in overcoming them.

In a jealousy crisis, you first need to determine what is at the heart of your jealousy. Is it fear of loss? Is it a feeling of humiliation? Is it feeling excluded? Is it something else? What is the most painful thought associated with your jealousy? Does it hurt you to know that your wife had a wonderful time with someone else, and you were excluded? Do you feel humiliated because your husband has flirted all night with a stunning woman, and everyone at the party saw it? Or do you feel a terrible pain of loss because you know you have lost your mate's love and the relationship? While feeling excluded is no doubt painful, it is not as painful as losing a love relationship. People who don't bother to clarify what hurts them most can respond to a trivial incident as if they have lost the relationship.

Once you've identified the focus of your jealousy, you need to figure out why you are responding the way you are. Is it a result of your sensitivity, or of a real threat to the relationship? Even if you're especially prone to jealousy, it's important to avoid thinking of yourself as a "jealous person" instead of as a person with a predisposition to jealousy. The predisposition can be a result of your family background, your cultural background, or your past history of intimate relationships.

After you've clarified for yourself what *exactly* you are experiencing and why, you can proceed to examine your different options for coping.

How Do You Cope with Jealousy?

Recall your most extreme experience or experiences of jealousy. To what extent did you use each one of the following coping strategies: never, only once or twice, rarely, occasionally, often, usually, or always?

- Talk to your mate about the situation and your response to it in a rational manner?

- Use sarcasm?

- Accept the situation because you felt you couldn't do anything about it?

- Avoid the issue and try not to think about it?

- Use "stony silence," clearly indicating that you were aware of the problem but refused to talk about it?

- Use denial (you knew that your mate was involved with someone, but you chose not to know)?

- Cry, either in front of your mate to make your suffering obvious, or when you were all alone?

- Use verbal assault, screaming at your mate, cursing, swearing?

- Retaliate, making your mate jealous either by flirting, having an affair, or by telling your mate about other lovers?

- Attack your mate physically, with fists, nails, dishes?

- Leave your mate, either temporarily or forever?

- Suffer silently and covertly, so neither your mate nor anyone else knew about your pain?

- Suffer silently but visibly (making a sad face and sighing whenever your mate was around)?

- Try to find the funny side as you thought about the situation?

- Make a joke of it to your mate or to others?

- Think through your role in the situation and assess rationally what you stood or feared to lose?

I presented the question "How do you cope with jealousy?" in two different studies.[5] In one of these studies, 285 men and 283 women were presented with a list of seven coping strategies and asked which one of these strategies they were most likely to use when feeling jealous. The response chosen most frequently was, "I talk about it with my mate." The least frequently chosen response was, "I respond with violence." Here are the percentages of the responses, in rank order:

- I talk about it with my mate—34 percent
- I let my mate know I'm hurt—25 percent
- I try to ignore it—22 percent

- I scream—7 percent

- I get away—5 percent

- I respond in some other way—5 percent

- I respond with violence—1 percent

The problem with these percentages is that they tell us only the primary strategy the person uses, when in many cases people use different strategies at different times, and even simultaneously. In the second study, 103 men and women were asked whether or not they use each of sixteen different coping strategies presented earlier. Once again, "rational discussion" was one of the two most frequent strategies, the second being "I think through my role in the situation and assess rationally what I stand or fear to lose." And again, "physical violence" was the least frequently mentioned strategy. Here are the percentages of people who answered "yes" when asked whether they use a particular strategy for coping with extreme jealousy:

- I think through my role in the situation and assess rationally what I stand or fear to lose—80 percent

- I use rational discussion—79 percent

- I use verbal assault—60 percent

- I use sarcasm—56 percent

- I accept the situation—55 percent

- I cry—44 percent

- I use stony silence—42 percent

- I suffer silently but visibly—36 percent

- I try to find the funny side of the situation—36 percent

- I avoid of the issue—33 percent

- I retaliate, making my mate jealous—33 percent

- I leave my mate—29 percent
- I suffer silently and covertly—27 percent
- I make a joke of it—26 percent
- I use denial—18 percent
- I resort to physical violence—7 percent

In two different studies, using two different groups of people and two different questions, the most frequent strategy reported for coping with jealousy was rational discussion; the least frequent strategy was violence.

Does this mean that people really are most likely to talk about their jealousy in a rational manner, or think through their role in the situation? Not necessarily. More likely, they answer according to what they know is the most acceptable way to deal with their jealousy—whether or not they actually do it.

If I were to ask you to recall the most intense jealousy you have ever experienced, and then ask how you would have liked to respond to the situation that triggered your jealousy, chances are you would say that you would have had a cool, rational discussion with your mate or thought through the situation and your role in it. Chances are also good that in fact you did something different—which is part of the reason you recall it until today as your most extreme experience of jealousy.

The fact is that talking with your mate and thinking through your role *are* indeed the best coping strategies for dealing with jealousy, because they are the most likely to produce positive results. The question is how to do it.

Since it is difficult to think clearly and compare options when you are in the midst of an emotional turmoil, it is best to get away temporarily from the person and the situation that triggered your jealousy. If at all possible, get out of town. It is important to be on your own and think—with or without the help of a friend or a professional.

When on your own, you need to consider several questions. These questions were mentioned before in this chapter and throughout the book, but they bear repeating:

- First, what is it exactly that's making you jealous? The fact that he's going out without you? That she seems to have more fun with him than with you do? That he had an affair?

- Second, what is at the heart of your jealousy? Envy of your rival? Fear of loss? Fear of abandonment? Humiliation? A threat to the relationship? A threat to your ego?

- Third, why are you experiencing that particular component of jealousy so intensely? Is it related to an old experience you might have had in your childhood? How is the old experience related to what you are experiencing now? Could the current threat be related to what you found most rewarding about your mate's love at the beginning of your relationship?

Once you've identified your own role in the jealousy problem, consider what your options are for responding. Consider, too, how your mate is likely to respond to each of those options, and what you want to happen. If you want more than anything else for the two of you to be close again, attacking your mate is not the best strategy. Expressing your love and pain is likely to have a much more positive outcome.

The best setting for that is an open and considerate discussion that gives you and your mate the opportunity to describe your feelings and explain whatever needs to be explained without being attacked. One way to do it is for each one of you to take exactly five minutes in which you can make one point (only!) as the other listens and tries to understand. The listener can only ask for clarification and, at the end of the five minutes, must repeat back the main point to the speaker's satisfaction.[6]

In all conversations, hurt feelings and counterattacks can be avoided if both you and your mate are careful to follow these three steps:

1. Describe what you think the other one is feeling. ("You must feel constrained when I'm with you at a party.")

2. Describe what you are feeling. ("I feel left out when you have long conversations with other people, especially when you are talking to an attractive person of the opposite sex.")

3. Express clearly what it is that you want. ("I would really appreciate it if you would include me in some conversations.")

When the situation is too explosive for any kind of talking, consider writing what you want to say to each other—in the form of a love letter.

If you feel overcome by jealousy and think you are likely to do "something crazy," remember the important distinction between what you feel and what you do. Even when you *feel* crazy, you don't have to *act* crazy; even if you *feel* out of control, you don't have to *act* that way. In fact, behavioral therapists believe that it is possible to change our feelings by changing the thoughts or actions associated with them.

We don't always realize, or want to admit, that we have a wide range of options for responding in a jealousy situation. We can show our mate how important the relationship is to us; we can get out of the situation or the relationship; we can ignore what is going on; we can show our mate how much we are suffering; we can laugh it off; we can make a scandal; or we can talk to our mate about our feelings and wishes.

THE BEHAVIORAL APPROACH TO JEALOUSY

The focus of the behavioral approach, as its name implies, is on observable behavior.[7] Unlike the psychodynamic approach and like the systems approach, the behavioral approach has no interest in the unconscious. Behaviorists assume that the causes for, and solutions to, a jealousy problem exist in the current environment, even if the jealousy-triggering event happened at another time and place.

To behaviorists, all psychological problems are a result of inappropriate learning. Like those who advocate open marriages, they disagree with the sociobiologists' view that jealousy is natural, instinctive, and inevitable. Since jealousy is learned, behaviorists maintain, it can also be unlearned and a new (and better) response can replace it.[8]

Behavioral therapists define a problem exactly the way the person who comes for treatment defines it. They do not assume that the therapist knows the "real" problem better than the person experiencing it. The treatment goal is to help the person change inappropriate responses and dysfunctional habits by unlearning them and replacing them with more appropriate responses. Treatment can accommodate either an individual or a couple.

According to behaviorists, in every interaction people try to get as many rewards as they can for the lowest possible cost. In couples therapy, couples are taught to negotiate contracts that enable each mate to get more rewards from the other. The only cost is doing something the other wants.

Desensitization is one of the behavioral techniques that can be used to treat jealousy.[9] The process comprises several steps. First, you are asked to make a list of the things that cause you jealousy and rank them according to the amount of jealousy they trigger in you. Second, you are taught progressive relaxation by learning to relax different parts of your body. Third, you are trained to remain relaxed as you imagine the different items on your list. You start by imagining the item at the bottom of the list, the one that triggers the least jealousy in you. Once you are able to think about this item and remain relaxed, you are asked to imagine the next item on your list. If you can't remain relaxed while imagining it, you return to your relaxation exercises and then try again. This way, you can gradually learn to confront the triggers that produce the most extreme jealousy in you, and remain calm.

In jealousy workshops I use a variation of this exercise, which involves revisiting your most intense experience of jealousy.

If you want to try the exercise, lie on the floor and make yourself as comfortable as possible. Imagine yourself in your favorite place (it can be in the house or outdoors); the day is sunny and you're relaxed and happy. Take a deep breath and imagine it bringing calm and comfort to every cell in your body. As you exhale, imagine all feelings of discomfort, tension, and pain leaving you. Concentrate on relaxing each part of your body separately, starting with your toes and moving up slowly to your face and head, until you feel completely relaxed.

Now flip through the pages of your personal history book until you reach the incident that triggered your most extreme jealousy. Try to remember as many details as you can about it. Who were the people involved? How did they look? What exactly happened? When? Where? What did you do in response? Don't try to escape the pain, the rage, the panic. Let them flood you. Stay with the pain for a minute, then take a deep breath, slowly bring your mind back to the present, and sit up.

Write down as many details of your experience as you can remember. (In workshops, the participants in this exercise tell each other the details of the experience.) For a behavioral therapist, accumulating such details is an essential step of treatment.

The second part of this exercise starts the same way as the first. Lie on the floor and imagine you're in your favorite place. Is it a beautiful, sandy beach? A stream in the forest? Imagine lying there, the sun warming you gently. The wonderful feeling of relaxation is back. But, this time, imagine that the sun is not only warming you, but also energizing and empowering you with its rays. You are feeling strong and in control. Time has passed since you experienced your most intense experience of jealousy, and during that time you have learned more about yourself, about relationships. You are wiser, more experienced, and more powerful now. Feel your inner power and wisdom. Hold on to them as you would to a shield, a magic weapon.

Now you are ready to go back in time and revisit your most intense experience of jealousy. Imagine you've been given a chance to go back to that incident and relive it any way you want. Remember that now you are armed with wisdom, experience, and power. What do you do? How do you respond this time? The same way you responded originally, because the experience taught you so much, despite the pain? Or differently, the way you have wished so many times you had responded—cool, gracious, in complete control of yourself and of the situation?

In workshops, after people have completed the guided imagery, they are given a chance to discuss their experiences and share insights they have gained. When you do the exercise on your own, be sure to write down both your experiences and your insights.

If you found yourself responding differently when you revisited the site of your most extreme jealousy, remember that the ability to respond in this new way is within you. The feelings of empowerment, of experience, wisdom, control, are a part of you. You can call them up at any time, even if this requires greater effort in times of stress. The next exercise is aimed at convincing you of this point.

Take a sheet of paper and fold it lengthwise. Write the letter *A* on top of one side, and *B* on top of the other side. Recall the thoughts that ran through your head during the first part of the exercise. List as many of them as you remember on the side of paper labeled *A*.

Next, recall your thoughts during the second part of the exercise. Write as many of them as you remember on the side of paper labeled *B*.

Now unfold the paper and compare the two columns. For example:

A	B
He doesn't love me, that's why he did it. I'm unlovable.	I know he loves me in his own way and he had his own reason for doing what he did.
I'm all alone. Nobody loves me.	I'm not alone. There are people I love who love me.
This is so painful, life is not worth living.	This is painful, so I'll do something nice for myself.
I'm in so much pain that I can't control what I do.	I'm in pain, but I'm strong and in control. I want to learn something from this.

Repeat the *B* sentences to yourself over and over again, every day, so that by the next time jealousy strikes they are familiar and easily accessible to you.

Albert Ellis uses a similar approach in the application of his Rational-Emotive Therapy to the treatment of jealousy.[10] Ellis differentiates between rational and irrational jealousy. Rational jealousy is reality-based, while irrational jealousy is the result of irrational thoughts such as "It's *awful* that my beloved is interested in someone else! I *can't stand* it!" Like all other emotional upsets, Ellis argues, jealousy follows an ABC scheme. At point A there is an *Activating* event: your beloved shows interest in or attention to someone else. At point B you feel an emotional *Consequence*—intense jealousy. Quite commonly you falsely attribute C to A—that is, you erroneously contend that "*Because* my mate is carrying on a hot affair with so-and-so, *that* makes me jealous." Actually, says Ellis, there is no magic by which any outside event, even a traumatic event such as your spouse's affair, can cause you to experience jealousy. Only your *Beliefs* (the B in the ABC scheme) can do that. *Disputing* the irrational beliefs is the D in rational emotive therapy. Instead of the irrational, and easily disputed beliefs such as "It's *awful*" and "*I can't stand* it!" you can *choose* to say to yourself, "I don't like this situation very much. I wish my beloved would be devoted only to me. What a pain in the ass this is!" If you chose to believe this, and nothing but this, promises Ellis, your emotional Consequence at point C may be disappointment, regret, or irritation, but not insane jealousy.

People tormented by jealousy almost always have a specific "traumatic scene" that causes them the sharpest pain each time they think of it. For men, it tends to be a sexual scene: "She is having sex with her new lover, and both of them are making fun of me." For women, it tends to be a scene of great intimacy: "They are walking together in the park with a baby carriage." "They are looking at each other lovingly after making love, smiling and touching tenderly." "He is offering her marriage." The behaviorist Zeev Wanderer believes that by eliminating the emotions associated with this traumatic scene, you eliminate the jealousy problem.

Wanderer developed a technique he calls Physiologically Monitored Implosion Therapy (PMIT).[11] PMIT is an improvement on a well-known behavioral technique called "implosion therapy" (or "flooding"), which has been used successfully in the treatment of phobias and post-traumatic stress syndrome. In implosion therapy, patients are asked to imagine their worst fear or most traumatic experience again and again until the fear is reduced. In PMIT, the therapist monitors the patient's blood pressure with an electronic instrument that records subtle changes. The patient talks about difficult situations, and the therapist keeps a tape recording of the scene the patient described just preceding a peak in blood pressure. This scene is considered the source of the problem. Repeated exposure to the recording reduces the scene's power over the patient, and blood pressure gradually returns to normal. Here is an example of how the process works:

A man in his mid-thirties with a job in radio broadcasting had a girlfriend who worked in his office. One day she terminated their relationship to start a romantic involvement with one of their co-workers. The man's job required that he interact frequently with both of them. His intense jealousy caused him to avoid this contact, to the detriment of his work.

During PMIT, the man was asked what he found most difficult about seeing his girlfriend with her new lover. "The fact that they are making love," he responded. What was it about their sex life that disturbed him most? Wanderer measured the man's blood pressure as he recounted his fantasies of the couple's sex life.

Analysis of the blood-pressure data indicated that the largest rise in blood pressure occurred when the man described the special sounds his ex-lover used to make when she reached orgasm. At the time of their own sexual involvement, he thought he was the only man who could make her produce these sounds. Now he was most tormented by the thought that she was making those sounds with her new lover.

The therapist recorded a session on tape in which the man was asked to imagine his ex-lover's new sexual liaison, dramatizing her orgasms, how "she's making those sounds with him. . . . He's touching her body in all the places that arouse her, they are laughing." The man was instructed to listen to the tape for an hour a day. After less than a week of listening to the tape, the scene no longer pained but bored him. He was able to have work-related contact with both his ex-lover and her new man without discomfort.

Another case that Wanderer treated involved a stockbroker who came to therapy because he felt he needed to stop being jealous. He said his jealousy had lost him several girlfriends. The last girlfriend, whom he liked a great deal, was especially nice and understanding, and he was pained by her loss, which he considered his own fault: "One day I saw her coming out of a movie house with a lawyer friend of hers, and I made a terrible scene. She was very angry, and told me she can't have a relationship with someone who behaves that way."

His PMIT revealed that the worst scene for him was imagining the girlfriend leaving him for that lawyer friend. The man was taught how to relax while imagining this terrible scenario over and over again. After several therapy sessions he saw his girlfriend again with the same lawyer. This time he felt calm. He approached them and said a polite, "Hello, how are you?" to both of them. His girlfriend was so impressed by the change in his behavior that she called him up and they started dating again.

In both examples Wanderer, describes, repeated exposure to the painful scene severed its connection to the jealous response and replaced it with a new connection between the scene and boredom.

The "Scrupulous Honesty" exercise described in chapter four (see page 94) is another version of implosion therapy.[12] In this technique, the non-jealous mate is instructed to "flood" the jealous mate with every detail of the day's experiences. The flooding inundates the jealous mate with information that helps dispel anxiety and insecurity.

Another version of implosion therapy used specifically for the treatment of jealousy is the "Dutch cow" technique described to me by therapist Tsafy Gilad.[13] Gilad used the technique in treating the jealousy problem of a middle-aged couple.

Jealousy became a problem after the wife discovered that her husband had had a year-long affair. Although the affair was long over, the wife couldn't stop thinking about it. During the process of therapy the couple realized that the wife's discovery of the affair devastated her sense of security in the marriage. Security was what she looked for when she married her husband, and was the most important thing the marriage gave her. To restore her sense of security, she wanted to know her husband's whereabouts every moment he was away from her, so she wouldn't worry that he might be spending time with the other woman.

The husband, who was ready to do anything to restore the marriage, was instructed to call his wife every hour whether she was at home, at work, with friends, or shopping. The instruction also meant, however, that the wife had to tell her husband where she would be every hour so he would know where to call her. The technique is nicknamed "Dutch cow," because the telephone calls serve the same function as the bells Dutch cows carry around their necks: they let their owner know where they are at every moment, so that no fences are needed.

After several weeks of this ordeal, the wife had had enough. She started dreading the phone calls, which intruded on her life. But her husband didn't mind them at all. He was ready to go on long after she said she couldn't take it anymore. While it is not clear whether the technique helped the wife genuinely trust her husband again, it clearly helped sever the connection between the husband's temporary absence and the wife's jealousy, and replaced it with a connection between his phone calls and annoyance.

Another example of a behavioral technique for helping a couple cope with the aftermath of an affair was developed by behavior therapist Bernie Zilbergeld.[14] It involves asking the betrayed spouse to write a convincing defense of the spouse who had the affair. When I use this technique, I also ask the spouse who had the affair to write a defense of the betrayed spouse's jealousy. These defenses are extremely difficult to write, but are effective in helping couples understand each other's perspective. Here, for example, is part of a defense written by a female attorney of her boyfriend's involvement with other women:

> A contract is not binding when one party has been coerced or fears negative repercussions for failure to enter the contract. Such is the case here. When Jack agreed to maintain an exclusive relationship with me, he believed that he must acquiesce to my terms or lose me. When the first breach occurred, I sent an ambiguous message: I hate your behavior, but I will never hate you, and so I will forgive you and put this behind us and resume our relationship. Again, I exacted the term of an agreement to remain exclusively committed to each other and added that truth was essential to the maintenance of the relationship. Repeatedly the pattern has been that promises are made, broken, forgiven, cajoled, questioned—unpleasant and painful for both, but put aside. Jack could easily have concluded that I was making empty threats to leave or to require him to leave. He saw how distressed I was, but saw, too, that I could bounce back and behave as if business as usual was the rule. When he was honest and revealed that he had been with a woman all night, coming home at five in the morning, my behavior didn't change. The pattern was so set that even then I did not act on my threats to end the relationship. These were storms we weathered. Since he prizes his autonomy and freedom above all else, he was willing to endure these painful confrontations because he knew that they would pass and he would be able to maintain his life according to his preferred pattern. The lies necessary to maintain that lifestyle were lies he told to protect me from hurt rather than to protect himself, he thought, and since

his affairs had nothing to do with his love for me, he told me about them to stabilize our life together.

After both mates read each other's defenses, they are more able and willing to see the other's point of view in the jealousy situation. This is a version of the role-reversal technique, described in chapter four (see page 94), in which mates take turns describing each other's point of view. At the basis of both the written defenses and the role-reversal techniques is the power of behaving "as if," which is also evident in a third technique, called "Pretend."[15]

In this technique, the jealous person is instructed to behave *as if* he or she were not jealous. The underlying assumption—one of the basic assumptions of the behavioral approach—is that if a jealous person can control his jealous behavior and act in a non-jealous manner, he can learn to perceive himself as a non-jealous person. In addition, behaving in a non-jealous manner is likely to evoke a more favorable response from the non-jealous partner. As systems therapists note, jealous behavior, with its attendant demands, interrogation, whining, and fault-finding, usually evokes a negative reaction from the partner. By behaving more reasonably and positively toward the partner, despite feelings to the contrary, couples can reverse their downward spiral of interaction.

The counterpart of the "Pretend" technique is another technique mentioned briefly in chapter four (see page 94), called "Turning the Tables," in which the non-jealous partner is instructed to act the part of the jealous partner.[16] Couples therapists Won-Gi Im, Stefanie Wilner, and Miranda Breit, who developed this technique, describe an example of its successful use.

The husband, a physician in his mid-forties, sought help because his marriage of twenty-one years was in trouble as a result of his wife's jealousy. His wife expressed her unfounded jealousy by raging at him and harassing him on the telephone at the hospital where he worked, which caused him a great deal of embarrassment.

The husband was instructed to act the part of a jealous spouse and to keep this strategy secret from his wife. Having learned over many years how a jealous person behaves, he was able to perform the role of the jealous husband so skillfully and subtly that his wife didn't realize he was only role-playing. While he had seldom called home in the past, he now called his wife frequently to check on her, to see whether she was home and to ask exactly what she was doing. He made critical and suspicious remarks about any new clothes she wore, and he expressed displeasure whenever she showed the slightest interest in another man.

The result was dramatic. The wife, now feeling flattered by her husband's attentiveness and newfound interest, stopped her jealous behavior completely. She became pleasant and loving toward her husband, and expressed remorse over her earlier behavior. At an eight-month follow-up, the husband reported that his wife continued to behave more lovingly toward him, but as a precaution he still played the role of the jealous husband from time to time.

In both the "Pretend" and the "Turning the Tables" techniques, one spouse is instructed to behave differently (more like the other spouse) as a way of changing the dynamics surrounding a jealousy problem. The following exercise is aimed at getting both mates to work on a jealousy problem together:[17]

Each of you will need three sheets of paper for this exercise. On top of the first page, write the heading, "Behaviors that Trigger my Jealousy" or "Jealous Behaviors that Get on My Nerves." Under this heading, if you are the jealous spouse, list all the things your mate does that trigger your jealousy; if you are the non-jealous spouse, list all the jealousy-related things your spouse does that make you feel angry, frustrated, caged, or hurt. For example, an item on a jealous spouse's list may be, "When you are honey-dripping sweet to every woman you meet on the street after being nasty to me." An item on the non-jealous spouse's list may be, "Your suspicion about every woman I happen to bump into on the street."

On top of the second page, write, "The Needs at the Base of My Jealousy" (if you are the jealous spouse) or "The Needs at the Base of My Annoyance" (if you are the non-jealous spouse). Under this second heading write the different needs at the heart of your jealousy or your annoyance. For example, at the heart of the jealousy triggered by seeing him act sweet to other women may be a need to feel special, to feel that you are his "one and only." At the heart of the anger at her suspicion may be a need to feel trusted.

At the top of the third page, write, "Wishes." Under this heading, write what your partner can do to fulfill your need. Don't ask for things that are too general, such as "Make me feel special" or "Show that you trust me." Ask for specific and concrete things your mate is able to do, things that have special significance for you. For example, "Take me out for a romantic dinner." "Tell me that you trust me." Note that both examples are positive statements—things to do, not things to avoid. Note, too, that both examples involve observable behavior, the focus of the behavioral approach.

After writing your lists of wishes, go over those lists and rank your requests from one to ten in terms of their importance to you, a score of ten means very important, a score of one means of minor importance. For example, how important is it that your husband take you out for a romantic dinner? Would you rank it 8? 6? 9? 3? What about his dancing a slow and intimate dance with you at a party? Is it more or less important? How important is it that your wife tell you that she trusts you?

Once both of you have ranked your requests, exchange your lists, examine your spouse's wishes, and then rank them in terms of your difficulty in fulfilling them. Again, the most difficult request gets the score of ten, the least difficult gets the score of one. How difficult it is for you to tell your husband that you trust him? 8? 6? 3? How difficult it is for you to to take your wife out for a romantic dinner? 9? 5? 2?

It is important to emphasize that requests are not demands, and should never be expressed or understood as such. They are wishes. When your partner fulfills your wish, it's a gift and should be perceived and received that way.

If you have a jealousy problem you are trying to overcome, try to give each other at least three gifts every week. This probably will not be easy; if it were easy, you would have done it before. The things your partner asks for may be difficult for you to give. It may be hard for you to look straight in your husband's eyes and tell him that you trust him, when deep in your heart you don't—which is why you respond with jealousy when he is too friendly toward other women. You don't *have* to give gifts you rated high in difficulty. Start with those you rated least difficult. As the relationship becomes more loving and trusting, you will find it easier to give your partner the more difficult gifts too.

Finally, a note about assumptions. One of the most damaging assumptions in couple relationships is that something asked for is worthless. ("If I have to ask for it, what kind of a gift is it?") Another dangerous assumption is that the gifts your mate wants are the same things *you* want. The exercise described above can help you break free of these assumptions and give each other what you *both* really want. This way, both of you will get more rewards from the relationship. You may recall that getting as many rewards as possible for the lowest possible cost is one of the goals of behavioral couples therapy.

AN EVALUATION OF THE BEHAVIORAL APPROACH TO JEALOUSY

One of the major contributions of the behavioral approach is its emphasis on observable behavior and its view of jealousy as a learned response that can be unlearned. The behavioral techniques and exercises described in this chapter have in common the assumption that if we change our behavior (even when we're only role-playing at first) we can change our feelings and attitudes. Such behavioral techniques can be very effective, and are far less time-consuming than psychodynamically oriented psychotherapy.

One of the major criticisms of the behavioral approach (similar to a criticism of the systems approach) is directed at its disregard of the role played by traumatic childhood experiences and unconscious processes in the development of psychological problems such as jealousy. According to psychodynamically oriented therapists, unless these childhood experiences are addressed and the unconscious processes brought to consciousness, the jealousy problem will not be cured. These critics see the changes brought about by behavioral techniques as superficial and temporary.

Behaviorists, however, believe that insight is not necessary for a lasting change in behavior to take place. Because behaviorists focus on observed behavior, their interventions can be studied and, indeed, have been proven effective.[18]

COPING STRATEGIES AND THEORETICAL APPROACHES

The coping strategies presented in this chapter are inspired primarily by the behavioral approach. Throughout the book, however, I've described exercises and coping strategies inspired by the other theoretical approaches to jealousy.

The psychodynamic approach, which views jealousy as occurring in the mind of the jealous individual, inspired the exercise called "Jealousy as the Shadow of Love." As you may recall from chapter one this exercise requires introspection with the goal of making a connection between the jealousy and childhood experiences. The systems approach, which views jealousy as occurring in the dynamic of a particular relationship, inspired the role-reversal exercise, requiring both mates to participate working on a jealousy problem. The social-psychological approach, which views jealousy as primarily influenced by the culture, inspired the shift from a dispositional to a situational attribution. The sociobiological approach, which views jealousy as innate and shaped by evolutionary forces, inspired the "relationship sociodrama," a technique designed to break our fallacy of uniqueness and discover the universal nature of jealousy. The behavioral approach, presented in this chapter, inspired a variety of techniques and exercises to help individuals and couples learn new responses to jealousy triggers. Each approach and every strategy can help us understand and cope with our jealousy more effectively.

FINAL WORDS ABOUT COPING

The exercises in this chapter assume that both of you truly want to be rid of your jealousy problem. This assumption may or may not be true. It is possible that, despite all appearances to the contrary, the jealousy problem serves an important function in your relationship—a function you would rather not acknowledge. If this is the case, chances are that the coping strategies recommended here will not work, and you may want to consider getting professional help.

Nevertheless, exercises that give you an opportunity to learn about yourself and about each other, and that increase the number of rewards you give each other, can only benefit the relationship, and therefore deserve a good try.

Even if the techniques and exercises recommended in this chapter don't solve your jealousy problem altogether, they are guaranteed to increase your self-knowledge and enhance your growth as an individual and as a couple.

CAN ANY GOOD
COME OUT OF
ROMANTIC JEALOUSY?

*Jealousy is always born together with love, but it
does not always die with love. . . . We are happier
in the passion we feel than in that we arouse.*

—LA ROCHEFOUCAULD, REFLECTIONS

*C*an any good come out of jealousy? If you have read the
preceding chapters of this book, you probably know that my answer
is a definite yes. Whether or not you have read the preceding chapters,
take a minute to rate your agreement with the following statements
on a one-to-seven scale:

1	2	3	4	5	6	7
DISAGREE						AGREE
STRONGLY			AGREE SOMEWHAT			STRONGLY

a. Jealousy is a sign of love.

b. Jealousy is an instrument for inducing commitment.

c. Jealousy brings excitement to listless relationships.

d. Jealousy teaches people not to take each other for granted.

e. Jealousy makes life more interesting.

f. Jealousy makes relationships last longer.

g. Jealousy makes our mate look more desirable.

h. Jealousy makes us feel alive.

i. Jealousy makes us examine our relationship.

I presented these statements to 103 men and women, and asked them to rate each one on the scale presented above.[1] Following is their mean rating for each statement, in descending order of agreement with the statements:

Jealousy makes us examine our relationship: 4.7

Jealousy teaches people not to take each other for granted: 3.1

Jealousy is a sign of love: 3.0

Jealousy is an instrument for inducing commitment: 2.8

Jealousy makes our mate look more desirable: 2.6

Jealousy brings excitement to listless relationships: 2.4

Jealousy makes life more interesting: 2.3

Jealousy makes us feel alive: 2.3

Jealousy makes relationships last longer: 1.5

The respondents agreed most with the statement that jealousy is positive in that it forces us to examine our relationship. Yet, as we can see by the mean rating (4.7), they agreed with it only to a certain extent. The same rating (4.7) was given to a statement describing a negative effect of jealousy with which the same respondents agreed *least*: that jealousy makes us feel guilty. They agreed much more strongly with statements about the other negative effects of jealousy:

Jealousy causes emotional distress: 5.9

Jealousy puts a strain on relationships: 5.9

Jealousy can block thought and distort emotions: 5.9

Jealousy wastes valuable time: 5.8

Jealousy causes physical distress: 5.5

Jealousy restricts the partner's freedom: 5.2

Jealousy may result in violence: 5.0

Jealousy can cause social embarrassment: 5.0

Jealousy drives our partner away: 4.8

Agreement about the negative effects of jealousy did not necessarily correlate with a respondent's own level of jealousy. In other words, whether or not one perceived oneself as a jealous person had no effect on one's rating of these negative effects of jealousy. On the other hand, agreement about the positive effects of jealousy was significantly correlated with self-perception—the more jealous one perceived oneself to be, the more likely one was to agree with the positive effects of jealousy. This means that while everyone agrees on the negative effects of jealousy, only people who perceive themselves as jealous agree that it has positive effects. There are several possible explanations for this.

People who perceive themselves as jealous may want to describe jealousy in a positive light. By the same token, people who perceive jealousy as a more positive experience may admit more readily to feeling jealous. It is also possible, of course, that when people have a traumatic experience with jealousy they need to convince themselves that something positive came out of it. The final possibility is that because people who describe themselves as jealous tend to experience jealousy more often, they have more occasions to discover its positive effects. While all four of these explanations have a grain of truth in them, for the remainder of this chapter I will take the approach suggested by the last explanation—namely, that some good *can* come out of jealousy. Let us examine this "good" more closely.

JEALOUSY MAKES US EXAMINE OUR RELATIONSHIPS

If you are like most people, chances are that after the first stage of courtship and romance you don't examine your relationship often, if at all. Similarly, you probably don't examine your work or your relationship with family members often. All this self-examination takes time and energy most of us don't have to spare. You may recall the common response of people who tried an open relationship and decided against it—it was too time-consuming: "You have to talk about the relationship all the time. You have to examine and reexamine rules you made for yourself that for some reason are not working. It is exhausting. It leaves no time or energy for anything else."

Jealousy, with all the emotional and physical turmoil it generates, provides us with an opportunity to examine our relationship without extra effort. To put it another way: If you've already suffered the pains of jealousy, don't waste the opportunity to learn something valuable about yourself and the relationship. Let the jealousy be your guide. Examine such questions as these: What does this experience tell me about myself? What does it tell me about the relationship? Examination of this sort is most productive if followed by more action-oriented questions such as, Is this the kind of relationship I want for myself? And if the answer is no, what can I do to change things?

JEALOUSY TEACHES PEOPLE NOT TO TAKE EACH OTHER FOR GRANTED

Romantic love is not an eternal flame. If fuel is not added to it, sooner or later the flame will burn out.[2] When we first fall in love and our love is reciprocated, we feel fortunate to have such a wonderful person return our love. When we're not sure whether or not our love is reciprocated, insecurity and doubt intensify our emotions. We are ready to do anything to have this wonderful person love us. Yet all too often, when we feel assured of our partner's love and commitment, we start to take this love for granted. We make demands we would not have made during the early stages of the relationship, and would never make of other people. Our partner becomes the one person in our life who is "supposed" to understand our work pressures, our all-absorbing involvement with our children, with our friends, with community work. "Who can I ask to be understanding and supportive if not my spouse?" we ask self-righteously. Dealing with continuous stress at work, with children, with a parent, with voluntary activities, in effect gives these concerns a higher priority than the marriage. No romantic relationship can withstand this kind of assault for long. Taking each other for granted erodes love.

Paradoxically, the threat of involvement with a third person stops this overinvolvement with people outside the relationship, and brings the focus back to the couple. Suddenly our security in our mate's love and commitment is shaken, as we wonder once again "does he [she] love me? Does he [she] not?"

JEALOUSY IS A SIGN OF LOVE

Whether or not romantic jealousy is seen as a sign of love varies in different cultures and in different periods of history. Therefore, whether or not we agree with the statement at the head of this section tends to be influenced by the norms of our own culture. Yet even people who don't see jealousy as a sign of love may still respond with jealousy when they perceive a threat to a valued love relationship. In this way, as noted in chapter one, jealousy is the shadow of love.

Perhaps you're thinking, "There's more self-love than love in jealousy," or, "Jealousy is caused by possessiveness and by a sense of inferiority, not by love." I would like to argue that even if self-love, possessiveness, and inferiority are a part of jealousy, couples can deal with these feelings more effectively if they focus on the love. If you are on the receiving end of your partner's jealousy and you're convinced that the jealousy results from your partner's possessiveness or inferiority complex, there is little you can do to change things. But if you see the jealousy as a sign of love, related to the things both of you found most attractive about each other initially, you are more likely to realize that jealousy is part of a dynamic in the relationship to which both of you contribute—and that both of you can work to change. As I noted before, viewing jealousy as a response to a perceived threat to a valued love relationship, or to its quality, eliminates guilt and blame, and frees energy for more constructive coping.

JEALOUSY IS AN INSTRUMENT FOR INDUCING COMMITMENT

When Gary reached forty, he felt that he had only a limited number of erections left. With this in mind, he wanted to enjoy as many of those erections as possible. Although he was happy in his fifteen-year marriage, he wanted the freedom to experience other women sexually. In turn, since he saw himself as an enlightened and liberated man, he was happy to allow his wife to have sex with other men, too. His wife, Sara, was not at all interested in an open marriage, and was jealous of every woman she thought Gary might be interested in. "When I walk down the street and I see these young, beautiful women, I panic," she said. But since she felt she had to be as enlightened and liberated as Gary was, she accepted his extramarital sexual liaisons. Months later, after much hesitation on her part and encouragement on Gary's part, she agreed to spend a weekend with a male friend. Afterward, to her surprise, Gary "freaked out." Sara recounted the strange experience: "He started following me around the house like a little puppy, begging me to assure him that I love him and would not leave him for that other man." To her great relief, he no longer wanted an open marriage.

A similar process often happens to people, most often men, who fear commitment.[3] A crisis of jealousy, which makes the person aware of competitors for his mate and the chance of losing the relationship, becomes the trigger that induces commitment. This might also explain why women try to induce jealousy more often than men do.

JEALOUSY INTENSIFIES EMOTIONS

As Gary discovered, jealousy makes one's mate look more desirable. At times this happens because, like the children we all were once, we find the toy we ourselves have neglected to be more interesting when someone else shows an interest in it. At other times our fear of losing what we have come to take for granted makes us realize just how desirable it is. Suddenly we notice the wonderful qualities that made us fall in love with our mate.

Jealousy can bring excitement to listless relationships. In the midst of a jealousy crisis, one thing people never complain about is boredom. They may talk about the pain of the experience, they may say it is infuriating, they may say it's humiliating—but they never say it's boring. And where there is emotional energy, there is an occasion for growth. The intense emotions serve as fuel for the exploration. You probably wouldn't do so much self-examination if you weren't in the midst of emotional turmoil.

If you are willing to explore intense emotions, positive as well as negative, you may even discover that jealousy can make life more passionate and interesting. As swingers know from their experience with sexual mate exchange, a sting of jealousy, if interpreted positively as a tease, can make you excited about your mate. The sphere in which all these positive effects can be seen most clearly is sex.

JEALOUSY ADDS PASSION TO SEX

Despite the great pain most people associate with jealousy, it sometimes has a positive effect on the quality of their sex lives.

I met Ben and Stacy at one of my intensive five-day jealousy workshops.[4] Ben was fifteen years older than Stacy. They had met as boss and employee, and Stacy continued to adore Ben and treat him as a mentor. Ben had been divorced for over five years when they became involved. Before that, he had been married for many years, and was monogamous the entire time. When he became single again, Ben wanted to make up for things he had missed in his youth (he married young), so he had many affairs.

Stacy had had several boyfriends prior to her involvement with Ben, but she was still a virgin when they met. The difference between them in age and sexual experience created problems in the relationship. The main problem, from Ben's point of view, was that sex had become boring. While he still loved Stacy, was flattered that such a young and beautiful woman was in love with him, and was committed to the relationship, her "lack of experience" made their sex life "unexciting." Ben wanted to be able to see some of his former girlfriends and have sex with them. He encouraged Stacy to get sexually involved with other men, which he said would be good for her, and good for the relationship. "It would help her become more experienced and sexually sophisticated," he argued.

Stacy, for her part, was jealous of Ben's former girlfriends and felt inferior to them. Although she was extremely attractive and had ample opportunities to date other men, she would have been happiest in a monogamous relationship with Ben. It was painful for her to realize that sex with her was not enough for him.

During the first days of the workshop, Ben brought Stacy's jealousy and insecurity to the group's attention on several occasions. On these occasions he presented himself as understanding of "Stacy's problem," while he flirted openly with other women in the group.

Then something happened that changed things dramatically. Following a particularly intense session in which one man in the group accused Stacy of being cold and emotionally unresponsive, Stacy broke down in tears and received warm feedback from the group. The man who initially attacked her—one of the more attractive men in the group—began to hug her and stroke her back.

The man had indicated his attraction to Stacy several times before, without a response from her. This was the real reason for his attack and accusation of "coldness." Now he was extremely sorry for the pain he had caused her, and was doing his best to comfort her. He was still hugging and stroking her when the session was over and the rest of the people in the group, including Ben, left the room.

His comforting gradually became more sexual. They both were emotionally aroused by the events that had taken place in the session, and physically aroused by their close contact. Their stroking and kissing became more passionate. Eventually they made love, right there on the carpet. Since they hadn't planned it, neither of them used contraceptives.

Ben was furious. He had seen Stacy and the man becoming physical with each other, and became extremely jealous. "How could you do this to me?" he demanded. The focus of his anger was not that Stacy had sex with another man, which was what he had claimed all along that he wanted her to do. Rather, he objected to her carelessness about contraception. "You hurt me more than any other woman has ever done," he said accusingly, "and I trusted you to protect my feelings."

Stacy, tears rolling down her cheeks, said that she'd never intended to hurt Ben's feelings. Nevertheless, she was stubborn in her insistence that she was not sorry for what she had done, and that it had been a wonderful experience.

While processing the experience with Ben and Stacy, examining his jealousy and her conflicting feelings, I asked them whether anything positive had come out of the incident. I was not surprised to hear Ben say, with great amazement, "When we made love afterward, it was the most passionate sex we ever had. It was unbelievably intense and exciting. I can't figure why." Stacy, still crying, nodded in agreement.

The reason their sex was so exciting was that it happened in the intensely emotional context of a jealousy crisis. For both Ben and Stacy, the security of a committed relationship had been shaken. Their perception of themselves and of each other suddenly changed. Ben, who until that time perceived himself as a "non-jealous" person, experienced many of the emotions associated with jealousy: anger, envy, rivalry, betrayal, fear of loss and of being excluded. Stacy, who until that time perceived herself as the one with the "jealousy problem," felt not only empathy for Ben's pain but also a new, powerful, and exciting experience of being desired by two attractive men.

Ben and Stacy's story is not unusual. I have seen many similar cases in which one partner pushed to open the relationship because sex had become boring, but who responded with great shock and jealousy when the other partner actually became involved with someone else. To the surprise of both partners, the painful shock helped revive the sexual passion in the relationship. Passionate sex depends on emotional arousal, and jealousy, as we well know, can be extremely arousing emotionally.

Jealousy doesn't always result in passionate sex, however. The jealous person may be terrified at the prospect of losing the relationship, and anxiety is the antithesis of passion. This tends to happen when jealousy is a chronic problem in the relationship.

When a relationship has strong roots of trust and security, a temporary jealousy crisis can remind both partners how important they are to each other. For mates who take each other for granted, or whose relationship has become boring and listless, jealousy can restore the relationship as the couple's number-one priority. Even if these changes are associated with the negative side of jealousy, they can intensify feelings between mates, and thus enhance the experience of sex.

On the other hand, when jealousy is a lasting problem, it threatens the fabric of security and trust at the foundation of a relationship. An example is a marriage in which the husband says he loves his wife, yet continues to have extramarital affairs. The wife responds to the affairs with jealous tantrums, yet remains in the marriage. The best thing that can result from this type of a jealousy problem is an occasion to examine the relationship and the role each partner plays in it: Why did you choose to marry someone who is interested in other people? Why are you staying in a relationship that doesn't satisfy your needs? Does it satisfy other needs— for example, a need for continuous drama? This kind of self-examination, as we saw in the previous chapter, is most beneficial if it leads to constructive action. The important question to address is, What can *you* do to change things?

JEALOUSY PROTECTS LOVE

At the beginning of the book I proposed that jealousy is a response to a perceived threat to a valued relationship or to its quality. In other words, jealousy aims to protect relationships. It is not a useless flight of irrationality, but a useful signal we can learn to interpret correctly. It is also a shock absorber that can facilitate both personal growth and relationship enrichment.[5] Every one of jealousy's positive effects, discussed in this chapter, can be seen as a love-protective function of jealousy.

Jealousy makes us examine our relationship, with the implicit hope that the relationship and its quality will remain intact. It teaches us not to take each other for granted; in this way it ensures that we continue to value our mate and to express this in our daily interactions with each other. It is a sign of love; it indicates that we value the relationship it protects. This is true even in those extreme situations in which jealousy leads to violence. It is an instrument for inducing commitment; it protects the boundaries of intimate relationships. It intensifies emotions—and thus keeps the spark alive in intimate relationships. It adds passion to sex; in this way it helps maintain the quality of sex in the relationship.

The next story demonstrates many of the positive effects of jealousy discussed in this chapter. It also demonstrates several of the issues discussed throughout the book.

A STORY OF LOVE AND JEALOUSY: ALAN AND LINDA AND GAIL

When Alan met Linda, she was in her first year of law school and he had a small house-painting business. Linda was a brilliant student and is an exceptionally attractive woman. Despite all her acknowledged success, however, she was very insecure. Alan, a virile, earthy, and affectionate man, calmed her. His love made her feel safe. No other man had ever made her feel that secure. Alan was the man who could take care of her and give her the loving attention her successful father never had time to give.

Alan, for his part, couldn't believe a woman like Linda would even look in the direction of a simple man like him, yet she was actually reciprocating his love. He was thrilled. He admired Linda's intelligence and identified with her academic success. She gave him an entrance into a world he had always considered beyond his reach. Their love for each other was passionate. Linda was the "wings" (intellectual, flighty, temperamental) and Alan the "roots" (simple, down to earth, stable). Together they felt complete. Things were going so well that they soon decided to get married.

Their marriage was passionate and turbulent. The areas in which they complemented each other intensified their mutual attraction, but the difference in their social status created a growing number of problems and conflicts. Linda complained that she couldn't talk to Alan the way she did to men in school. Alan complained that she was too involved with her studies.

With a moment's reflection it becomes clear that Alan's and Linda's complaints about each other were related to the things they found most attractive when they first met. Linda was attracted to Alan's earthiness and simplicity, but now he was too earthy and simple. Alan was attracted to Linda's intelligence and academic involvement; now he thought she was too involved academically.

Alan's complaints made Linda feel that he was criticizing her career goals. His lack of support made her withdraw even further into her academic world. At the same time, Linda's complaints hurt Alan's pride. He became increasingly uncomfortable in social situations that involved Linda's fellow students and law professors, and tried to avoid these situations as much as he could.

Given the growing distance between Alan and Linda, and the intensity built into the relationships among law students, who spend long hours studying together, what happened was almost inevitable: Linda had an affair with another student in her program. She felt that this man, unlike Alan, was her equal. They shared similar goals and she could talk with him about things she could never talk about with Alan.

Alan was terribly hurt by Linda's affair and responded with tremendous jealousy. The affair was particularly painful for him, because it took away what he found most rewarding about Linda's love: her acceptance of him as an equal.

Linda's lover was someone with whom Alan felt unable to compete; he wasn't enough as a man or as a mate. The "wings" Linda's love gave him had been clipped. Now she shared with someone else what he considered an even greater intimacy than the intimacy she had with him—the intimacy of minds. Alan's pain was unbearable.

To help himself overcome the pain, Alan started playing tennis several times a week. His good looks and excellent skills made him a desirable tennis partner. After tennis, the players often would go to a nearby coffee shop. Alan found himself talking with the attractive women he had played tennis with. Unlike Linda, these women seemed to appreciate him, to share his values, and to delight in his company. It didn't take him long to get sexually involved with one of them, and later on with two more. These sexual liaisons restored his self-confidence.

Now it was Linda's turn to experience the pain of jealousy. By this time her own affair was over. The law student had returned to a committed relationship he had with someone else; his affair with Linda turned out to be only a diversion. Linda was crushed. She had failed with a man who was her equal. This reinforced her belief that anyone she found desirable would never want her in the long run. She longed for the security of Alan's love, but now Alan was giving his love to other women. Linda couldn't bear it, even though she considered the other women "stupid fools."

Linda's jealousy focused on the most important thing Alan's love gave her, the thing she was now most afraid to lose: the feeling of secure ground under her feet. If she lost Alan's love, her life would not be worth living.

Linda started to woo Alan back, using every charm she knew would attract him. Alan was delighted, and happy to return to her. His encounters with women who were "less liberated" than Linda, however, made him aware of his need for a home—not the kind of home that Linda provided, but a "real home" complete with a hot meal waiting when he came home from work. They decided to hire a live-in housekeeper who would stay in a spare room in exchange for cleaning and cooking. That housekeeper was Gail.

Gail was new in town and almost penniless. For her, the arrangement with Alan and Linda, which gave her a roof over her head in addition to a job, was ideal. As a hardworking woman, she had no problem with the cleaning and cooking her job required.

The new arrangement worked wonderfully for everyone. Alan felt that now the house was a real home. He loved Gail's cooking and tidiness. On nights when Linda studied in the library, he and Gail sat at the kitchen table and talked. Gail, who had a history of troubled relationships with men, found Alan to be similar to herself. They became good friends. Like Alan, Linda appreciated having a neat house and great meals to come home to. She and Gail were also becoming good friends.

All three seemed happy with the arrangement. It ended only because Gail decided it was time to go back to her hometown.

After Gail left, Alan and Linda discovered that her presence had been hiding a growing estrangement between them. Linda once again complained about Alan's intellectual inadequacies, and Alan once again felt that this was not the "home" he wanted. They decided on a trial separation, and Linda moved to another apartment in their building. Despite the separation, they continued to see each other.

When Linda left for a professional convention one week, Alan decided to go out of town too. It happened that the relatives he wanted to visit lived close to Gail's hometown, so he called her up and suggested that they meet. The meeting was more moving and emotional than either of them expected. Both of them discovered how much they really meant to each other. Alan told Gail that he and Linda were separated and seriously contemplating divorce.

Gail, who had held back her feelings for Alan out of loyalty to Linda, gave in after hearing about the planned divorce. What hadn't happened during all the time they had shared a household happened now; they became lovers. Alan felt that this time he had found a woman who was truly perfect for him. They were so much alike. It felt so comfortable, so easy, so different from the eternal struggles in his marriage.

Gail, too, felt that she had found her "match made in heaven." Unlike the men she had known in the past, Alan was a friend and kindred spirit. She could talk to him. She could trust him. And now that he and Linda were separated, she could let herself feel passion for him, something she had never let herself experience before.

When Alan returned from the trip, he told Linda he wanted a divorce and that Gail was coming back to live with him. Linda, who until then had been searching for a more appropriate mate, was overcome with jealousy. It was "the most awful, consuming, heart-wrenching pain" she had ever experienced. She felt betrayed by Alan and by Gail. She telephoned Gail, weeping and screaming, "How can you do this to me? And I thought you were my friend!" "This is not something I did," Gail responded. "You were going to divorce Alan anyway. I had nothing to do with the problems between you two." The verbal brutality of Linda's attack made Gail even more determined to stay in the relationship with Alan.

Linda was inconsolable. She couldn't accept that she had lost Alan to a woman she cared for and trusted. She cried incessantly and was ready to promise Alan anything he wanted. She threatened: "I'll never let the two of you be alone in peace. I'll never let you make love. I'm going to stand at the window, scream, and throw stones. When I see Gail, I'm going to bash her face." Alan was patient and understanding. He held Linda in his arms when she cried. Yet he remained determined to give his relationship with Gail a chance.

On their way home from the airport, Alan started talking to Gail about getting married and having children. Gail had to slow him down and remind him that they needed to find out whether they could live together as a couple before deciding to have a family. But his enthusiasm was contagious.

The idyll between Alan and Gail was shorter than anyone could have anticipated. Almost immediately after she moved in with Alan, Gail sensed his change of attitude. At first she tried to ignore it, but soon things became intolerable and the confrontation unavoidable. "What is going on with you?" she asked, afraid to hear his answer.

"This is not working out for me. It's not the way I imagined it would be," said Alan.

"How can you say that, when I've been here only two days?" Gail said. "You need to give us a chance to make it work."

"I'm sorry. I think this is all one big mistake," Alan said quietly, and left.

Gail sank to the floor. This was a nightmare come true. This was exactly what had kept her from getting involved in relationships with men before. How had she let Alan get through her defenses? Why did she think that being kindred spirits was an assurance for anything? What was she going to do? She couldn't go back home—the humiliation would be too great. She couldn't stay. Maybe it would be better to finish it all right now. Life wasn't worth living with so much pain.

When the phone rang, Gail hesitated, but thinking Alan might have changed his mind again, she picked up the receiver. It was Linda.

Since her arrival, Gail had called Linda several times. She had left messages for her at home and at school, but Linda hadn't returned her calls. Now, in her hour of despair, she was on the line.

Linda knew what was going on because Alan had told her about his change of heart the minute it happened. Now that she had Alan back, she could allow herself to feel empathy with Gail's pain. She knew that pain intimately.

The two women started talking. After starting, it was difficult to stop. Both of them had so much to talk about, so much that needed to be said, to be clarified. Suddenly Linda said, "I have this weekend off. How about us going skiing? That will give us a chance to talk as much as we need to." Gail couldn't imagine anything she would rather do.

At the ski resort, Linda and Gail had a chance to compare notes. What had Alan told Gail to convince her that his relationship with Linda was over? What had he told Linda at the same time to keep her tied to him? Two women had been betrayed by the same dishonest and undeserving man—"and to think that he almost managed to turn us against each other."

Carried away by their excitement over renewing their friendship and sharing the pain they each experienced, they became affectionate with each other.

In the romantic atmosphere of the ski resort, hugs and kisses of excitement gradually turned more passionate. Finally they made love. For both, it was their first sexual encounter with a woman.

Gail fell in love with Linda in a way she had never loved before. She had never opened up to a man the way she did to Linda. She had never felt so understood. She adored Linda. She wanted to take care of her. She moved in with Linda and started once again cleaning the apartment and cooking Linda's favorite meals. When Linda was exhausted after a long day at court, Gail would drive her home.

While this was going on, Alan was wild with jealousy and was doing what Linda and Gail described as "crazy things." He came to Linda's apartment raving and raging, threw her clothes out the window, screamed at the top of his lungs that they were "filthy, disgusting sluts." Now it was Alan's turn to feel betrayed, rejected, and left out by two women he loved and considered his best friends. But he also felt he was competing against something beyond him, beyond his comprehension. Only perverts were doing the kind of things Linda and Gail were doing. How could they do it? How could they do it to *him?*

Linda and Gail felt sorry for Alan, yet felt united in their womanhood against this man whom both of them had loved, trusted, and felt betrayed by.

The joy of sharing their love, their pain, and their power as women fueled Linda and Gail's relationship for a while. It was not, however, enough of a foundation for a long-term relationship—not for Linda, that is. Soon she started longing for the safety of Alan's arms. Gail's arms weren't strong enough to make her feel safe, to calm her fears and insecurities. Eventually, Linda went back to Alan.

Once again Gail had a chance to experience jealousy. This time she was not jealous of Linda for having Alan, but of Alan for having Linda. The loss of Linda's love was far more painful than the loss of Alan's love. Gail had never allowed herself to be as vulnerable with a man as she had been with Linda. The loss was devastating.

Linda was supportive and understanding of Gail, yet clear about wanting to make her marriage work. After a while she found Gail's pain and emotional dependency increasingly more difficult to handle.

She suggested that Gail go to therapy, and told her she was willing to help her cover the cost.

Through therapy, Gail was able to understand her obsession with Linda and the reasons for her problematic relationships with men. A year and a half later she moved in with another woman, with whom she now has a satisfying relationship. Yet she still cared deeply about Linda and wanted to be a part of her life. When Linda had a baby, Alan, Linda's doctor, *and* Gail were with her in the delivery room.

Alan came to realize the impact his lack of formal education had on his self-image and on his relationship with Linda, and decided to go to college—something he had dreamed about all his life.

A CASE ANALYSIS

For purpose of this chapter, the most important point this complicated case demonstrates is that something good can indeed come out of jealousy. In the study mentioned earlier, the effect of jealousy that people found most positive was that jealousy could make us examine our relationships. Did jealousy cause Alan, Linda, and Gail to examine their relationship? Most definitely yes. As a result of their different jealousy crises, all three of them spent hours talking about themselves and about their relationship.

Although the results of such an exploration can be rewarding, the process it involves can be difficult and emotionally demanding. It points to the personal vulnerabilities that make us susceptible to jealousy, and to the repeated patterns that keep jealousy alive in our relationships. Some couples can explore their jealousy problem on their own; others need the professional help and support of a therapist.

By examining the love they felt for each other—the qualities that had initially attracted them to each other, and the most important thing they gained from the relationship—and by examining the shadow this love had cast when threatened—the threat or the loss that triggered their jealousy—Alan, Linda, and Gail were able to identify the function that the love and the jealousy served in their inner lives, and in the dynamics of their relationship.

Regardless of the approach, or combination of approaches, we use to analyze this complicated relationship, the story portrays jealousy as the shadow of love. Let's look at Linda's love and jealousy of Alan. Both of Linda's parents were intellectuals and successful professionals. They were also very close to each other, and their closeness didn't leave much space for Linda. In addition, Linda's emotional life was marked by competition with a brilliant and cold older brother, and by identification with her mother's unhappiness. As a result of these childhood experiences, Linda was sophisticated intellectually, but full of emotional insecurities. Alan, a simple man, gave her the adoration and intimacy she was longing for because of her childhood deprivation. Only after Alan met her deeper emotional needs was Linda able to look for someone more like herself (and like her father and brother). When Linda had the affair, Alan's jealousy focused on his intellectual inferiority to her lover.

Alan's parents were farmers and uncomplicated, practical people. Alan felt loved, yet was desperate to get away from the world they represented. When Linda had her affair, he not only felt devastated by the betrayal of the woman he adored, but also rejected by the world she represented. Alan wanted to be comforted by someone more like himself. He needed someone who would appreciate him, and his female tennis partners met that need. During the second crisis in his marriage he was looking for the same thing, and found it in his relationship with Gail.

Linda's jealousy was dominated by the feeling of exclusion she had experienced often in her childhood: "the two of them" (her parents) shared a wonderful intimacy that did not include her. The security of being loved and adored by a stable man like Alan was gone. She no longer felt safe and special. He was giving to other women (especially to Gail) what she considered as hers alone: the affirmation she was not able to get as a child, the assurance that she was "number one."

A different kind of love bound Alan and Gail. They were two of a kind; their family backgrounds were similar, and an easy friendship developed between them long before they felt any passion. When Alan went back to Linda, Gail's jealousy focused on the loss of this friendship. Alan's romantic betrayal was especially painful for Gail because he was someone she had considered a trusted friend and a kindred spirit.

The love between Gail and Linda was fueled by sharing powerful emotions: love, jealousy, rage at Alan, and camaraderie as women. It also had another powerful element: Gail and Linda complemented each other in much the same way Linda and Alan did. Gail was the "roots" and Linda the "wings." This proved, once again, a powerful combination. The combination, however, was much more powerful for Gail than for Linda, because Alan, with whom Linda had a similar relationship, was physically stronger and more able to make her feel secure.

When Linda returned to Alan, Gail's jealousy focused on the loss of the intimate bond the two women had shared. She was certain she would never have this kind of a bond again. She later discovered that while she couldn't have such a bond with a man, she could have it with another woman.

A psychodynamic analysis of the relationship between Alan, Linda, and Gail focuses on the unconscious needs brought out by their jealousy, and on the childhood experiences at the root of both their jealousy and their love.

Looking at jealousy as a couple issue (in all three permutations) is an example of the systems approach. In Linda and Alan's case, for example, they fell in love because each represented a lost part in the other (Linda was Alan's "wings" and Alan was Linda's "roots"). With time, however, the missing part in the other became a source of repeated conflicts. Each wanted the thing the other was least able to provide: Linda wanted Alan to become more intellectual, and Alan wanted Linda to become less career-oriented. When Alan and Linda recognized this destructive pattern, they were able to work on developing the lost parts in themselves. For Linda, motherhood provided an especially rewarding opportunity to develop her "roots"; for Alan, the possibility of going to college provided an opportunity to develop his "wings." Once they took steps to develop the "missing parts" in themselves, they no longer depended on each other to provide them.

From the sociobiological point of view, the differences between Linda's relationships with Gail and Alan demonstrate the inherent difference between the male and the female response to jealousy. When Gail and Linda were jealous, they felt devastated and responded with desperate attempts to save the relationship. When it was Alan's turn to experience jealousy, however, he responded in the typical masculine way: with rage and lashing out, protecting his ego more than the relationship.

According to the social-psychological perspective, the threesome's need for exclusive monogamous relationships reflects the North American value of monogamy. In another culture the threesome could have found a solution in the form of a triangle family. In a polygamous society, Alan could have taken both Linda and Gail as wives. Jealousy is a culturally accepted reaction to many of the situations described in the story. None of the same jealous reactions would have happened in a culture such as the Toda.

Returning to the definition of jealousy offered in chapter one, I think most readers will agree that every time Alan, Linda, or Gail experienced jealousy, each was responding to what he or she perceived as a threat to a valued relationship. Jealousy, as the story demonstrates, is a complex response with many influences: childhood experiences, the dynamics of relationships, learned responses, cultural norms, and inherent differences between the sexes.

POSTSCRIPT

The jealousy crisis taught Linda not to take Alan for granted and also gave her the incentive to commit herself to the relationship—both very positive effects. While their marriage had never been listless, jealousy brought so much excitement into it that once the crisis passed, both Linda and Alan were ready for some peace and quiet.

Since they no longer needed jealousy to make life more interesting, Linda and Alan arrived at a relatively calm stage of their relationship. Instead of using jealousy to fuel their passion and intensify the emotions in their relationship, they could focus their energy on their young child and therefore delight in something positive and hopeful. Alan is a doting father who built the baby's crib and first toys with his own hands. Linda appreciates Alan's help and devotion. She too adores her beautiful child and has discovered that she can be a good mother. Linda finds motherhood a rich and rewarding experience.

Working on their jealousy problem made Alan and Linda aware of each other's needs and vulnerabilities. Both are trying hard to be sensitive to these needs. Although they are not always successful, the overall atmosphere in their little family is one of warmth and caring. Linda concludes, "All this taught Alan and me how much we really care about each other. We decided to stop hurting each other and just enjoy the good thing that we have. And we do."

Gail, who started therapy as a result of the jealousy crisis, has made important discoveries about herself that have enabled her to live a more honest and satisfying life. As an introverted woman who grew up in a blue-collar family, self-examination was something she had never before considered. The therapy offered her the chance to work through her relationship with Linda and discover the roots of her problem in relationships with men. If it were not for the crisis prompted by her jealousy of Linda and Alan, she probably would have continued to avoid this painful but ultimately helpful process.

Since Alan no longer perceived Gail as a threat to his relationship with Linda, he didn't object to her presence in their life. With time, some of his warm feelings toward Gail returned. Linda continues to maintain a close friendship with Gail.

Jealousy itself did not cause these positive changes in Alan, Linda, and Gail. The changes came from the way they coped with their jealousy. Instead of treating it as a traumatic experience they had to get over as quickly as possible, they used it as an opportunity for growth.

My goal in writing this book has been to give individuals and couples the information, tools, and examples they need to turn jealousy into a positive experience. The preceding case is one such example.

A FINAL WORD ABOUT THE FIVE APPROACHES TO JEALOUSY

In describing the five basic approaches to jealousy, I have underplayed the aspects in which they contradict each other. I value and use each one of the five approaches, but part company with them when they dismiss each other—which they routinely do. Many of the theoreticians and practitioners of each approach would be extremely uncomfortable at the prospect of being lumped together with approaches they oppose.

For a psychodynamically oriented therapist, behavioral techniques can't possibly cure the "real issue" underlying a jealousy problem. To a behaviorist, the psychodynamic preoccupation with the unconscious and with childhood experiences is unnecessary and can't possibly help cure a jealousy problem. To a systems therapist, the focus of both behavioral and psychodynamically oriented therapists on the individual makes no sense in the treatment of such obvious "couple" issues as jealousy. To a social psychologist, the notion that jealousy is a product of a particular individual mind or a particular relationship is absurd when it is so clearly determined by cultural norms and mores. In addition, the sociobiologist's notion that jealousy is innate and that sex differences in jealousy have evolved in an evolutionary process sounds not only ridiculous, but dangerous as well. Sociobiologists don't understand how anyone can deny the existence of an innate component in jealousy when the evidence for it seems so overwhelming.

The picture of jealousy that I have tried to paint incorporates the views of the five approaches in expanding concentric circles. In the center is the individual who experiences jealousy. The individual's jealousy is related to childhood experiences and his or her personal history of intimate relationships. It is expressed in learned responses. The next circle is the couple, of which the jealous individual is a part. The couple's dynamic determines whether and how a jealousy problem will be expressed. The third circle is the situation. It includes the culture in which the couple lives, which in turn determines how jealousy is experienced and expressed. The fourth circle is the genetic programming that is different for men and women.

My discussion of the five approaches has focused on those aspects that are most relevant for coping with jealousy. Each approach has something valuable to offer. It is illuminating to discover how our jealousy is related to unresolved childhood experiences. It is helpful to discover how our jealousy is maintained by the dynamics of our relationship. Sometimes we need to unlearn inappropriate responses to jealousy triggers and learn more appropriate responses. We can take comfort in knowing that no matter how crazy we sometimes think we are when jealous, we are not unique; other people respond the way we do, and there may be a culture that considers our response the most appropriate. It is also comforting to realize that some of the troublesome differences between one's own sex and the opposite sex in response to jealousy are related to different genetic programming.

People who assume that there is only one way to cope with jealousy deprive themselves of the benefits that other approaches can offer. Even if a particular coping strategy is successful in a certain situation, we don't have to use this strategy exclusively. As noted in chapter nine, the person best able to cope has many arrows in the quiver, is able to deal with a jealousy problem in a variety of ways, and uses the most effective strategy or combination of strategies for each situation.

APPENDIX.
EXPLORING YOUR
ROMANTIC JEALOUSY: A
QUESTIONNAIRE

If you are interested in exploring your romantic jealousy, you can benefit from responding to this questionnaire. There are no right or wrong answers. It would be best to answer the questions before you read the book. Then, after you read the book, you can go back and examine how your responses compare to those of other people. (If you have borrowed this book, please photocopy the questionnaire, or write your answers on a separate sheet of paper.)

A. BACKGROUND INFORMATION
(If you wish to send me your responses to the questionnaire [see page 264], please answer the questions in this section. If not, you can skip to part B.)

Sex: _____ Age: _____
Last grade/degree completed in school: _____
Occupation: _____
Race: Asian ____ Black ____ Hispanic ____ White ____

Other (please specify) _____
Religion: None/atheist ____ Catholic ____ Jewish ____
Protestant ____ Other (please specify) _____
Number of older brothers: ____ Older sisters: ____
Younger brothers: ____ Younger sisters: ____

B.   HOME/CHILDHOOD

1. Who was primarily responsible for rearing you?
    a. mother and father (state reason)
    b. mother only (state reason)
    c. father only (state reason)
    d. other relative (explain who and why)
    e. other person (explain who and why)

2. Are your parents currently together?
    a. yes
    b. no

3. If your parents are not together, what is the reason?
    a. death
    b. divorce
    c. other (please explain)

4. If your parents are separated, how old were you when the separation occurred? _____

5. Were either of your natural parents absent from the home while you were growing up? (If so, please state the reason.)
    a. no
    b. father absent part of the time
    c. mother absent part of the time
    d. both father and mother absent part of the time
    e. father absent all the time
    f. mother absent all the time
    g. both father and mother absent all the time

6. How would you describe your family's financial situation while you were growing up?

   1   2   3   4   5   6   7
   poor   managed to get by   rich

7. How would you describe your relationship with your mother while you were growing up?

   1   2   3   4   5   6   7
   terrible   mixed   excellent

8. How would you describe your relationship with your father while you were growing up?

   1   2   3   4   5   6   7
   terrible   mixed   excellent

9. How would you describe your home life while you were growing up?

   1   2   3   4   5   6   7
   terrible,   mixed,   excellent,
   abusive   O.K.   loving

10. How would you describe the relationship between your father (or father figure) and your mother (or mother figure) while you were growing up?

    1   2   3   4   5   6   7
    terrible   mixed   excellent

11. Was you father ever physically violent with your mother?

    1   2   3   4   5   6   7
    never   once a month   every day

12. Was your mother ever physically violent with your father?

    1   2   3   4   5   6   7
    never   once a month   every day

13. Were you ever beaten while growing up?

1	2	3	4	5	6	7
never			once a month			every day

14. If you were beaten, what was the usual excuse?
    a. something you did (If so, what?)
    b. something the beater did (If so, what?)
    c. no apparent reason

15. Was/is your father (or father figure) a jealous man?

1	2	3	4	5	6	7
not at all			average			extremely

16. Was/is your mother (or mother figure) a jealous woman?

1	2	3	4	5	6	7
not at all			average			extremely

17. Were there jealousy scenes between your parents?

1	2	3	4	5	6	7
never			several times			regularly

18. While growing up, did you have a very close (best) friend?

1	2	3	4	5	6	7
never			part of the time			always

19. While growing up, were you ever rejected by a group of kids you wanted to belong to?

1	2	3	4	5	6	7
always			several times			never

    (Please describe any such incidents.)

20. While growing up, were you ever rejected by a boy/girl you loved?

1	2	3	4	5	6	7
always			several times			never

    (Please describe any such incidents.)

21. How did you feel about yourself, most of the time, while growing up?

1	2	3	4	5	6	7
terrible			average			great

C. CURRENT SITUATION

1. How would you describe your financial situation?

1	2	3	4	5	6	7
insecure		manage to get by				secure

2. How would you describe your physical condition?

1	2	3	4	5	6	7
terrible			average			excellent

3. How would you describe your emotional condition?

1	2	3	4	5	6	7
terrible			average			excellent

4. How do you feel about your life in general?

1	2	3	4	5	6	7
dissatisfied			average or ambivalent			very satisfied

5. How do you feel about yourself in general?

1	2	3	4	5	6	7
terrible			average			great

6. How do you feel about your looks in general?

1	2	3	4	5	6	7
dissatisfied			average or ambivalent			very satisfied

7. How do you feel about your general desirability as a sexual partner?

1	2	3	4	5	6	7
very dissatisfied			average or ambivalent			very satisfied

The next series of questions will address your most significant intimate relationship. If you are currently not involved in such a relationship, please answer all the following questions as they relate to your most important past relationship.

D. INTIMATE RELATIONSHIP

1. Are you currently in an intimate relationship?
   a. yes
   b. no

2. How long, in years and months, have you been with your partner? _____ years _____ months

3. How long do/did you expect the relationship to last?

1	2	3	4	5	6	7
short time			several years			forever

4. How would you describe the relationship?

1	2	3	4	5	6	7
bad			mixed or average			excellent

5. Who has/had the control in the relationship?

1	2	3	4	5	6	7
your partner			equal control			you

6. How secure do/did you feel about the relationship?

1	2	3	4	5	6	7
very insecure			moderately secure			very secure

7. How do/did you feel about your partner in general?

   1   2   3   4   5   6   7

   very   very

   dissatisfied   average or ambivalent   satisfied

8. How physically attracted are/were you to your partner?

   1   2   3   4   5   6   7

   not at all   moderately   very

9. How emotionally attracted are/were you to your partner?

   1   2   3   4   5   6   7

   not at all   moderately   very

10. How sexually desirable do you feel your partner is/was?

    1   2   3   4   5   6   7

    not at all   moderately   very

11. If you found someone else, would you leave your partner?

    1   2   3   4   5   6   7

    definitely not   possibly   definitely

E. ATTITUDES AND FEELINGS RELATED TO JEALOUSY

1. Do you believe in monogamous (one-on-one) relationships for yourself?

   1   2   3   4   5   6   7

   definitely not   to a certain degree   definitely

2. Have you ever been sexual with someone else while in the relationship?

   1   2   3   4   5   6   7

   never   a few times   all the time

3. If so, did your partner know about it?

   a.   yes

   b.   no

4. If yes, how did your partner respond?

1	2	3	4	5	6	7
badly			mixed			very well

5. Have you ever been unfaithful to your partner in any other way?

1	2	3	4	5	6	7
never			a few times			all the time

(If so, please explain in what way.)

6. Has your partner ever been sexual with someone else while in the relationship with you?

1	2	3	4	5	6	7
never			a few times			all the time

7. If so, how did you feel about it?

1	2	3	4	5	6	7
bad			mixed			good

8. Has your partner ever been unfaithful to you in any other way?

1	2	3	4	5	6	7
never			a few times			all the time

(If so, please explain in what way.)

9. Would you be (or were you) open with your partner about other sexual experiences?

1	2	3	4	5	6	7
definitely not		to a certain degree				definitely

10. Would your partner be (or was your partner) open with you about other sexual experiences?

1	2	3	4	5	6	7
definitely not		to a certain degree				definitely

11. How jealous is your partner?

    1   2   3   4   5   6   7

    not at all   moderately   extremely

12. To what extent is jealousy a problem in your relationship?

    1   2   3   4   5   6   7

    not at all   moderately   extremely

13. How often has jealousy been a problem in previous relation-ships you had?

    1   2   3   4   5   6   7

    never   a few times   always

F. JEALOUSY PREVALENCE

1. How jealous are you?

   1   2   3   4   5   6   7

   not at all   moderately   extremely

2. Do you consider yourself a jealous person?
   a. yes
   b. no

3. How jealous were you during childhood?

   1   2   3   4   5   6   7

   not at all   moderately   extremely

4. How jealous were you during adolescence?

   1   2   3   4   5   6   7

   not at all   moderately   extremely

5. Do people with whom you were intimate consider you jealous?

   1   2   3   4   5   6   7

   not at all   moderately   extremely

G. JEALOUSY TRIGGERS

Please use the following jealousy scale for all the questions in this section:

1	2	3	4	5	6	7
no jealousy at all			moderate jealousy			extreme jealousy

1. How much jealousy would you experience if you found out that your partner had been having a sexual relationship with:
   a. someone you don't know personally, and of whom you have a low opinion? _____
   b. someone you don't know personally and know nothing about? _____
   c. a family member? _____
   d. someone you don't know personally and of whom you think highly? _____
   e. someone you know personally and distrust? _____
   f. someone you know and find to be similar to you? _____
   g. someone you know, trust, and consider a friend? _____
   h. your best friend and confidant? _____
   i. someone you know and envy? _____

2. How much jealousy would you experience in each of the following situations?
   a. Your partner is being flirtatious and spends a great deal of time during a party dancing intimately and behaving provocatively with someone else. _____
   b. Your partner spends a great deal of time during a party dancing with someone else. _____
   c. Your partner spends a great deal of time during a party talking to someone else. _____
   d. Your partner disappears for a long time during a party. _____

e. Your partner disappears briefly during a party. ——

f. You answer your phone, and the caller hangs up after hearing your voice. ——

3. How much jealousy would/did you experience if/when your partner . . .
   a. had another lover? ——
   b. had a close friend of your sex who was single and eligible? ——
   c. had a close friend of your sex? ——
   d. was friendly with single and eligible people? ——
   e. expressed appreciation of, and interest in, someone s/he knows casually? ——
   f. expressed appreciation of an attractive stranger passing by? ——
   g. expressed appreciation of a movie or television star? ——

4. How much jealousy would you experience if your partner . . .
   a. announced s/he had fallen in love with someone else and was thinking about leaving you? ——
   b. had a serious long-term affair? ——
   c. had an affair, but was open about it and assured you it was caused by a need for variety that in no way would affect your relationship? ——
   d. was open to, and frequently had, casual sexual experiences? ——
   e. recently had a casual one-night affair? ——
   f. had a love affair a long time ago, when already partnered with you? ——
   g. had a love affair many years ago, before being partnered with you? ——
   h. had an affair many years ago, when already partnered with you, with someone who is now deceased? ——
   i. had an affair many years ago, before being partnered with you, with someone who is now deceased? ——

5. How much jealousy would you experience if you discovered that your partner was having a love affair and . . .

   a. was extremely indiscreet about it; a scandal erupts in the middle of a big party, you are cast in the role of the betrayed lover and are expected to respond? ＿＿＿

   b. was extremely indiscreet about it; a scandal erupts, you are cast in the role of the betrayed lover, but you hear about it when you are alone? ＿＿＿

   c. everyone but you has known about it for a long time, but no one has said anything? ＿＿＿

   d. everyone knows about it? ＿＿＿

   e. only you and a few close and trusted friends know about it? ＿＿＿

   f. your partner is discreet, the three of you are the only ones who know about it, and they know that you know? ＿＿＿

   g. your partner is discreet, no one knows about it, and your partner doesn't know that you know? ＿＿＿

Try to recall, in as much detail as possible, your most extreme experience of jealousy. For example, who were the people involved? How did they look and act? What was the situation? How did you feel? What did you do? Please describe the experience.

H. REACTIONS TO JEALOUSY

1. Recalling your most extreme experience of jealousy, to what extent did you experience each one of the following physical and emotional reactions? Please use the following scale to respond to all items.

1	2	3	4	5	6	7
not at all			moderately			extremely

PHYSICAL REACTIONS:

a. heat ＿＿＿   c. shakiness ＿＿＿

b. headaches ＿＿＿   d. empty stomach ＿＿＿

e. shortness of
breath ＿＿

f. blood rushing ＿＿

g. high energy ＿＿

h. coldness ＿＿

i. fainting ＿＿

j. nausea ＿＿

k. cramps ＿＿

l. nightmares ＿＿

m. feeling of impending
nervous breakdown ＿＿

n. exhaustion ＿＿

o. dizziness ＿＿

p. no appetite ＿＿

q. hands/legs trembling ＿＿

r. fast heart ＿＿

s. insomnia ＿＿

t. sexual arousal ＿＿

EMOTIONAL REACTIONS:

a. rage ＿＿

b. humiliation ＿＿

c. self-pity ＿＿

d. confusion ＿＿

e. pain ＿＿

f. possessiveness ＿＿

g. blame ＿＿

h. feeling of being
excluded ＿＿

i. inferiority ＿＿

j. frustration ＿＿

k. fear of loss ＿＿

l. envy ＿＿

m. anger ＿＿

n. aggression ＿＿

o. passion ＿＿

p. understanding
＿＿

q. anxiety ＿＿

r. depression ＿＿

s. guilt ＿＿

t. grief ＿＿

u. helplessness ＿＿

v. vulnerability ＿＿

w. excitement ＿＿

x. emotional
exhaustion ＿＿

COGNITIVE REACTIONS:

a. "How could you do this to me?" ＿＿

b. "Everybody must be laughing at me." ＿＿

c. "You couldn't possibly love me and still do this." ＿＿

d. "You lied to me!" ＿＿

e. "Where have I gone wrong?" ＿＿

f. "I knew something was going on." ＿＿

g. "How could I not notice that something like that was going on?" ＿＿

h. "I would never have done such a terrible thing to you." ＿＿

i. "This is the end of the relationship." ＿＿

j. "What is missing in me that you're looking for in someone else?" ＿＿

k. "I wish I were as attractive, smart, sexy." ＿＿

l. "If you leave me I'm going to die." ____

m. "How dare you treat me this way." ____

n. "I wish you [or the other person] were dead." ____

o. "I can't take this much pain." ____

p. "I wish I were dead." ____

(Please give any other thoughts you may have had.)

2. How long did your most extreme jealousy last?

1	2	3	4	5	6	7
seconds	minutes	hours	days	weeks	months	years

3. How long does your most common jealousy last?

1	2	3	4	5	6	7
seconds	minutes	hours	days	weeks	months	years

4. How often do you experience extreme jealousy?

1	2	3	4	5	6	7
never	once	rarely	occasionally	often	usually	always

I. COPING WITH JEALOUSY

1. Recalling your most extreme experience of jealousy, how well do you think you coped with it?

1	2	3	4	5	6	7
poorly			average			very well

2. If you could rewrite history, would you have acted differently?

1	2	3	4	5	6	7
definitely			not sure			definitely not

3. How have you coped with jealousy? Please use the following scale to respond to all items:

1	2	3	4	5	6	7
never	once	rarely	occasionally	often	usually	always

a. rational discussion ____   c. avoiding the issue ____

b. screaming ____   d. "stony silence" ____

e. crying ____

f. physical violence ____

g. suffering silently and covertly ____

h. finding the funny side ____

i. using the occasion for thinking through my role in the situation and what it is I stand or fear to lose ____

j. sarcasm ____

k. acceptance ____

l. throwing things ____

m. denial ____

n. retaliating—making partner jealous ____

o. leaving partner ____

p. suffering silently and visibly ____

q. making a joke of it ____

J. EFFECTS OF JEALOUSY

1. Do you consider your jealousy a problem?

1	2	3	4	5	6	7
not at all			moderately so		very much so	

2. Do you like being jealous?

1	2	3	4	5	6	7
not at all			moderately so		very much so	

3. If you could get rid of your jealousy completely, would you like to?

1	2	3	4	5	6	7
definitely no			not sure		definitely yes	

4. Do you like your partner to be jealous?

1	2	3	4	5	6	7
definitely no			not sure		definitely yes	

5. Do you think jealousy is a normal response in certain situations?

1	2	3	4	5	6	7
definitely no			somewhat		definitely yes	

6. Do you consider your own jealousy in extreme situations an appropriate response?

1	2	3	4	5	6	7
definitely no			somewhat			definitely yes

7. Would you believe someone who will told you s/he is not jealous in such an extreme situation?

1	2	3	4	5	6	7
definitely no			somewhat			definitely yes

8. How desirable do you think jealousy is as a personal characteristic?

1	2	3	4	5	6	7
undesirable			mixed			desirable

9. Can you make yourself stop being jealous?

1	2	3	4	5	6	7
definitely no		to a certain degree			definitely yes

10. What are some of the positive and negative effects of jealousy? Please use the following scale to rate all items:

1	2	3	4	5	6	7
definitely no		to a certain degree			definitely yes

POSITIVE EFFECTS OF JEALOUSY:

a. Jealousy is a sign of love. _____
b. Jealousy is an instrument for inducing commitment. _____
c. Jealousy brings excitement to listless relationships. _____
d. Jealousy teaches people not to take each other for granted. _____
e. Jealousy makes one's partner look more desirable. _____
f. Jealousy makes life more interesting. _____
g. Jealousy makes relationships last longer. _____
h. Jealousy makes one examine one's relationship. _____

NEGATIVE EFFECTS OF JEALOUSY:
    a. Jealousy drives one's partner away. ____
    b. Jealousy causes physical and emotional distress. ____
    c. Jealousy may result in violence. ____
    d. Jealousy puts a strain on relationships. ____
    e. Jealousy wastes time that could be spent more enjoyably. ____
    f. Jealousy restricts partners' freedom. ____
    g. Jealousy can block thoughts and distort emotions. ____

11. Have you ever been the object of someone's jealousy?

    1   2   3   4   5   6   7
    never   a few times   all the time

12. Did you like the experience?

    1   2   3   4   5   6   7
    not at all   somewhat   very much

K. REASONS FOR JEALOUSY

1. What do you think causes people in general to experience jealousy? Please use the following scale to rate all items:

    1   2   3   4   5   6   7
    definitely not   to a certain degree   definitely

Jealousy is:
    a. a normal reaction accompanying love ____
    b. the result of personal insecurity ____
    c. the result of feeling excluded and left out ____
    d. the result of weakness in the relationship ____
    e. the result of fear and loss ____
    f. the result of being afraid to lose face ____
    g. the result of being afraid to lose control ____
    h. reaction to grief and pain over losing partner's love ____
    i. an instinctive reaction to threat to a love relationship ____
    j. a result of one's own impulses toward infidelity ____

    k.   a result of feeling inadequate as a woman or man _____
    l.   a result of childhood deprivation and abandonment _____
   m.   a fear of being considered inadequate by others _____
    n.   the result of self-blame, feeling that if your partner is attracted to someone else or having an affair, you probably deserve it because you brought it on yourself _____
    o.   the result of feeling envious resentment of another's success or advantage _____
    p.   the result of a threat to the privacy of your intimate relationship (intimate acts, secrets, and so on) _____

2.   After answering this questionnaire, what is your own definition of jealousy?

3.   Using your own definition, how jealous are you?

1	2	3	4	5	6	7
not jealous at all			moderately jealous			extremely jealous

After you finish reading the book, go over the questionnaire one more time. Would you answer the questions the same way?

I would love to get your responses to this questionnaire. Please mail me a copy of your responses in care of St. Martin's Press, 175 Fifth Avenue, New York, NY 10010.

NOTES

CHAPTER 1. THE GREEN-EYED MONSTER OR THE SHADOW OF LOVE?

1. This definition was influenced by my work with sociologist Gordon Clanton, and Dr. Clanton's writings, especially "Frontiers of Jealousy Research: Introduction to the Special Issue on Jealousy," in *Alternative Lifestyles* 4 (1981), no. 3, 373–92. Also see Gordon Clanton and Lynn G. Smith, eds., *Jealousy* (Lanham, MD: University Press of America, 1986).

2. Robert Anderson, "Envy and Jealousy," *Journal of College Student Psychotherapy* 1 (1987), no. 4, 49–81.

There are other writers who discuss the differences between envy and jealousy, including the following:

Betsy Cohen, *The Snow White Syndrome: All About Envy* (New York: Jove, 1989).

Nancy Friday, *Jealousy* (New York: Bantam, 1987). Nancy Friday relies heavily on Melanie Klein's analysis of the dynamics of envy in her book. Friday's book, in fact, deals mostly with envy and not with jealousy.

Gerrod W. Parrott, "The Emotional Experience of Envy and Jealousy," *The Psychology of Jealousy and Envy*, edited by Peter Salovey (New York: Guilford Press, 1991).

Richard H. Smith, Sung-Hee Kim, and Gerrod W. Parrott, "Envy and Jealousy:

Semantic Problems and Experiential Distinctions," *Personality and Social Psychology Bulletin* 14 (1988), no. 2, 401–09.

Philip M. Spielman, "Envy and Jealousy: An Attempt at Clarification," *Psychoanalytic Quarterly* 40 (1971), 59–82.

3. Betty Joseph, "Envy in Everyday Life," *Psychoanalytic Psychotherapy* 2 (1986), no. 1, 13–22.

4. Ralph B. Hupka et al., "Romantic Jealousy and Romantic Envy: A Seven-Nation Study," *Journal of Cross Cultural Psychology* 16 (1985), no. 4, 423–46.

5. Sigmund Freud, "Certain Neurotic Mechanisms in Jealousy, Paranoia and Homosexuality" (1922), in *Complete Psychological Works of Sigmund Freud*, vol. 18 (London: Hogarth Press, 1955).

6. Melanie Klein, "A Study of Envy and Gratitude," in *The Selected Melanie Klein*, edited by Juliet Mitchell (New York: Free Press, 1986), 211–29.

7. Ibid., 212.

8. A study on jealousy as a trigger of family murder followed by suicide:

Robert D. Goldney, "Family Murder Followed by Suicide," *Forensic Science* 9 (1977), no. 3, 219–28.

Reports on jealousy as a trigger of murder:

Michel Benezech, "Homicide by Psychotics in France," *Journal of Clinical Psychiatry* 45 (1984), no. 2, 85–86.

William East, *Society and the Criminal* (London: H.M.S.O., 1949), 53–280.

Ronald Rae Mowat, *Morbid Jealousy and Murder* (London: Tavistock Publications, 1966).

Gregory White and Paul Mullen, *Jealousy: Theory, Research and Clinical Strategies* (New York: Guilford Press, 1990) chapter 8. White and Mullen report that up to one in five murders is motivated by jealousy.

On jealousy as a trigger of wife battering:

David Adams, "Identifying the Assaultive Husband in Court: You Could Be the Judge," *Response to the Victimization of Women and Children* 13 (1990), no. 1, 13–16.

Jerry Finn, "The Stresses and Coping Behavior of Battered Women," *Social Casework* 66 (1985), no. 6, 341–49.

Daniel G. Saunders and Darald Hanusa, "Cognitive-Behavioral Treatment of Men Who Batter," *Journal of Family Violence* 1 (1986), no. 4, 357–72.

On jealousy as a trigger of marital problems and divorce:

John Docherty and Jean Ellis, "A New Concept and Findings in Morbid Jealousy," *American Journal of Psychiatry* 133 (1976), no. 6, 679–83.

On jealousy as a cause for the destruction of romantic relationships:

Larry Constantine, "Managing Jealousy," in *Treating Relationships*, edited by D. H. Olson (Lake Mills, IA: Graphic Publishers, 1976).

On the relationship between jealousy and depression, suicidal thoughts, loss of self-esteem, anxiety, and anger:

Norma D. Carson and Rhoda E. Johnson, "Suicidal Thoughts and Problem-

Solving Preparation Among College Students," *Journal of College Student Personnel* 26 (1985), no. 6, 484–87.

Eugene W. Mathes, Heather E. Adams, and Ruth M. Davies, "Jealousy, Loss of Relationship Reward, Loss of Self-Esteem, Depression, Anxiety and Anger," *Journal of Personality and Social Psychology* 48 (1985), no. 6, 1552–61.

G. McIntosh Everton and Douglass T. Tate, "Correlates of Jealous Behavior," *Psychological Reports* 66 (1990), no. 2, 601–02.

Robert A. Stewart and Michael J. Beatty, "Jealousy and Self-Esteem," *Perceptual and Motor Skills* 60 (1985), no. 1, 153–54.

On jealousy as a trigger of aggression, criminal behavior, hatred, and violence: Mary R. Laner, "Violence and Its Precipitators: Which Is More Likely to be Identified as a Dating Problem?" *Deviant Behavior* 11 (1990), no. 4, 319–29.

Robert N. Whitehurst, "Violence Potential in Extramarital Sexual Responses," *Journal of Marriage and the Family* 33 (1971), 683–91.

9. Gregory L. White and Kathy Devine, "Romantic Jealousy: Therapists' Perception of Causes, Consequences and Treatment," *Family Process*, in press.

10. In seven studies involving 847 people, all of the respondents, including those who described themselves as not jealous, said that they experienced jealousy in some stage of their life. The first study (described in Aronson and Pines, 1980) involved 54 people. The second (described in Pines and Aronson, 1983) involved 103 people. The third (described in Pines, 1987) involved fifteen commune members. The fourth (described in Pines, 1983) involved twenty-two male inmates. The fifth (described in Pines, 1987) involved fifty-eight people. The sixth (described in Pines, 1987a) involved 571 people. The seventh (described in chapter 8) involved 12 female inmates and 12 female non-inmates.

Elliot Aronson and Ayala M. Pines, "Exploring Sexual Jealousy," paper presented at the annual meeting of the Western Psychological Association, Honolulu, 1980.

Ayala M. Pines, *Keeping the Spark Alive: Preventing Burnout in Love and Marriage* (New York: St. Martin's Press, 1988), 164.

———, "Polyfidelity—An Alternative to Monogamous Marriage?" in *Communal Life*, edited by Yusef Gorni, Yaacouv Oved and Idit Paz (Yad Tabenkin, Israel: Transaction Books, 1987), 622–26.

———, "Sexual Jealousy," *Chadashot* (Tel Aviv), 5 April 1987a, 3–11.

———, "Sexual Jealousy as a Cause of Violence," paper presented at the annual convention of the American Psychological Association, Anaheim, California, August 1983.

———, and Elliot Aronson, "Antecedents, Correlates and Consequences of Sexual Jealousy," *Journal of Personality* 51 (1983), no. 1, 108–36.

11. For a discussion of pathological jealousy, see Stanley J. Coen, "Pathological Jealousy," *International Journal of Psychoanalysis* 68 (1987), no. 1, 99–108.

For a discussion of pathological tolerance to jealousy, see Emil Pinta, "Pathological Tolerance," *American Journal of Psychiatry* 135 (1978), no. 6, 698–701.

12. Sigmund Freud, "Certain Neurotic Mechanisms in Jealousy, Paranoia and Homosexuality" (1922), in *Complete Psychological Works of Sigmund Freud*, vol. 18 (London: Hogarth Press, 1955), 223–340.

13. Ralph B. Hupka, et al., "Romantic Jealousy and Romantic Envy: A Seven-Nation Study," *Journal of Cross-Cultural Psychology* 16 (1985), no. 4, 423–46.

Ralph B. Hupka, "Cultural Determinants of Romantic Jealousy," paper presented at the annual convention of the American Psychological Association, San Francisco, 1977.

————, "Cultural Determinants of Jealousy," *Alternative Lifestyles* 4 (1981), no. 3, 310–56.

14. David R. Mace, "Two Faces of Jealousy," *McCall's*, May 1962.

15. A normal distribution is bell-shaped:

LOW   HIGH

Normalcy is defined as a characteristic of the majority that falls within two standard deviations above and below the mean. The middle range (the wide part of the bell) constitutes 95 percent of cases. This part is defined as normal. The lowest part of the scale (the edge of the bell) comprises 2.5 percent of cases, and is defined as abnormally low. Similarly, 2.5 percent of cases fall in the highest part of the scale and are defined as abnormally high. If we think of a similar bell curve in relation to height, 95 percent of the population are of "normal" height, 2.5 percent are "abnormally" short, and 2.5 percent are "abnormally" tall. "Abnormal" in this case simply means the lowest and the highest ends of the scale.

16. This literature was first presented in my book, *Keeping the Spark Alive*, chapter 2. Additional references include the following:

Avshalom Caspi and Ellen S. Herbener, "Continuity and Change: Assortative Marriage and the Consistency of Personality in Adulthood," *Journal of Personality and Social Psychology* 58 (1990), no. 2, 250–58.

Philip Kay, David W. Fulker, Gregory Carey, and Craig T. Nagoshi, "Direct Marital Assortment for Cognitive and Personality Variables," *Behavior Genetics* 18 (1988), no. 3, 347–56.

Kathleen R. Marikagas, Myrna M. Weissman, Briggitte A. Prusoff, and K. John, "Assortative Mating and Affective Disorders," *Psychiatry* 51 (1988), no. 1, 48–57.

C. G. Mascie-Taylor, "Spouse Similarity for IQ and Personality Convergence," *Behavior Genetics* 19 (1989), no. 2, 223–27.

C. G. Mascie-Taylor and S. G. Vandenberg, "Assortative Mating for IQ and Personality Due to Propinquity and Personal Preference," *Behavior Genetics* 18 (1988), no. 3, 339–45.

Warner Wilson, "Brief Resolution of the Issue of Similarity Versus Complementarity in Mate Selection Using Height Preference as a Model," *Psychological Reports* 65 (1989), no. 2, 387–93.

17. I first introduced the concept of "romantic image" in chapter 2 of *Keeping the Spark Alive.*

18. Harville Hendrix, *Getting the Love You Want* (New York: Henry Holt, 1988).

19. David Lester, George Deluca, William Hellinghausen, and David Scribner, "Jealousy and Irrationality in Love," *Psychological Reports* 56 (1985), no. 1, 210.

20. Vic Pestrak, Don Martin and Maggie Martin, "A Brief Model of Jealousy: A Threat of Loss of Power and Identity," *Counseling and Values* 31 (1986), no. 1, 97–100.

21. Anand-Veereshwar Swami, "Jealousy and the Abyss," *Journal of Humanistic Psychology* 23 (1983), no. 2, 70–84.

CHAPTER 2. ARE YOU A JEALOUS PERSON?

1. Seven hundred and twenty-eight people answered the question "Are you a jealous person?" They took part in three different studies on which this chapter is based. The first study (described in Aronson and Pines, 1980) was a pilot study involving 54 men and women. The second (described in Pines and Aronson 1983) involved 103 men and women. The third (described in Pines, 1987) involved 571 men and women.

A study of the convergent validity of the Pines and Aronson Jealousy Question, together with five other jealousy scales, appears in Mathes et al. It reports a significant correlation between the question and variables: Interpersonal Jealousy ($r = .33$); Chronic Jealousy ($r = .61$); Self-Reported Jealousy ($r = .31$); Projective Jealousy ($r = .52$); Neuroticism ($r = .42$) and Insecurity ($r = .45$). ("r" is a symbol of correlation. The higher the correlation, the more two variables tend to vary together.)

Elliot Aronson and Ayala M. Pines, "Exploring Sexual Jealousy," paper presented at the annual meeting of the Western Psychological Association, Honolulu, 1980.

Eugene W. Mathes, Petra M. Roter, and Steven M. Joerger, "A Convergent Validity Study of Six Jealousy Scales," *Psychological Reports* 59 (1982), 1143–47.

Ayala Pines, "Sexual Jealousy," *Chadashot* (Tel Aviv) 5 April 1987, 3–11.

———, and Elliot Aronson, "Antecedents, Correlates and Consequences of Sexual Jealousy," *Journal of Personality* 51 (1983), no. 1, 108–36.

2. The research is reported by Frank Pittman in his book *Private Lies: Infidelity and the Betrayal of Intimacy* (New York: W. W. Norton, 1989).

3. James Joyce, "The Dead," in *Dubliners* (New York: Viking Press, 1969).

4. Pittman, *Private Lies.*

5. The finding of positive correlation between belief in monogamy and jealousy seems to contradict the findings of a recent study by David L. Weis and Judith Felton, "Marital Exclusivity and the Potential for Future Marital Conflict"

(*Social Work* 32 [1987], no. 1, 45–49), in which it was found that single undergraduate females with most exclusive extramarital activities (those who rejected a higher number of extramarital activities) were most likely to score high on a measure of jealousy, to associate sex and love, to view themselves as conservative, and to attend church frequently. The results of our study suggest that when such women marry, they tend to marry men with conservative attitudes similar to their own, and thus create unions in which jealousy is less likely to be triggered.

6. Sigmund Freud, "Certain Neurotic Mechanisms in Jealousy, Paranoia and Homosexuality" (1922), *The Complete Psychological Works of Sigmund Freud*, standard edition, vol. 18 (London: Hogarth Press, 1955), 223–340.

7. Other researchers have also noted the relationship between dispositional proneness to experience romantic jealousy and perception of jealousy in others. For example, see Jeff Greenberg, "Proneness to Romantic Jealousy and Proneness to Jealousy in Others," *Journal of Personality* 53 (1985), no. 3, 468–79. Mathes, et al. (see note 1, above) report a significant correlation between the Pines and Aronson Jealousy Question and Projective Jealousy ($r = .52$).

8. Robert G. Bringle and Scott Evenbeck, "The Study of Jealousy as a Dispositional Characteristic," in *Love and Attribution*, edited by M. Cook and G. Wilson (Oxford, England: Pergamon Press, 1979). Bringle is one of the theorists who view jealousy as a stable personality trait.

Robert G. Bringle and Larry J. Williams, "Parental-Offspring Similarity on Jealousy and Related Personality Dimensions," *Motivation and Emotion* 3 (1979), 265–86.

Other scholars also have noted that such traits as jealousy have a "family history." For example, see George Vinokur, "Classification of Chronic Psychoses Including Delusional Disorders and Schizophrenias," *Psychopathology* 19 (1986), 30–34.

9. The results of a 1987 study, for example, suggest that decreased jealousy in older people results from increased maturity and self-esteem. See Jerrold L. Downey and William F. Vitulli, "Self-Report Measures of Behavioral Attributions Related to Interpersonal Flirtation Situations," *Psychological Reports* 61 (1987), no. 3, 899 –904.

10. Jessie Bernard, "Jealousy and Marriage," in *Jealousy*, edited by Gordon Clanton and Lynn G. Smith (Lanham, MD: University Press of America, 1986). The noted sociologist Jessie Bernard suggests that because of changes in the institution of marriage, jealousy is declining.

11. For example, see Alexander S. Neill, "Jealousy at Summerhill," in *Summerhill: A Radical Approach to Child-Rearing* (New York: Hart, 1960), 317–22.

12. Other scholars have also noted the effect of the family constellation on the child's jealousy. Peter B. Neubauer, for example, contends that differences in the development of rivalry, jealousy, and envy depend on whether the child is an older or younger sibling, and that the sibling position may be significant. See his "The Importance of the Sibling Experience," *The Psychoanalytic Study of the Child* 38 (1983), 325–36.

13. Other researchers have also noted the relationship between jealousy and low self-esteem. For example, see Robert A. Stewart and Michael J. Beatty, "Jealousy and Self-Esteem," *Perceptual and Motor Skills* 60 (1985), no. 1, 153–54. Mathes et al. (see note 1, above) report a significant correlation between the Pines and Aronson Jealousy Question and Insecurity (r = .45). Other scholars, such as Gordon Clanton, claim that the direction of the relationship between jealousy and self-esteem is not clear.

14. The correlation between jealousy and one's mental state has been noted in other studies as well. For example:

Norma D. Carson and Rhoda E. Johnson, "Suicidal Thoughts and Problem-Solving Preparation Among College Students," *Journal of College Student Personnel* 26 (1985), no. 6, 484–87.

Eugene W. Mathes, Heather E. Adams, and Ruth M. Davies, "Jealousy, Loss of Relationship Reward, Loss of Self-Esteem, Depression, Anxiety and Anger," *Journal of Personality and Social Psychology* 48 (1985), no. 6, 1552–61.

Nicholas Tarrier, Richard Becket, Susan Harwood, and Yasmin Ahmed, "Comparison of a Morbidly Jealous and a Normal Female Population," *Personality and Individual Differences* 10 (1989), no. 12, 1327–28.

15. Ayala M. Pines, *Keeping the Spark Alive: Preventing Burnout in Love and Marriage* (New York: St. Martin's Press, 1988), 164.

16. Jon Wagner, "Jealousy, Extended Intimacies and Sexual Affirmation," *E.T.C.* 33 (1976), no. 13, 269–88.

CHAPTER 3. THE UNCONSCIOUS ROOTS OF ROMANTIC JEALOUSY

1. Sigmund Freud, "Certain Neurotic Mechanisms in Jealousy, Paranoia and Homosexuality" (1922), in *The Complete Psychological Works of Sigmund Freud*, standard edition, vol. 18 (London: Hogarth Press, 1955), 223–340.

2. Emil R. Pinta, "Pathological Tolerance," *American Journal of Psychiatry* 135 (1978), no. 6, 698–701.

3. Freud, "Certain Neurotic Mechanisms," 223.

4. At the later stages of his writing, Freud gave up the idea of an Electra complex for girls, and talked about Oedipus complex for both boys and girls.

5. Freud, "Certain Neurotic Mechanisms," 224.

6. Pinta, "Pathological Tolerance."

7. Robert L. Spitzer, Andrew E. Skodol, Miriam Gibbon, and Janet B. W. Williams, *DSM-III Case Book* (American Psychiatric Association, 1981), 103–4.

8. John P. Docherty and Jean Ellis, "A New Concept and Finding in Morbid Jealousy," *American Journal of Psychiatry* 133 (1976), no. 6, 679–83.

9. Ibid., 681.

10. Gregory White and Paul Mullen, *Jealousy* (New York: Guilford Press, 1989), 78–79.

11. Mary V. Seeman, "Pathological Jealousy," *Psychiatry* 42 (1979), 351–61.

12. John Todd, J. R. Mackie, and Kenneth Dewhurst, "Real or Imagined Hypophallism: A Cause of Inferiority Feelings and Morbid Sexual Jealousy," *British Journal of Psychiatry* 119 (1971), 315–18.

13. Rodrigo Gonzales, Arrillga Pinto, and Gonzalez Asuncion, "Morbid Jealousy in Chronic Alcoholics," *Psiquis* (Spain) 5 (1984), no. 3, 140–42.

14. Delusional jealousy has been treated by various pharmacological interventions, including those specified in the following reports:

Alan Byrne and Lakshmi N. Yatham, "Pimozide in Pathological Jealousy," *British Journal of Psychiatry* 155 (1989), 249–51.

Neda Herceg, "Successful Use of Thiothirene in Two Cases of Pathological Jealousy," *Medical Journal of Australia* 1 (1976), no. 16, 569–70.

Richard D. Lane, "Successful Fluoxetine Treatment of Pathological Jealousy," *Journal of Clinical Psychiatry* 51 (1990), no. 8, 345–46.

Alistair Munro, James V. O'Brien, and Dawn D. Ross, "Two Cases of 'Pure' or 'Primary' Erotomania Successfully Treated with Pimozide," *Canadian Journal of Psychiatry* 30 (1985), no. 8, 619–22.

15. An example of the successful treatment of delusional jealousy with a combination of drug therapy and psychotherapy is provided by Thierry Pereira in "Melancholia or Jealousy," *Perspectives Psychiatriques* 23 (1985), no. 3, 237–41.

16. Papers describing individual psychotherapy for the treatment of delusional jealousy include the following:

Stanley J. Coen, "Pathological Jealousy," *International Journal of Psychoanalysis* 68 (1987), no. 1, 99–108.

Docherty and Ellis, "Morbid Jealousy," 679–83.

Freud, "Certain Neurotic Mechanisms."

Ping-Nie Pao, "Pathological Jealousy," *Psychoanalytic Quarterly* 34 (1969), no. 4, 617–701.

17. For example, see Karen Horney, *The Neurotic Personality of Our Time* (New York: Norton, 1937), 129.

18. Chris Downing, "Jealousy: A Depth-Psychological Perspective."

CHAPTER 4. TREATING THE COUPLE, NOT THE JEALOUS MATE

1. Writings on the systems approach to treating marital problems include the following:

Philip J. Guerin, Leo F. Fay, Susan L. Burden, and Judith G. Kautto, *The Evaluation and Treatment of Marital Conflict: A Four-Stage Approach* (New York: Basic Books, 1987).

Alan S. Gurman and David P. Kniskem, eds., "Part IV: Systems Theory Approaches," in *Handbook of Family Therapy* (New York: Brunner/Mazel, 1981).

Carlos E. Sluzki, "Marital Therapy from a Systems Theory Perspective," in

Marriage and Marital Therapy, edited by Thomas J. Paolino and Barbara S. McRady (New York: Brunner/Mazel, 1978).

Peter Steinglass, "The Conceptualization of Marriage from a Systems Theory Perspective," in *Marriage and Marital Therapy*, edited by Thomas J. Paolino and Barbara S. McRady (New York: Brunner/Mazel, 1978).

Paul Watzlawick, John Weakland, and Richard Fisch, *Change: Principles of Problem Formation and Problem Resolution* (New York: W. W. Norton, 1974).

Writings on the systems approach to jealousy include the following:

Steven Friedman, "Strategic Reframing in a Case of Delusional Jealousy," *Journal of Strategic and Systemic Therapies* 8 (1989), no. 2–3, 1–4.

Philip J. Guerin, et al., *Marital Conflict*, 64–80.

Won-Gi Im, Sephanie R. Wilner, and Miranda Breit, "Jealousy: Interventions in Couples Therapy," *Family Process* 22 (1983), 211–19.

Gayla Margolin, "Building Marital Trust and Treating Sexual Problems," in *Casebook of Marital Therapy*, edited by Alan S. Gurman (New York: Guilford Press, 1985), 271–301.

Carlos E. Sluzki, "Jealousy," *Networker* May/June 1989: 53–55.

Mark W. Teisman, "Jealousy: Systemic Problem-Solving Therapy with Couples," *Family Process* 18 (1979), 151–160.

2. Michael Nichols, *Family Therapy: Concepts and Methods* (New York: Gardner Press, 1984), 127.

3. White and Mullen, *Jealousy: Theory*, 14–17.

4. A shorter version of this case was presented in chapter 6 of my book *Keeping the Spark Alive: Preventing Burnout in Love and Marriage* (New York: St. Martin's Press, 1988).

5. Guerin et al., *Marital Conflict*, 64–80.

6. Ibid., 77.

7. Robert L. Barker, *The Green-Eyed Marriage: Surviving Jealous Relationships* (New York: Free Press, 1987), 79–81.

8. I would like to thank Professor Murry Bilmes for his contribution to my understanding of the psychoanalytic perspective in general, and this case in particular.

9. Role-reversal was used as a technique for treating jealousy by others as well. For example, see Padmal De-Silva, "An Unusual Case of Morbid Jealousy Treated with Role Reversal," *Sexual and Marital Therapy* 2 (1987), no. 2, 179–82; also Im et al., "Jealousy: Interventions."

10. Watzlawick et al., *Change*.

11. Im et al., "Jealousy: Interventions."

12. Reframing was recommended by some psychologists as a technique for treating jealousy. For example, see Im et al., "Jealousy: Interventions," and Teisman, "Jealousy: Systemic Problem-Solving."

13. Margolin, "Building Marital Trust."

14. Sluzki, "Jealousy."

274 • *Notes*

CHAPTER 5. MEN GET ANGRY, WOMEN GET DEPRESSED

1. Bernie Zilbergeld, *The New Male Sexuality* (New York: Bantam, 1992).

2. Jean Baker Miller, *Toward a New Psychology of Women*, second edition (Boston: Beacon Press, 1987).

3. Susan A. Basow, *Gender Stereotypes: Traditions and Alternatives* (Monterey, Calif.: Brooks/Cole, 1986), 80–81.

4. Lillian Rubin, *Intimate Strangers: Men and Women Together* (New York: Harper and Row, 1983).

5. David M. Buss, M. Abbott, A. Angleitner, and A. Asherian, "International Preferences in Selecting Mates: A Study of Thirty-seven Cultures," *Journal of Cross-Cultural Psychology* 21 (1990), no. 1, 5–47.

David M. Buss and A. Angleitner, "Mate Selection Preferences in Germany and the United States," *Personality and Individual Differences* 10 (1989), no. 12, 1269–80.

Martin Daly and Margo Wilson, *Sex, Evolution and Behavior* (North Scituate, Mass.: Duxbury Press, 1978).

Donald Symons, *The Evolution of Human Sexuality* (Oxford, England: Oxford University Press, 1979). See especially chapters 4, 6, and 7.

6. Elliot Aronson and Ayala M. Pines, "Exploring Sexual Jealousy," paper presented at the annual meeting of the Western Psychological Association, Honolulu, 1980.

Ayala M. Pines, "Jealousy," *Chadashot* (Tel Aviv), 5 April 1987, 3–5.

Ayala M. Pines and Elliot Aronson, "Antecedents, Correlates and Consequences of Sexual Jealousy," *Journal of Personality* 51 (1983), no. 1, 108–36.

7. In a study done by Gary L. Hansen, "Dating Jealousy Among College Students" (*Sex Roles* 12 [1985]: 713–21), it was found that there were no sex differences in response to jealousy-provoking situations. On the other hand, sex-role orientation was consistently related to dating jealousy—with traditional men and women being the most jealous.

In their book, *Jealousy* (New York: Guilford Press, 1989), Gregory White and Paul Mullen report (pp. 713–21) that most studies did not find sex differences in jealousy, and that those studies in which a sex difference was found were not consistent in finding one gender to be more jealous than the other.

8. For both men and women, the most frequent response (38 percent of the men and 30 percent of the women) was "talking." For women, the second most frequent response (26 percent) was "ignoring." For men it was a far less frequent response (18 percent). Men and women "let their mate know they are hurt" to a surprisingly similar degree (25 percent for the men and 24 percent for the women). For both men and women these three responses (talking, ignoring, and showing hurt) accounted for the major part of the total responses (81 percent for the men and 80 percent for the women). Only a very small percentage of both men and women described themselves as either shouting (8 percent of the women and 5

percent of the men), getting away (5 percent of the men and 4 percent of the women), or using violence (only three of the men and one of the women out of the 568 who responded).

9. Nancy Henley and Barrie Thorne, "Womanspeak and Manspeak: Sex Differences and Sexism in Communication, Verbal and Nonverbal," in *Beyond Sex Roles*, edited by A. Sargent (St. Paul: West, 1977), 201–18.

Deborah Tannen, *You Just Don't Understand: Women and Men in Conversation* (New York: William Morrow, 1990).

10. Basow, *Gender Stereotypes*.

11. Jan E. Stets and Maureen A. Good-Pirog, "Violence in Dating Relationships," *Social Psychology Quarterly* 50 (1987), no. 5, 237–46.

In a study by Bram Buunk, "Jealousy as Related to Attributions for the Partner's Behavior" (*Social Psychology Quarterly* 47 [1984], no. 1, 107–12), it was found that the attribution of aggression was significantly related to jealousy among males, but not among females.

12. This observation is based on my own clinical work, as well as the work of others. See, for example:

Bram Buunk, "Strategies of Jealousy: Styles of Coping with Extramarital Involvement of the Spouse," *Family Relations* 31 (1982), 13–18.

Gordon Clanton and Lynn G. Smith, eds., *Jealousy* (Landham, MD: University Press of America, 1986).

Gregory L. White and Paul Mullen, *Jealousy* (New York: Guilford Press, 1989), 126–131.

13. Jeffrey B. Bryson, "Situational Determinants of the Expression of Jealousy," paper presented at the annual convention of the American Psychological Association, San Francisco, 1977.

14. Gregory L. White, "Coping with Romantic Jealousy: Comparison to Rival, Perceived Motives, and Alternative Assessment," paper presented at the annual convention of the American Psychological Association, Los Angeles, 1981.

15. Lillian B. Rubin, *Intimate Strangers: Men and Women Together* (New York: Harper and Row, 1983).

16. This conclusion is based on both my research (Pines and Aronson, 1983) and clinical work.

17. Gregory White, "Inducing Jealousy: A Power Perspective," *Personality and Social Psychology Bulletin* 6 (1980), 222–27.

18. Charles Darwin, *The Descent of Man and Selection in Relation to Sex* (New York: W. W. Norton, [1871] 1970).

———, *The Expression of Emotions in Man and Animals* (Chicago: University of Chicago Press, [1888] 1965).

19. Daly and Wilson, *Sex, Evolution and Behavior*.

Richard Dawkins, *The Selfish Gene* (Oxford, England: Oxford University Press, 1976). Of special interest for our subject is chapter 9, "The Battle of the Sexes."

Symons, *Evolution of Human Sexuality*, especially chapters 4, 6, and 7.

Bernard Campbell, ed., *Sexual Selection and the Descent of Man* (Chicago: Aldine, 1972).

Edward O. Wilson, *On Human Nature* (Cambridge, MA: Harvard University Press, 1978), especially chapter 6.

20. Grenville Goodwin, *The Social Organization of the Western Apache* (Chicago: University of Chicago Press, 1942); quoted in Ralph Hupka, "Cultural Determinants of Jealousy," 1977, 1981.

21. A lecture on this topic, "Jealousy from a Sociobiological Perspective," was given by Yochanan Peres, professor of sociology and social work at Tel Aviv University, in January 1989.

22. David M. Buss, "Conflict Between the Sexes: Events Evoking Anger and Jealousy," paper presented at the annual convention of the American Psychological Association, San Francisco, 1991.

23. Ada Lumpart, "Parental Investment, Relative Vulnerability and Adjustment Difficulties," Ph.D. dissertation, Tel Aviv University, 1981.

24. This point was also made by Peres (see note 21, above).

25. George Peter Murdock, *Social Structure* (New York: Macmillan, 1949).

26. White and Mullen, *Jealousy*, 63–64.

27. The power perspective was discussed by Gregory White in several of his writings, including "Inequality of Emotional Involvement, Power, and Jealousy in Romantic Couples," a paper presented at the annual convention of the American Psychological Association, San Francisco, 1977; "Inducing Jealousy" (see note 17 above); and (with Paul Mullen) *Jealousy*.

28. White and Mullen, *Jealousy*, 58.

29. Clanton and Smith, *Jealousy*.

CHAPTER 6. ROMANTIC JEALOUSY IN DIFFERENT CULTURES

1. Ralph B. Hupka, a cross-cultural psychologist at California State University, Long Beach, summarized many of the anthropological reports relating to jealousy in his paper "Cultural Determinants of Romantic Jealousy," probably the best work written on the subject. The paper was presented at the annual meeting of the American Psychological Association, San Francisco, 1977. A later version, "Cultural Determinants of Jealousy," appeared in *Alternative Lifestyles* 4 (1981), 310–56. Many of the examples quoted in this chapter are from these two papers.

Another source was an article written by the noted anthropologist Margaret Mead when she was thirty: "Jealousy, Primitive and Civilized," first published in *Women Coming of Age*, edited by Samuel D. Schalhausen and V. F. Calverton (New York: Liveright, 1931) and reprinted in *Jealousy*, edited by Gordon Clanton and Lynn G. Smith (Lanham, MD: University Press of America, 1986). The sociological contribution to the chapter is mainly that of Gordon Clanton in his introduction to his book, as well as his recent article "Jealousy in American Culture, 1945–1985," in *The Sociology of Emotions*, edited by David D. Franks and E. Doyle McCarthy (Greenwich, CT: JAI Press, 1989).

2. John H. Weeks, *Among the Primitive Bakongo* (London: Seeley Service Co., 1914).

3. George Turner, *Samoa* (London: Macmillan, 1884).

4. Clanton, "Jealousy in American Culture."

5. Collen Gouldsbury and Hubert Sheane, *The Great Plateau of Northern Rhodesia* (London: Edward Arnold, 1911).

6. Hupka, "Cultural Determinants of Romantic Jealousy."

———, "Cultural Determinants of Jealousy."

7. Stephen Powers, *Tribes of California* (Washington, DC: Government Printing Office, 1877).

Gene Weltfish, *The Lost Universe* (New York: Basic Books, 1967).

8. Jeannette Mirski, "The Eskimo of Greenland," in *Cooperation and Competition Among Primitive Peoples*, edited by Margaret Mead (New York: McGraw-Hill, 1937).

9. Mead, "Jealousy: Primitive and Civilized."

10. F. Fawcett, "On the Saoras (or Savaras)," *Journal of the Anthropological Society of Bombay* 1 (1886–89), 206–72.

11. Ruth Benedict, *Patterns of Culture* (Boston: Houghton Mifflin, 1934).

12. Gouldsbury and Sheane, *The Great Plateau.*

13. Ayala M. Pines and Elliot Aronson, "Antecedents, Correlates and Consequences of Sexual Jealousy," *Journal of Personality* 51 (1983), no. 1, 108–36.

Elliot Aronson and Ayala M. Pines, "Exploring Sexual Jealousy," paper presented at the annual meeting of the Western Psychological Association, Honolulu, 1980.

Ayala Pines, "Sexual Jealousy," *Chadashot* (Tel Aviv) 5 April 1987, 3–11.

14. Benedict, *Patterns of Culture.*

15. William Irons, "Investment and Primary Social Dyads," in *Evolutionary Biology and Human Social Behavior*, edited by Napoleon A. Chagnon and William Irons (North Scituate, Mass.: Duxbury Press, 1979), 181–221.

J. A. Kurland, "Paternity, Mother's Brothers, and Human Society," in Chagnon and Irons, *Evolutionary Biology*, 145–80.

Mead, "Jealousy: Primitive and Civilized."

Marc J. Swartz and David K. Jordan, *Culture: The Anthropological Perspective* (New York: Wiley, 1980).

16. Mead, "Jealousy: Primitive and Civilized."

17. Hupka, "Cultural Determinants."

18. Mirski, "Eskimo of Greenland."

19. Mead, "Jealousy: Primitive and Civilized."

20. Warner, *A Black Civilization* (New York: Harper and Row, 1937).

21. R. Karsten, "The Toba Indians of the Bolivian Gran Chaco," *Acta Academiae Aboensis* 4 (1925), no. 4, 1–126.

22. Gregory L. White and Paul E. Mullen, *Jealousy: Theory, Research and Clinical Strategies* (New York: Guilford Press, 1989), 231–235.

23. George Taplin, ed. *The Folklore, Manners, Customs and Languages of the South Australian Aborigines* (Adelaide: E. Spiller, 1879).

24. Georg Heinrich Von Langsdorff, *Voyages and Travels in Various Parts of the World* (London: H. Colburn, 1813).

25. Daniel Williams Harmon, *"A Journal of Voyages and Travels in the Interior of North America"* (Andover, MA: Flagg & Gould, 1820).

26. Arthur Saunders Thompson, *The Story of New Zealand*, vol. 1 (London: John Murray, 1859).

27. Bernard Mishkin, "The Maori of New Zealand," in Mead, *Cooperation and Competition*.

28. Kingsley Davis, "Jealousy and Sexual Property," in *Jealousy*, edited by G. Clanton and L. Smith (Lanham, MD: University Press of America, 1986).

29. Gouldsbury and Sheane, *The Great Plateau*.

30. Washington Matthews, *Ethnography and Philology of the Hidatsa Indians* (Washington, DC: Government Printing Office, 1877).

31. William Halse Rivers, *The Todas* (London: Macmillan, 1906).

32. Grenville Goodwin, *The Social Organization of the Western Apache* (Chicago: University of Chicago Press, 1942). The comparison between the Toda and the Apache was done by Ralph Hupka in "Cultural Determinants of Romantic Jealousy."

33. Clanton, "Jealousy in American Culture."

34. Jessie Bernard, "Jealousy and Marriage," in Clanton and Smith, *Jealousy*.

35. Daniel Yankelovich, "New Rules in American Life: Searching for Self- Fulfillment in a World Turned Upside Down," *Psychology Today*, April 1981, 35–92.

36. James Prochaska and Janice Prochaska, "Twentieth-Century Trends in Marriage and Marital Therapy," in *Marriage and Marital Therapy*, edited by Thomas J. Paolino and Barbara S. McCrady (New York: Brunner/Mazel, 1978).

37. Elaine Crovitz and Anne Steinman, "A Decade Later: Black-White Attitudes Toward Women's Familial Role," *Psychology of Women Quarterly* 5 (1980): 170–76.

38. The results of the Harris poll are quoted in Susan Basow, *Gender Stereotypes: Traditions and Alternatives* (Monterey, CA: Brooks/Cole, 1986).

39. Ibid., 212.

40. Davis, "Jealousy and Sexual Property."

41. Lillian Rubin, *Erotic Wars* (New York: Farrar, Straus and Giroux, 1990).

42. Anthony Thompson, "Extramarital Sex: A Review of the Research Literature," *The Journal of Sex Research* 19 (1983), no. 1, 1–22.

43. Philip Blumstein and Pepper Schwartz, *American Couples* (New York: William Morrow, 1983).

Similar findings about high rates of infidelity combined with a belief in monogamy are reported by Frank Pittman in his book *Private Lies: Infidelity and the Betrayal of Intimacy* (New York: W. W. Norton, 1989).

44. Robert N. Whitehurst, "Jealousy and American Values," in Clanton and Smith, *Jealousy*.

45. Paul L. Harris, T. Jeert Olthof, Mary Terwogt, and Charlotte E. Hardman,

"Children's Knowledge of the Situations that Provoke Emotion," *International Journal of Behavioral Development* 10 (1987), no. 3, 319–43.

46. Bram Buunk and Ralph B. Hupka, "Cross-Cultural Differences in the Elicitation of Sexual Jealousy," *Journal of Sex Research* 23 (1987), no. 1, 12–22.

47. *The Holy Bible* (author's translation from the Hebrew), Exodus 19: 3–5.

48. Chris Downing, "Jealousy: A Depth-Psychological Perspective," in Clanton and Smith, *Jealousy*, 72–79.

49. Clanton, "Jealousy in American Culture."

50. John Harvey and Gifford Weary, "Current Issues in Attribution Theory and Research," *Annual Review of Psychology* 35 (1984): 427–59.

Judith S. Thompson and Douglas K. Snyder, "Attribution Theory in Intimate Relationships: A Methodological Review," *The American Journal of Family Therapy* 14 (1986), no. 2, 123–38.

For more basic issues in attribution theory, see Edward E. Jones and Richard E. Nisbett, "The Actor and the Observer: Divergent Perceptions of the Causes of Behavior," in *Attribution: Perceiving the Causes of Behavior*, edited by Edward Jones et al. (Morristown, NJ: General Learning Press, 1972); also Susan V. Eisen, "Actor-Observer Differences in Information Inferences and Causal Attributions," *Journal of Personality and Social Psychology* 37 (1979): 261–72.

51. Hupka, "Cultural Determinants."

CHAPTER 7. ROMANTIC JEALOUSY IN OPEN RELATIONSHIPS

1. Brian G. Gilmartin, "Jealousy among the Swingers," in *Jealousy*, edited by Gordon Clanton and Lynn Smith (Lanham, MD: University Press of America, 1986).

"Sexual mate exchange" was formerly called "wife swapping." The new term avoids the sexist connotations of the older one.

2. Richard J. Jenks, "Swinging: A Test of Two Theories and a Proposed New Model," *Archives of Sexual Behavior* 14 (1985): 517–27. Richard J. Jenks found that swingers rated themselves as less jealous than did nonswingers.

3. George and Nena O'Neill, *Open Marriage: A New Lifestyle for Couples* (New York: Evans, 1972).

4. Albert Ellis, *The American Sexual Tragedy* (New York: Grove Press, 1962).

5. James R. Smith and Lynn G. Smith, "Co-marital Sex and the Sexual Freedom Movement," *Journal of Sex Research* 6 (1973): 131–42.

6. Gregory White and Paul Mullen, *Jealousy* (New York: Guilford Press, 1989), 122.

7. Ayala M. Pines, "Polyfidelity—An Alternative to Monogamous Marriage?" *Communal Life*, edited by Josef Y. Gorni, Yaacov Oved, and Idit Paz (Yad Tabenkin, Israel: Transaction Books, 1987), 622–26.

8. Ayala M. Pines, "Polyfidelity: A Lifestyle Without Jealousy," paper presented at the annual convention of the American Psychological Association, Los Angeles, August 1981.

9. Marguerite Beecher and Willard Beecher, *The Mark of Cain: An Anatomy of Jealousy* (New York: Harper and Row, 1971).

White and Mullen, *Jealousy*.

This position is elaborated in chapter 6 (pp. 000–000) of the present work.

10. Kingsley Davis, "Jealousy and Sexual Property," *Social Forces* 14 (1936): 395–405, reprinted in Clanton and Smith, *Jealousy*. Davis's position is elaborated in chapter 6 of the present work.

11. Alexander S. Neill, *Summerhill: A Radical Approach to Child Rearing* (New York: Hart, 1960).

12. Ayala M. Pines and Elliot Aronson, "Polyfidelity: An Alternative Lifestyle Without Jealousy," *Alternative Lifestyles* 4 (1981), no. 3, 373–92.

13. Rosabeth M. Kanter, *Commitment and Community* (Cambridge, Mass.: Harvard University Press, 1972).

White and Mullen, *Jealousy*, 122–23.

14. Bram Buunk, "Jealousy in Sexually Open Marriages," *Alternative Lifestyles* 4 (1981), no. 3, 357–72.

Larry L. Constantine and Joan M. Constantine, "Sexual Aspects of Multilateral Relations," in *Beyond Monogamy*, edited by James R. Smith and Lynn G. Smith (Baltimore: Johns Hopkins University Press, 1974), 268–90.

15. Duane Denfeld, "Dropouts from Swinging: The Marriage Counselor as Informant," in Smith and Smith, *Beyond Monogamy*, 260–67.

16. Gilbert D. Bartell, "Group Sex Among Mid-Americans," *Journal of Sex Research* 6 (1970), 113–30.

17. Gilmartin, "Jealousy Among the Swingers."

18. Barbara DeBuono, Stephen Zinner, Maxim Daamen, and William M. McCormack, "Sexual Behavior of College Women in 1975, 1986 and 1989," *New England Journal of Medicine* 322 (1990), no. 12, 821–25.

19. Ayala M. Pines, *Keeping the Spark Alive: Preventing Burnout in Love and Marriage* (New York: St. Martin's Press, 1988), chapter 6.

20. Gilmartin, "Jealousy Among the Swingers."

21. Ibid. Similar findings were also reported in a special session devoted to the subject of infidelity in the annual convention of the American Association of Marriage and Family Therapists, San Francisco, October 1989. See also Frank Pittman, *Private Lies* (New York: W. W. Norton, 1989).

CHAPTER 8. CRIMES OF PASSION

1. For example, see Robert D. Goldney, "Family Murder Followed by Suicide," *Forensic Science* 9 (1977) no. 3, 219–28. Also see Ronald Rae Mowat, *Morbid Jealousy and Murder* (London: Tavistock Publications, 1966). In Mowat's British study, of the seventy-one murders and thirty-nine attempted murders triggered by jealousy that he analyzed, 85 percent involved the loved one.

In a more recent analysis of 138 crimes of passion, 51 percent involved an attack on the loved one. See Paul E. Mullen and L. H. Maack, "Jealousy: Pathological Jealousy and Aggression," in *Aggression and Dangerousness*, edited by David P. Farrington and John Gunn (New York: Wiley, 1985), 103–26.

2. Federal Bureau of Investigation, *Uniform Crime Reports of the United States* (Washington, DC: Department of Justice, 1986).

In an analysis almost forty years earlier of two hundred murders committed in England, it was found that jealousy was the underlying motive in 23 percent of the cases. See William East, *Society and the Criminal* (London: H.M.S.O., 1949), 53–280.

In another analysis of 195 murders, jealousy was the underlying motive in 22 percent of the cases. See T. C. N. Gibbens, "Sane and Insane Homicide," *Journal of Criminal Law, Criminology and Police Science* 49 (1958), 110–15.

3. Richard Goodstein and Ann A. Page, "The Battered Wife Syndrome: Overview of the Dynamics and Treatment," *American Journal of Psychiatry* 138 (August 1981), 65–77.

Heinz Hafner and Wolfgang Boker, *Crimes of Violence by Mentally Abnormal Offenders* (Cambridge, England: Cambridge University Press, 1982).

Ayala M. Pines, "Sexual Jealousy as a Cause of Violence," paper presented at the annual convention of the American Psychological Association, Anaheim, California, 1983.

White and Mullen, *Jealousy*, chapter 8.

Robert N. Whitehurst, "Violence Potential in Extramarital Sexual Responses," *Journal of Marriage and the Family* 33 (1971), 681–83.

4. The study involving 603 people is described in Ayala Pines, "Jealousy," *Chadashot*, (Tel Aviv) 5 April 1987.

The study involving 103 people is described in Ayala M. Pines and Elliot Aronson, "The Antecedents, Correlates and Consequences of Sexual Jealousy," *Journal of Personality* 51 (1983), no. 1, 108–36.

5. In two different studies of homicide, jealousy was found to be the third most common cause. See D. J. West, "A Note on Murders in Manhattan" (*Medicine, Science and the Law* 8 [1968], 249–55); also Marvin E. Wolfgang, *Patterns in Criminal Homicide* (Philadelphia: University of Pennsylvania Press, 1958).

6. Pines, "Sexual Jealousy."

7. For the characteristics of violent offenders, see Murray A. Straus, Richard Gelles, and Suzanne K. Steinmetz, *Behind Closed Doors: Violence in the American Family* (Garden City, NY: Doubleday, 1980), 32.

Murray Straus and Gerard T. Hotaling, eds., *The Social Causes of Husband-Wife Violence* (Minneapolis: University of Minnesota Press, 1980).

Pamela J. Taylor, "Motives for Offending Among Violent and Psychotic Men," *British Journal of Psychiatry* 147 (1985): 491–98.

Walter R. Gove, "The Effect of Sex and Gender on Deviant Behavior," in *Gender and the Life Course*, edited by Alice S. Rossi (New York: Adeline, 1985), 115–44.

For characteristics of the violently jealous, see Gregory White and Paul Mullen, *Jealousy* (New York: Guilford Press, 1989), 227–30.

8. A. D. Psarska, "Jealousy Factor in Homicide in Forensic Material," *Polish Medical Journal* 1970, 1504–10.

9. Shana Alexander, *Very Much a Lady: The Untold Story of Jean Harris and Dr. Herman Tarnower* (Boston: Little, Brown, 1983).

10. Ibid.

11. I discuss our romantic images extensively in chapter 1 of the present work, as well as in the second chapter of my book *Keeping the Spark Alive: Preventing Burnout in Love and Marriage* (New York: St. Martin's Press, 1988).

12. This point was nicely articulated by Harville Hendrix in his book *Getting the Love You Want* (New York: Henry Holt, 1988).

13. This point is also made in White and Mullen, *Jealousy*, 223–27.

14. Studies of individuals who committed crimes related to jealousy show that most often the crimes are committed by males on female victims. For example, see Ronald Rae Mowat, *Morbid Jealousy and Murder* (London: Tavistock Publications, 1966); also Paul Mullen and L. H. Maack, "Jealousy, Pathological Jealousy and Aggression," in *Aggression and Dangerousness*, edited by David P. Farrington and John Gunn (New York: Wiley, 1985), 103–26.

For other characteristics of violent offenders, see Walter R. Gove, "The Effect of Sex and Gender on Deviant Behavior," in *Gender and the Life Course*, edited by A. Rossi (New York: Adeline, 1985), 115–44.

For other characteristics of the violently jealous, see White and Mullen, *Jealousy*, 227–30.

15. Pines, "Sexual Jealousy."

16. The study was conducted in a women's prison in California, with the help of specially trained UC Berkeley students.

17. The results of the comparison indicated that the women in prison described themselves as more jealous (3.4 vs. 2.7) and as perceived by their intimate partners as far more jealous (4.9 vs. 2.7) than did the control group. When describing their most intense experiences of jealousy, the women in prison reported feeling more rage (6.9 vs. 4.9), anxiety (5.1 vs. 4.4), humiliation (5.2 vs. 4.5), frustration (6.2 vs. 5.5), depression (6.0 vs. 4.9), grief (4.2 vs. 3.8), pain (6.5 vs. 5.1), and aggression (6.5 vs. 4.7). They also felt more possessive (6.0 vs. 4.3), self-righteous (5.7 vs. 3.8), and close to a nervous breakdown (3.1 vs. 2.8). When asked how they coped with their jealousy, they were far more likely to say that they used violence (3.4 vs. 1.6). They also reported being more likely to suffer silently but visibly (4.0 vs. 2.8) or to leave their mate (3.3 vs. 2.5). When asked about their childhoods, the women in prison described a more troubled home life (3.7 vs. 4.9), a troubled relationship between the parents (2.9 vs. 4.6) marked by violence of father toward mother (2.8 vs. 1.2), having a jealous mother (4.3 vs. 2.1), and being beaten while growing up (2.8 vs. 1.1). They were also likely to feel less secure in their current intimate relationships (4.7 vs. 5.5).

18. Paul Mullen and L. H. Maack, "Jealousy, Pathological Jealousy and Aggres-

sion," in *Aggression and Dangerousness*, edited by D. P. Farrington and J. Gunn (New York: Wiley, 1985), 103–26.

19. Ibid.

20. White and Mullen, *Jealousy*, 226.

21. For example, Zeev Wanderer, *Letting Go* (New York: Warner Books, 1989). For a discussion of coping with jealousy see White and Mullen, *Jealousy*, chapter 9.

CHAPTER 9. COPING WITH ROMANTIC JEALOUSY

1. For an example of the treatment of jealousy with self-hypnosis, see Gordon Milne, "Horse Sense in Pyschotherapy," *Australian Journal of Clinical and Experimental Hypnosis* 13 (1985), no. 2, 132–34. For examples of treating jealousy with drug therapy, see the following:

Alan Byrne and Lakshmi N. Yatham, "Pimozide in Pathological Jealousy," *British Journal of Psychiatry* 155 (1989), 249–51.

Neda Herceg, "Successful Use of Thothirene in Two Cases of Pathological Jealousy," *Medical Journal of Australia* 1 (1976), no. 16, 569–70.

Richard D. Lane, "Successful Fluoxetine Treatment of Pathological Jealousy," *Journal of Clinical Psychiatry* 51 (1990), no. 8, 345–46.

Alistair Munro, James V. Obrien, and Dawn Ross, "Two Cases of 'Pure' and 'Primary' Erotomania Successfully Treated with Pimozide," *Canadian Journal of Psychiatry* 30 (1985), no. 8, 619–22.

For examples of the treatment of jealousy with cognitive behavioral therapy, see the following:

Nagy A. Bishay, Neil Petersen, and Nicholas Tarrier, "An Uncontrolled Study of Cognitive Therapy for Morbid Jealousy," *British Journal of Psychiatry* 154 (1989), 386–89.

Ernest Feist, "An Innovative Programme for the Treatment of Panic Attacks: A Case Study," *Australian Journal of Clinical Hypnotherapy and Hypnosis* 7 (1986), no. 2, 122–26.

For examples of the use of couples therapy for the treatment of jealousy, see the following:

Steven Friedman, "Strategic Reframing in a Case of Delusional Jealousy," *Journal of Strategic and Systemic Therapies* 8 (1989), no. 2–3, 1–4.

Won-Gi Im, Stephanie R. Wilner, and Miranda Breit, "Jealousy: Interventions in Couples Therapy," *Family Process* 22 (1983), 211–19.

Gayla Margolin, "Building Marital Trust and Treating Sexual Problems," in *Casebook of Marital Therapy*, edited by Alan S. Gurman (New York: Guilford Press, 1985), 271–301.

Mark W. Teisman, "Jealousy: Systemic Problem-Solving Therapy with Couples," *Family Process* 18 (1979), 151–60.

Johan M. Verhulst, "The Jealous Spouse," *Medical Aspects of Human Sexuality* 19 (1985), no. 5, 110–20.

For examples of the use of systems therapy to treat a jealousy problem, see the following:

Padmal De-Silva, "An Unusual Case of Morbid Jealousy Treated With Role Reversal," *Sexual and Marital Therapy* 2 (1987), no. 2, 179–82.

S. Green and M. Bobele, "An Interactional Approach to Marital Infidelity," *Journal of Strategic and Systemic Therapies* 7 (1988), 35–47.

The most famous treatment of jealousy using psychoanalysis is, of course, the work of Sigmund Freud. Other works on this subject include the following:

Otto Fenichel, "A Contribution to the Psychology of Jealousy," in *Collected Papers of Otto Fenichel*, collected and edited by Hanna Fenichel and David Rapaport (New York: W. W. Norton, 1953), 349–62.

Ernest Jones, "Jealousy" (1929), in *Papers on Psychoanalysis* (London: Baillieve, Tindall, and Cox, 1950).

Joan Riviere, "Jealousy as a Mechanism of Defense," *The International Journal of Psychoanalysis* 13 (1932), 414–29.

The psychodynamic approach is described in the treatment of the jealous spouse by Robert I. Barker in his book *The Green-Eyed Marriage: Surviving Jealous Relationships* (New York: Free Press, 1987).

A combination of couples and psychodynamic therapy is described by Hildegard Baumgart in her book *Jealousy: Experiences and Solutions* (Chicago: University of Chicago Press, 1990).

For an example of treating jealousy with rational-emotive therapy, see A. Ellis, "Rational and Irrational Jealousy," in *Jealousy*, edited by Gordon Clanton and Lynn G. Smith (Lanham, MD: University Press of America, 1986).

Arline M. Rubin and James R. Adams, "Outcomes of Sexually Open Marriages," *Journal of Sex Research* 22 (1986), 311–19.

2. Alan Monat and Richard S. Lazarus, *Stress and Coping* (New York: Columbia University Press, 1985).

3. Ayala M. Pines and Elliot Aronson, *Career Burnout: Causes and Cures* (New York: Free Press, 1988), chapter 7.

4. Anand Veereshwar Swami, "Jealousy and the Abyss," *Journal of Humanistic Psychology* 23 (1983), no. 2, 70–84.

5. The study involving 571 men and women was described in Ayala Pines, "Sexual Jealousy," *Chadashot* (Tel Aviv) 5 April 1987, 3–11.

The study involving 103 men and women was described in Ayala M. Pines and Elliot Aronson, "Antecedents, Correlates and Consequences of Sexual Jealousy," *Journal of Personality* 51 (1983), no. 1, 108–36.

6. A version of this "talk and listen" exercise is offered by Bernie Zilbergeld in his book *The New Male Sexuality* (New York: Bantam, 1992).

7. B. F. Skinner, *Science and Human Behavior* (New York: Macmillan, 1953). Skinner is considered the father of the behavioral approach.

8. J. P. Cobb and I. M. Marks, "Morbid Jealousy Featuring an Obsessive Compulsive Neurosis: Treatment by Behavioral Psychotherapy," *British Journal of Psychiatry* 134 (1979): 301–5.

Isaac M. Marks, "The Current Status of Behavioral Psychotherapy, Theory and Practice," *American Journal of Psychiatry* 133 (1976): 253–61.

9. Joseph Wolpe, *Psychotherapy by Reciprocal Inhibition* (Stanford, CA: Stanford University Press, 1958).

10. A. Ellis, "Rational and Irrational Jealousy," in *Jealousy*, edited by Gordon Clanton and Lynn G. Smith (Lanham, MD: University Press of America, 1986).

11. Zeev Wanderer and B. L. Ingram, "Treatment of Phobias with Physiologically Monitored Implosion Therapy (PMIT)," *Journal of Behavior Therapy and Experimental Psychiatry*, in press.

12. Won-Gi Im, Stephanie R. Wilner, and Miranda Breit, "Jealousy: Interventions in Couples Therapy," *Family Process* 22 (1983): 211–19.

13. Tsafy Gilad, personal communication with the author.

14. Bernie Zilbergeld, personal communication with the author.

15. Im, et al., "Jealousy: Interventions."

16. Ibid.

17. This exercise was inspired by Harville Hendrix's book *Getting the Love You Want* (New York: Henry Holt, 1988).

18. Neil S. Jacobson, "Specific and Nonspecific Factors in the Effectiveness of a Behavioral Approach to the Treatment of Marital Discord," *Journal of Consulting and Clinical Psychology* 46 (1978): 442–52.

Neil S. Jacobson, "When and Why Couples Change in Marital Therapy," paper presented at the annual convention of the American Psychological Association, San Francisco 1991.

CHAPTER 10. CAN ANY GOOD COME OUT OF ROMANTIC JEALOUSY?

1. Other parts of this research were described in Ayala M. Pines and Elliot Aronson, "Antecedents, Correlates and Consequences of Sexual Jealousy," *Journal of Personality* 51 (1983), no. 1, 108–36.

2. Ayala M. Pines, *Keeping the Spark Alive: Preventing Burnout in Love and Marriage* (New York: St. Martin's Press, 1988).

3. Steven Carter and Julia Sokol, *Men Who Can't Love* (New York: Berkley Books, 1988).

4. The case was first described in my book *Keeping the Spark Alive,* chapter 6.

5. This view of jealousy was the basis for workshops I led with Gordon Clanton.

REFERENCES

BOOKS

Alexander, Shana. *Very Much a Lady: The Untold Story of Jean Harris and Dr. Herman Tarnower.* Boston: Little Brown, 1983.

Barker, Robert L. *The Green-Eyed Marriage: Surviving Jealous Relationships.* New York: Free Press, 1987.

Basow, Susan A. *Gender Stereotypes: Traditions and Alternatives.* Monterey, CA: Brooks/Cole, 1986.

Baumgart, Hildegard. *Jealousy: Experiences and Solutions.* Chicago: University of Chicago Press, 1990.

Beecher, Marguerite, and Willard Beecher. *The Mark of Cain: An Anatomy of Jealousy.* New York: Harper and Row, 1971.

Benedict, Ruth. *Patterns of Culture.* Boston: Houghton Mifflin, 1934.

Blumstein, Philip, and Pepper Schwartz. *American Couples.* New York: William Morrow, 1983.

Campbell, Bernard, ed. *Sexual Selection and the Descent of Man.* Chicago: Aldine, 1972.

Carter, Steven, and Julia Sokol. *Men Who Can't Love.* New York: Berkley Books, 1988.

Chagnon, Napoleon A., and William Irons, eds. *Evolutionary Biology and Human Social Behavior.* North Scituate, MA: Duxbury Press, 1979.

Clanton, Gordon, and Lynn G. Smith, eds. *Jealousy*. Lanham, MD: University Press of America, 1986.

Cohen, Betsy. *The Snow White Syndrome: All About Envy*. New York: Jove, 1989.

Cook, M., and G. Wilson, eds. *Love and Attribution*. Oxford, England: Pergamon Press, 1979.

Daly, Martin, and Margo Wilson. *Sex, Evolution and Behavior*. North Scituate, MA: Duxbury Press, 1978.

Darwin, Charles. *The Descent of Man and Selection in Relation to Sex*. New York: W. W. Norton, [1871] 1970.

———. *The Expression of Emotions in Man and Animals*. Chicago: University of Chicago Press, [1888] 1965.

East, William. *Society and the Criminal*. London: H.M.S.O., 1949.

Ellis, Albert. *American Sexual Tragedy*. New York: Grove Press, 1962.

Farrington, David P., and John Gunn, eds. *Aggression and Dangerousness*. New York: Wiley, 1985.

Fenichel, Otto. *Collected Papers of Otto Fenichel*. Collected and edited by Hanna Fenichel and David Rapaport. New York: W. W. Norton, 1953.

Freud, Sigmund. *Complete Psychological Works of Sigmund Freud*. Standard Edition. London: Hogarth Press, [1922] 1955.

Friday, Nancy. *Jealousy*. New York: Bantam, 1987.

Goodwin, Grenville. *The Social Organization of the Western Apache*. Chicago: University of Chicago Press, 1942.

Gorni, Josef Y., Yaacov Oved, and Idit Paz. *Communal Life*. Yad Tabenkin, Israel: Transaction Books, 1987.

Guerin, Philip J., Leo F. Fay, Susan L. Burdeu, and Judith G. Kautto. *The Evaluation and Treatment of Marital Conflict: A Four-Stage Approach*. New York: Basic Books, 1987.

Gurman, Alan, ed. *Casebook of Marital Therapy*. New York: Guilford Press, 1985.

———, and David P. Kniskem, eds. *Handbook of Family Therapy*. New York: Brunner/Mazel, 1981.

Hendrix, Harville. *Getting the Love You Want*. New York: Henry Holt, 1988.

Jones, Edward, ed. *Attribution: Perceiving the Causes of Behavior*. Morristown, NJ: General Learning Press, 1972.

Kanter, Rosabeth M. *Commitment and Community*. Cambridge, MA: Harvard University Press, 1972.

Klein, Melanie. *The Selected Melanie Klein*. Edited by Juliet Mitchell. New York: Free Press, 1986.

Miller, Jean Baker. *Toward a New Psychology of Women*. Second Edition. Boston: Beacon Press, 1987.

Monat, Alan, and Richard S. Lazarus. *Stress and Coping*. New York: Columbia University Press, 1985.

Mowat, Ronald Rae. *Morbid Jealousy and Murder*. London: Tavistock Publications, 1966.

Murdock, George Peter. *Social Structure*. New York: Macmillan, 1949.

Neill, Alexander S. *Summerhill: A Radical Approach to Child-Rearing.* New York: Hart, 1960.

Nichols, Michael. *Family Therapy: Concepts and Methods.* New York: Gardner Press, 1984.

Olson, D. H., ed. *Treating Relationships.* Lake Mills, IA: Graphic Publishers, 1976.

O'Neill, George and Nena. *Open Marriage: A New Lifestyle for Couples.* New York: Evans, 1972.

Paolino, Thomas J., and Barbara S. McRady, eds. *Marriage and Marital Therapy.* New York: Brunner/Mazel, 1981.

Pines, Ayala M., and Elliot Aronson. *Career Burnout: Causes and Cures.* New York: Free Press, 1988.

Pines, Ayala M. *Keeping the Spark Alive: Preventing Burnout in Love and Marriage.* New York: St. Martin's Press, 1988.

Pittman, Frank. *Private Lies: Infidelity and the Betrayal of Intimacy.* New York: W. W. Norton, 1989.

Rossi, Alice S., ed. *Gender and the Life Course.* New York: Adeline, 1985.

Rubin, Lillian. *Erotic Wars.* New York: Farrar, Straus & Giroux, 1990.

Rubin, Lillian. *Intimate Strangers: Men and Women Together.* New York: Harper and Row, 1983.

Salovey, Peter, ed. *The Psychology of Jealousy and Envy.* New York: Guilford Press, 1991.

Sargent, A., ed. *Beyond Sex Roles.* St. Paul: West, 1977.

Skinner, B. F. *Science and Human Behavior.* New York: Macmillan, 1953.

Smith, James R., and Lynn G. Smith, eds. *Beyond Monogamy.* Baltimore: Johns Hopkins University Press, 1974.

Straus, Murray, Richard Gelles, and Suzanne Steinmetz. *Behind Closed Doors: Violence in the American Family.* Garden City, NY: Doubleday Anchor Books, 1980.

Swartz, Marc, and David Jordan. *Culture: The Anthropological Perspective.* New York: Wiley, 1980.

Symons, Donald. *The Evolution of Human Sexuality.* Oxford, England: Oxford University Press, 1979.

Tannen, Deborah. *You Just Don't Understand: Women and Men in Conversation.* New York: William Morrow, 1990.

Wanderer, Zeev. *Letting Go.* New York: Warner Books, 1989.

Warner, William Lloyd. *A Black Civilization.* New York: Harper and Row, 1937.

Watzlawick, Paul, John Weakland, and Richard Fish. *Change: Principles of Problem Formation and Problem Resolution.* New York: W. W. Norton, 1974.

Weltfish, Gene. *The Lost Universe.* New York: Basic Books, 1967.

White Gregory, and Paul Mullen. *Jealousy: Theory, Research and Clinical Strategies.* New York: Guilford Press, 1990.

Wilson, Edward O. *On Human Nature.* Cambridge, MA: Harvard University Press, 1978.

Wolfgang, Marvin. *Patterns in Criminal Homicide.* Philadelphia: University of Pennsylvania Press, 1958.

Wolpe, Joseph. *Psychotherapy by Reciprocal Inhibition.* Stanford, CA: Stanford University Press, 1958.

Zilbergeld, Bernie. *The New Male Sexuality.* New York: Bantam, 1992.

ARTICLES

Adams, David. "Identifying the Assaultive Husband in Court: You Could Be the Judge." *Response to the Victimization of Women and Children* 13 (1990), no. 1, 13–16.

Anderson, Robert. "Envy and Jealousy." *Journal of College Student Psychotherapy* 1 (1987), no. 4, 49–81.

Aronson, Elliot, and Ayala M. Pines. "Exploring Sexual Jealousy." Paper presented at the annual meeting of the Western Psychological Association, Honolulu, 1980.

Bishay, Nagy A., Neil Petersen, and Nicholas Tarrier. "An Uncontrolled Study of Cognitive Therapy for Morbid Jealousy." *British Journal of Psychiatry* 154 (1989): 386–89.

Bringle, Robert G., and Larry J. Williams. "Parental-Offspring Similarity on Jealousy and Related Personality Dimensions." *Motivation and Emotion* 3 (1979): 265–86.

Bryson, Jeffrey B. "Situational Determinants of the Expression of Jealousy." Paper presented at the annual convention of the American Psychological Association, San Francisco, 1977.

Buss, David M. "Conflict Between the Sexes: Events Evoking Anger and Jealousy." Paper presented at the annual convention of the American Psychological Association, San Francisco, 1991.

Buss, David M., M. Abbott, A. Angleitner, and A. Asherian. "International Preferences in Selecting Mates: A Study of 37 Cultures." *Journal of Cross Cultural Psychology* 21 (1990), no. 1, 5–47.

Buss, David M., and A. Angleitner. "Mate Selection Preferences in Germany and the United States." *Personality and Individual Differences* 10 (1989), no. 12, 1269–80.

Buunk, Bram. "Jealousy as Related to Attributions for the Partner's Behavior." *Social Psychology Quarterly* 47 (1984), no. 1, 107–12.

Buunk, Bram. "Jealousy in Sexually Open Marriages." *Alternative Lifestyles* 4 (1981), no. 3, 357–72.

Buunk, Bram. "Strategies of Jealousy: Styles of Coping with Extramarital Involvement of the Spouse." *Family Relations* 31 (1982): 13–18.

Buunk, Bram, and Ralph B. Hupka. "Cross-Cultural Differences in the Elicitation of Sexual Jealousy." *Journal of Sex Research* 23 (1987), no. 1, 12–22.

Byrne, Alan, and Lakshmi N. Yatham, "Pimozide in Pathological Jealousy." *British Journal of Psychiatry* 155 (1989): 249–51.

Caspi, Avshalom, and Ellen S. Herbener. "Continuity and Change: Assortative Marriage and the Consistency of Personality in Adulthood." *Journal of Personality and Social Psychology* 58 (1990), no. 2, 250–58.

Cobb, J. P., and I. M. Marks. "Morbid Jealousy Featuring an Obsessive Compulsive Neurosis: Treatment by Behavioral Psychotherapy." *British Journal of Psychiatry* 134 (1979): 301–5.

Coen, Stanley J. "Pathological Jealousy." *International Journal of Psychoanalysis* 68 (1987), no. 1, 99–108.

Clanton, Gordon. "Frontiers of Jealousy Research: Introduction to the Special Issue on Jealousy." *Alternative Lifestyles* 4 (1981), no. 3, 373–92.

Davis, Kinsley. "Jealousy and Sexual Property." *Social Forces* 14 (1936): 395–405.

De-Silva, Padmal. "An Unusual Case of Morbid Jealousy Treated with Role Reversal." *Sexual and Marital Therapy* 2 (1987), no. 2, 179–82.

Docherty, John, and Jean Ellis. "A New Concept and Findings in Morbid Jealousy." *American Journal of Psychiatry* 133 (1976), no. 6, 679–83.

Downey, Jerrold L., and William F. Vitulli. "Self-Report Measures of Behavioral Attributions Related to Interpersonal Flirtation Situations." *Psychological Reports* 61 (1987), no. 3, 899–904.

Eisen, Susan. "Actor-Observer Differences in Information Inferences and Causal Attributions." *Journal of Personality and Social Psychology* 37 (1979): 427–59.

Everton, G. McIntosh, and Douglass T. Tate. "Correlates of Jealous Behavior." *Psychological Reports* 66 (1990), no. 2, 153–54.

Friedman, Steven. "Strategic Reframing in a Case of Delusional Jealousy." *Journal of Strategic and Systemic Therapies* 8 (1989), no. 2–3, 1–4.

Gonzales, Rodrigo, Arrillga Pinto, and Gonzalez Ascuncion. "Morbid Jealousy in Chronic Alcoholics." *Psiquis* (Spain) 5 (1984), no. 3, 140–42.

Greenberg, Jeff. "Proneness to Romantic Jealousy and Proneness to Jealousy in Others." *Journal of Personality* 53 (1985), no. 3, 468–79.

Hansen, Gary L. "Dating Jealousy Among College Students." *Sex Roles* 12 (1985): 713–21.

Harris, Paul, L. Olthof, T. Jeert, Mark M. Terwogt, and Charlotte E. Hardman, "Children's Knowledge of the Situations that Provoke Emotion." *International Journal of Behavioral Development* 10 (1987), no. 3, 319–43.

Harvey, John H., and Gifford Weary, "Current Issues in Attribution Theory and Research." *Annual Review of Psychology* 35 (1984): 427–59.

Herceg, Neda. "Successful Use of Thiothirene in Two Cases of Pathological Jealousy." *Medical Journal of Australia* 1 (1976), no. 16, 569–70.

Hupka, Ralph. "Cultural Determinants of Jealousy." *Alternative Lifestyles* 4 (1981), no. 3, 310–56.

———. "Romantic Jealousy and Romantic Envy: A Seven-Nation Study." *Journal of Cross Cultural Psychology* 16 (1985), no. 4, 423–46.

Im, Won-Gi, Stephanie R. Wilner, and Miranda Breit. "Jealousy: Interventions in Couples Therapy." *Family Process* 22 (1983): 211–19.

Jacobson, Neil S. "Specific and Nonspecific Factors in the Effectiveness of a Behavioral Approach to the Treatment of Marital Discord." *Journal of Consulting and Clinical Psychology* 46 (1978): 442–52.

Jenks, Richard J. "Swinging: A Test of Two Theories and a Proposed New Model." *Archives of Sexual Behavior* 14 (1985): 517–27.

Joseph, Betty. "Envy in Everyday Life." *Psychoanalytic Psychotherapy* 2 (1986), no. 1, 13–22.

Kay, P., D. W. Fulker, G. Carey, and C. T. Nagoshi, "Direct Marital Assortment for Cognitive and Personality Variables." *Behavior Genetics* 18 (1988), no. 3, 347–56.

Lane, Richard D. "Successful Fluoxetine Treatment of Pathological Jealousy." *Journal of Clinical Psychiatry* 51 (1990), no. 8, 345–46.

Lester, David, George Deluca, William Hellinghausen, and David Scribner. "Jealousy and Irrationality in Love." *Psychological Reports* 56 (1985), no. 1, 97–100.

Lumpart, Ada. "Parental Investment, Relative Vulnerability and Adjustment Difficulties." Ph.D. dissertation, Tel Aviv University, 1981.

Mace, David R. "Two Faces of Jealousy." *McCall's*, May 1962.

Marikagas, Kathleen R., Myrna M. Weissman, Briggitte A. Prusoff, and K. John. "Assortative Mating and Affective Disorders." *Psychiatry* 51 (1988), no. 1, 48–57.

Marks, Issac M. "The Current Status of Behavioral Psychotherapy, Theory and Practice." *American Journal of Psychiatry* 133 (1976), 253–61.

Mascie-Taylor, C. G., and S. G. Vanderberg. "Assortative Mating for IQ and Personality Due to Propinquity and Personal Preference." *Behavior Genetics* 18 (1988), no. 3, 339–45.

Mascie-Taylor, C. G. "Spouse Similarity for IQ and Personality Convergence." *Behavior Genetics* 19 (1989), no. 2, 223–27.

Mathes, Eugene W., Heather E. Adams, and Ruth M. Davies. "Jealousy, Loss of Relationship Reward, Loss of Self-Esteem, Depression, Anxiety and Anger." *Journal of Personality and Social Psychology* 48 (1985), no. 6, 1552–61.

Munro, Alistair, James V. O'Brien, and Dawn D. Ross. "Two Cases of 'Pure' or 'Primary' Erotomania Successfully Treated with Pimozide." *Canadian Journal of Psychiatry* 30 (1985), no. 8, 619–22.

Neubauer, Peter B. "The Importance of the Sibling Experience." *The Psychoanalytic Study of the Child* 38 (1983): 325–36.

Pao, Ping-Nie. "Pathological Jealousy." *Psychoanalytic Quarterly* 34 (1969), no. 4, 617–701.

Pereira, Thierry. "Melancholia or Jealousy." *Perspectives Psychiatriques* 23 (1985), no. 3, 237–41.

Pestrak, Vic, Don Martin, and Maggie Martin. "A Brief Model of Jealousy: A Threat of Loss of Power and Identity." *Counseling and Values* 31 (1986), no. 1, 97–100.

Pines, Ayala M., and Elliot Aronson. "Antecedents, Correlates and Consequences of Sexual Jealousy." *Journal of Personality* 51 (1983), no. 1, 108–36.

———. "Polyfidelity: An Alternative Lifestyle Without Jealousy." *Alternative Lifestyles* 4 (1981), no. 3, 373–92.

Pines, Ayala M. "Polyfidelity: A Lifestyle Without Jealousy." Paper presented at the annual convention of the American Psychological Association, Los Angeles, August 1981.

——. "Sexual Jealousy as a Cause of Violence." Paper presented at the annual convention of the American Psychological Association, Anaheim, California, August, 1983.

——. "Sexual Jealousy." *Chadashot* (Tel Aviv), 5 April 1987: 3–11.

Pinta, Emil. "Pathological Tolerance." *American Journal of Psychiatry* 135 (1978), no. 6, 698–701.

Riviere, Joan. "Jealousy as a Mechanism of Defense." *The International Journal of Psychoanalysis* 13 (1932): 414–29.

Rubin, Arline M., and James R. Adams. "Outcomes of Sexually Open Marriages." *Journal of Sex Research* 22 (1986), 311–19.

Seeman, Mary V. "Pathological Jealousy." *Psychiatry* 42 (1979): 351–61.

Smith, James R., and Lynn G. Smith. "Co-marital Sex and the Sexual Freedom Movement." *Journal of Sex Research* 6 (1973), 131–42.

Smith, Richard H., Sung-Hee Kim, and Gerrod W. Parrott. "Envy and Jealousy: Semantic Problems and Experiential Distinctions." *Personality and Social Psychology Bulletin* 14 (1988), no. 2, 401–9.

Spielman, Philip M. "Envy and Jealousy: An Attempt at Clarification." *Psychoanalytic Quarterly* 40 (1971): 59–82.

Stets, Jan E., and Maureen A. Good-Pirog. "Violence in Dating Relationships." *Social Psychology Quarterly* 50 (1987), no. 5, 237–46.

Stewart, Robert A., and Michael J. Beatty. "Jealousy and Self-Esteem." *Perceptual and Motor Skills* 60 (1985), no. 1, 153–54.

Swami, Anand-Veereshwar. "Jealousy and the Abyss." *Journal of Humanistic Psychology* 23 (1983), no. 2, 70–84.

Tarrier, Nicholas, Richard Becket, Susan Harwood, and Yasmin Ahmend. "Comparison of a Morbidly Jealous and a Normal Female Population." *Personality and Individual Differences* 10 (1989), no. 12, 1327–28.

Teisman, Mark W. "Jealousy: Systemic Problem-Solving Therapy with Couples." *Family Process* 18 (1979): 151–60.

Thompson, Anthony. "Extramarital Sex: A Review of the Research Literature." *The Journal of Sex Research* 19 (1983), no. 1, 1–22.

Todd, John, J. R. Mackie, and Kenneth Dewhurst. "Real or Imagined Hypophallism: A Cause of Inferiority Feelings and Morbid Sexual Jealousy." *British Journal of Psychiatry* 119 (1971): 315–18.

Vinkour, George. "Classification of Chronic Psychoses Including Delusional Disorders and Schizophrenias." *Psychopathology* 19 (1986): 30–34.

Wagner, Jon. "Jealousy, Extended Intimacies and Sexual Affirmation." *E.T.C.* 33 (1976), no. 13, 269–88.

Wanderer, Zeev, and B. L. Ingram. "Treatment of Phobias with Physiologically Monitored Implosion Therapy (PMIT)." *Journal of Behavior Therapy and Experimental Psychiatry*, in press.

Weis, David L., and Judith Felton. "Marital Exclusivity and the Potential for Future Marital Conflict." *Social Work* 32 (1987), no. 1, 45–49.

White, Gregory L. "Coping with Romantic Jealousy: Comparison to Rival, Perceived Motives, and Alternative Assessment." Paper presented at the annual convention of the American Psychological Association, Los Angeles, 1981.

————. "Inducing Jealousy: A Power Perspective." *Personality and Social Psychology Bulletin* 6 (1980), 222–27.

————. "Inequality of Emotional Involvement, Power, and Jealousy in Romantic Couples." Paper presented at the annual convention of the American Psychological Association, San Francisco, 1977.

————, and Kathy Devine. "Romantic Jealousy: Therapists' Perception of Causes, Consequences and Treatment." *Family Process*, in press.

Whitehurst, Robert N. "Violence Potential in Extramarital Sexual Responses." *Journal of Marriage and the Family* 33 (1971): 683–91.

Wilson, Warner. "Brief Resolution of the Issue of Similarity Versus Complementarity in Mate Selection Using Height Preference as a Model." *Psychological Reports* 65 (1989), no. 2, 387–93.

Yankelovich, Daniel. "New Rules in American Life: Searching for Self-Fulfillment in a World Turned Upside Down." *Psychology Today*, April 1981: 35–92.

INDEX